The Dance with Community

American Political Thought
edited by
Wilson Carey McWilliams and Lance Banning

The Dance
with Community

The Contemporary Debate
in American Political Thought

Robert Booth Fowler

 University Press of Kansas

© 1991 by the University Press of Kansas
All rights reserved.

Published by the University Press of Kansas (Lawrence, Kansas 66049), which was organized by the Kansas Board of Regents and is operated and funded by Emporia State University, Fort Hays State University, Kansas State University, Pittsburg State University, the University of Kansas, and Wichita State University

Library of Congress Cataloging-in-Publication Data

Fowler, Robert Booth, 1940–
    The dance with community : the contemporary debate in
American political thought / Robert Booth Fowler.
        p.   cm. — (American political thought)
    Includes bibliographical references and index.
    ISBN 0-7006-0493-6 (cloth)   ISBN 0-7006-0623-8 (pbk.)
    1. Political science—United States.   2. Community.   I. Title.
II. Series.
JA84.U5F683   1991
320′.01′1—dc20   90-23001

British Library Cataloguing in Publication Data is available.

Printed in the United States of America

10   9   8   7   6   5   4   3   2

The paper used in this publication meets the minimum requirements of the American National Standard for Permanence of Paper for Printed Library Materials Z39.48-1984.

For Alice

Contents

Preface

This book is a journey in contemporary intellectual history. It explores the current engagement with community among many American political intellectuals writing and thinking about public ideas and problems. The book is written with the assumption that this journey in search of community is now too popular and too central to an understanding of contemporary political thinking in the United States for us to ignore the opportunity to study and learn from this powerful impulse.

Of course my assumption is not that the theme of community is the only significant development in contemporary political thinking in the United States. Far from it. But there is little doubt that interest in community is *a* major turn in current thinking, if not somehow *the* turn. I am less interested in establishing whether or not community is the dominant theme than I am in exploring its expressions, recognizing that community is very much on the agenda at present.

The book proceeds through four stages. It examines the chorus of complaint that constitutes so much of our intellectual political discourse. It follows contemporary discussion on another characteristic route, the journey into history—especially American history—in search of community. Both tasks are not just preliminary. They are integral to current considerations of community, though they are sometimes a substitute for rigorous reflection about that concept. Then the book turns onto the main path; the visions of community that currently animate so much intellectual aspiration. Originating in present-day complaints and grounded in analyses of history, they are the central issue and the substance of my explication of American political thought today. The book concludes with my reflections as a participant in the conversation, the views of a sympathetic traveler.

I write this book, however, not as a contribution to the normative debates over community, its meaning, its value, or its implementation. The book is meant not as an essay in normative political philosophy but as a discussion of the present-day developments in American political thought as they focus on community. I seek to tell the story of the coming of age of community (however defined) in American political thought and along the way to provide some measured analysis and reflection on some of the many directions in which thinking about community has proceeded.

An almost bewildering variety of conceptions of community floats through American intellectual life today. Most are far from complete, much less polished, even from a generous perspective. They parallel the diversity in the current mood of complaint among American political intellectuals. That mood is broadly inclusive, and it can be intense. It is not unusual to learn that ahead lie "coming ages of barbarism and darkness," and it is routine to be told that we face the decisive "turning point."[1]

Yet on reflection the ideas of community pervading our intellectual life are boundless neither in number, history, nor conception. The field is not small, but it is not unlimited. To be sure there is no consensus. Such a phenomenon, if it ever existed in American intellectual life, is very much in the past. As we shall see, the absence of consensus in intellectual opinion regarding the need for community is even more pointed with regard to alternative ideas of community. No vision commands the field, though some are formidable in appeal. To explore them is to open the door to much of contemporary political thought; this is the mission of my book. The examples I examine are not exhaustive, nor are they intended to be. Arguably, they are not even representative. But they do range over different arenas of intellectual discourse and they are intended to do so. My aim is to look at the interest in community in a variety of conversations about our present and our future.

Along the way in pursuing this project I have received much help. Of all those I have called on, Charlie Anderson has, as always, been a most steadfast colleague. Supportive yet skeptical, he has been of great assistance to me. Kathy Sell got me serious about community; Jim Farr and Erik Olsen helped in my thinking about republicanism; Mary Dietz provoked me to think about community and feminism through her work; Eric Gorham aided me on participatory democracy; Evan Ringquist prompted and then Joe Bowersox and Adolf Gunderson worked with my views on the globalists; Michael Dubin tried to straighten me out about Louis Hartz, among other things; Suzanne Jacobitti came through at a difficult point; Lance Banning and Carey McWilliams, among others, read the entire manuscript and offered me numerous suggestions that were of great benefit in my enterprise; the list could justifiably go on. I am grateful even as I am certain none of these souls would be willing to share my responsibility for what follows! Finally the folks at the University of Kansas were wonderfully helpful in making this book become a reality; I especially thank them.

Chapter One

Introduction: The Meaning of Community

The 1960s echo on. Their influence is not always direct, but they loom large in current American intellectual life. One way present attention to community reflects this is in the considerable number of political intellectuals to whom community can really be understood only as expanding participatory democracy. This perspective is directed toward a greater inclusion in and seriousness about participation in politics. Participatory intellectuals lament that in the United States today the citizen all but "disappears from view" due to the "eclipse of community."[1] A community-oriented society would be different. Its members would be a "citizenry that is educated, organized, and empowered."[2] Moreover, in some versions, participation would go beyond the political as we know it today and encompass economic life and institutions as part of the community.[3]

Intellectuals who look to community through republican lenses represent another perspective. Sensitive to American history and previous historical experience of republican community, they emphasize the fostering of virtuous citizens, above all public-regarding citizens. Republicans stress that a community devoted to a common good fashioned by public-spirited individuals is the model. Like participatory democrats, they do not want just any community whatever its form, and often they are skeptical of participatory democracy.[4]

Another focus is on community in the more traditional and private sides of life. Those who engage its vocabulary and categories include conservatives of a multitude of hues, feminists and antifeminists, enthusiasts and critics of any traditional communities in human experience such as family and neighborhood. They may not agree with

1

each other as to what kind of "family" they favor, but they share a recognition of the power of traditional and not entirely public realms of community in human existence. They know these communities are important, and that is why the intellectual struggle over them now is so intense.[5]

More than ever, calls for community today refer to global community. Inevitably urgent in tone, this mode of thinking about community often speaks from a text devoted to survival of the human species, often all of life, indeed of the planet itself. Survival is not the only motivator, however. There is a considerable mystical and perhaps a romantic strain here as well, an orientation toward something called nature that is as deeply loved as it is variously defined. This understanding of community has received too little attention in formal reflection on the subject, yet it may well be—perhaps it must be—the wave of our future.[6]

Finally, even as appeals for global community soar, appeals that are frequently couched in distinctly secular language, intellectual reawakening regarding the possibilities of religious community proceeds apace. Of course, community has always been a favorite word in almost all religious vocabularies.[7] But the apparent recent increase in community understood in religious categories—which allows and achieves a myriad of possibilities—has much to do with the unexpected and grudging growth of fascination with religion on the part of some political intellectuals.[8]

And there are other perspectives. One is an existential view, community defined as our human longing for a union that inevitably lies beyond our reach. This vision of human fate, perhaps a tragic one, exerts considerable appeal now despite, or perhaps because of, the energy directed toward community in contemporary intellectual life. Where others hurry, its proponents amble, frequently avoiding the main paths. Yet there are few gleeful skeptics among the existentialists (as I shall call them). In their dreams they are enthusiasts for community too.[9]

Not one of these understandings of community dominates the whole. Nor is any one of them, or any of the central arguments, exclusive one from another. The intellectual engagement with community bursts across boundaries with abandon. It displays all the creative freedom that intellectual life and demanding moral agendas require. What is evident, however, is the reality of the project. Community, its nature, and its desirability are now a part of the conversation of many political intellectuals in the United States; it has become a watchword of the age.

The strength and the diversity of the appeal of community in contemporary American intellectual life guarantees that no definition of the term, no matter how spacious, will easily enclose or tame it. A study of thirty years ago spoke of a hundred definitions; we now recognize that there are hundreds.[10] Some of these are the product of the fallacy of misplaced concreteness among modern social scientists. Many others originate in the popularity of the idea of community today, which necessarily taps a multitude of springs of definition.

It is undeniable too that community is a "contested concept."[11] Intellectuals are embroiled in arguments over its meaning because major issues are at stake—issues of principle, practice, and policy. Many of these areas of dispute may properly be called definitional controversies; I will return to several such examples. The picture is thus confused and complicated. The meaning of community is elusive, a word without an essence or a text without meaning, as so many appear to be in this day of pluralism, Wittgenstein, deconstruction, and contested concepts.

Yet this judgment need not lead to utter despair. Though not wrong, it may perhaps be too pessimistic. Some definitional themes are present in most discussions of community. It is a loose-bounded concept, but that is not at all the same thing as a concept with no boundaries. Thus though my use will be broad at times, enough so to be contested, it is far from a residual category into which anything and everything may be or will be placed. Community is contested and its contours can be altered, but there are still limits.

The concept of community invariably invokes the notion of commonality, of sharing in common, being and experiencing together. This is the root concept implied in most uses of the word. On the whole, contemporary versions of community distinguish themselves one from another by the specific forms or types of commonality emphasized, participatory democracy, for example, as differentiated from a global community. That the sharing implies an affective or emotional dimension is a usual assumption. It is not that advocates of community spurn rationality (some do, but most do not); it is, rather, that com-

community is and must be a deeply felt experience. That is inherent to what it is.[12] In fact, most communitarians analyze this necessity as incorporating a rational aspect. As Michael Sandel puts it, strong community involves "fraternal sentiments and fellow-feeling," but it is also a communal "mode of self-understanding" partly constitutive of the agent's identity.[13] Community goes deep into our souls, and in the process helps us to understand ourselves in quite (but far from exclusively) rational terms. For its denizens community must be seen, chosen, and experienced. Indeed, it really is "shared self-understanding of the participants."[14] A common life is crucial, but it is not sufficient. A shared life, self-consciously accepted, is required.[15]

Beyond these lightposts of definition, there is no certain signal in the modern conversation about community. Perhaps this is one reason why so much of the effort of the protagonists of our story is spent in denouncing part or all of liberal America and not on defining or even defending community. Analyses differ here too—as do degrees of denunciation. But there is no disagreement over the fact and legitimacy of considerable (intellectual) dissatisfaction.[16] And to that world of complaint, unease, and anger we now turn.

Part One

The Context

Chapter Two

Present Discontents

Community is the goal, a goal that comes in many shapes. To understand the urge toward community, we have to appreciate the broader mood among many contemporary American political intellectuals: a mood of unease, complaint, concern at best and panic and desperation at worst. The Reagan era relieved some of the alienation of many Americans.[1] However, intellectual dissatisfactions burned bright through the 1980s and into the 1990s. Perhaps political intellectuals tend by nature to be dissatisfied. Certainly they often have been in recent times.

The attraction of community has not simply happened magically; it is directly related to the intellectual mood of complaint. Yet widespread complaints need not lead in a straight line to affirmations of community. Thus the specific nature of the present discontents is crucial because if we understand this, the current rush to affirm community loses much of its mystery.

Of course the category "intellectual" is imprecise; it must be, and this reality cannot be overlooked. There are many attempts to define intellectual, but here I shall define the category culturally and treat as intellectuals those who are presented in journals of ideas and discussion as serious thinkers in the realm of political thought today. This definition is inclusive, and that, perhaps, is its most troubling feature. There are an incredible number of such intellectuals, and the diversity of those who meet the definitional standard and are engaged in the political concerns this book addresses is substantial. The list of well-known figures is considerable and the variety of ideas they advance seems endless. Given this fact, I have to choose whom to include and exclude in examining intellectual discontents today. Moreover, I certainly do not propose that there is consensus on the current unease or on its causes, much less on how to address present discontents. Many perspectives exist, no doubt of it, and I make my choices in terms of where emphasis should fall.

Caveats aside, this book must begin with a sense of the considerable intellectual dissatisfaction in our age and with the characteristics of that unease. Although by no means does everyone incline to a portentous pessimism—"the new dark ages . . . are already upon us"—or an almost casual pessimism—"how very grim things are in this country"[2]—pessimism and criticism are the foundation for all that follows. So much effort concentrates on sounding the charge against so much of the United States, its values, and its institutions that one may wonder if complaint does not overwhelm or sometimes substitute for the formulation and defense of a vision of community. No doubt it sometimes does.

The intellectual climate from the 1970s to the 1980s has been negative and critical. This is obviously true if one compares it with the 1950s and also, in a way, with the 1960s. There was no dearth of angry intellectual criticism in that unforgettable time, to be sure, but underneath it almost to the end was a confidence and a hope that is plainly absent in many intellectual circles today. Many political intellectuals are sunk in their unhappiness, unable to do much but be negative. Yet for others the irresponsibility of free-floating negativity clearly appeals as a form of liberation. This is especially the case with some of the postmoderns, dedicated to deconstructing anything and everything.[3] Either way this age is not an era of bliss among prominent political intellectuals.

Yet there is much more here than sheer negativity. At first the complaints overwhelm one, but on reflection one finds a more interesting story, the presence of a substantial, creative element in recent political thought.[4] It is the movement toward ideas about the origin and the healing of modern dissatisfactions. Driven by intellectual discontent, political theory is now alive and well in the United States.

When one wades through the flood of complaint pouring from political intellectuals, the sheer volume is impressive. There is almost no limit to what is wrong. Yet great volume does not mean formlessness. Though they cannot be categorized neatly, the present discontents are surprisingly tightly focused and not just in their aspiration toward community. Three themes predominate, and two others are closely connected. First is the emphasis on the American crisis as one of meaning, a spiritual crisis, if you will, the assumption that there is no inner life in modern society. The image is of an America without goals, without explanations. Second is the tremendous concern with the crisis over values that many political intellectuals identify as endemic to the U.S., one generally perceived as woeful and as of great significance. This crisis is sometimes connected to the larger metaphysical condition. Third, worry over crises of meaning and value lead to the attack on their offspring, the rampant individualism that critics believe afflicts our age. It is routine for political intellectuals to trace everything they perceive as wrong with the U.S.—a formidable list indeed—to American individualism (and liberalism). In the process, emphasis shifts from general ailments to the specific carriers of disease (the particular contribution) and to the noxious manifestations of the disease (the corruption and collapse of American lives and American institutions).

Daniel Bell has proclaimed that the "real problem of *modernity* is the problem of belief . . . it is a spiritual crisis." Though hardly unanimously shared, this sober judgment is popular.[5] The underlying assumption is expressed by Richard J. Neuhaus: Our missing "language of communal meaning," our absent "public ethic," our lost "sense of shared responsibility" once drew their strength from and had their origins in religion. The decline of religion in society, or among elites, explains much of the crisis and leaves us adrift.[6]

For some the remedy is obvious. We must turn toward God if we wish to alleviate our spiritual exhaustion. Only through God working with us can we build community.[7] Nonbelievers lack this faith, but as with Michael Harrington, often note the "disappearance of the traditional Western God" and bemoan the costs of spiritual emptiness: "The work day world . . . has become empty and alienated, without a transcendent justification or preserve. . . . There are private escapes from this fate, such as the religion of sexuality. But these can hardly hold a community together."[8] Thus, Harrington urges, we have a need to develop "transcendental common values" which are, somehow, not grounded in the "supernatural."[9] Bell also encourages us to search for a solution to the spiritual crisis.[10] Modern political thought in the U.S. is from one angle exactly about this search.

Of course, the crisis of meaning is not discussed only in terms of the (alleged) decline of religion. Nor is it unusual for a thinker to argue that preoccupation with religion or any form of answers—including obsessive concern with their absence—is yet another problem for a liberalism that today fails to appeal to a surprising number of political intellectuals.[11] More typical though are dissatisfactions similar to the perception of meaninglessness but not directed at the problem of decaying religious foundations. After all, what Bell describes as the (now absent) "rational cosmos"[12] had other underpinnings besides religion, certainly in Western intellectual life. Alasdair MacIntyre is, to say the least, another worried student of the crisis of meaning. He notes that the efforts of Kant and the Utilitarians to build a "rational secular account" for moral life did not succeed. They "have in fact failed."[13] Michael Sandel contributes to the same anxious mood as he contemplates liberalism and problems of justification.[14]

Meanwhile, Nietzsche has increasingly attained status as the greatest postmodern thinker. For theorists such as MacIntyre and Allan Bloom, Nietzsche's brilliance and influence are overwhelming —and devastating. Their Nietzsche announces the triumph of modernism and the loss of foundations. He ushers in the twentieth century and its spiritual crisis.[15] The consequences are as numerous as they are crushing, but two in particular get the most attention. Relativism has seized the stage, as Bloom argues so insistently in *The Closing of the American Mind*. People float with "no common object, no common good, no natural complementarity."[16] No wonder our civilization loves sincerity; it substitutes for missing truths.[17] We have become, says Irving Kristol, a decadent society whose cultural life is in another metaphor, nothing more than "a vast and variegated cultural supermarket."[18] And even among those who in the postmodern or deconstructionist spirit applaud such a breakdown, there is no sympathy or even charity for the resulting crisis in the United States.[19]

This does not mean we are in imminent danger of collapse yet. As Bloom describes the situation, "American nihilism is . . . a vague disquiet . . . nihilism without the abyss."[20] More directly the consequence is unchecked self-interest: hedonistic, rapacious, ruthless.

Those who no longer have an idea of evil or those for whom "the sacred is destroyed" naturally exist in a fashion any society might find frightening. As Bell says, "we are left with the shambles of appetite and self-interest and the destruction of the moral circle which engirds mankind."[21] The nonreligious Benjamin Barber concludes it is obvious that we have "a collection rather than a collectivity" as our society.[22] Less pessimistic, Robert Bellah and his associates in *Habits of the Heart* nonetheless insist on an honest acknowledgment of the results of our spiritual situation. People are not out of control on the whole, but they are often lost and we pay no mean price for that.[23]

All this invocation of spiritual crisis shades quickly (and inevitably in American political thought) into a discourse on the destructive sway of the relativism of values. There is plenty of agreement (ironically) that the "new language is that of *value* relativism."[24] Shared morality has been submerged by modernism which has torn apart boundaries.[25] We are increasingly a "culture of separation," wondering how we can be a society and, ironically, how we can ever be individuals, requiring as we do others to define ourselves.[26] In human relationships and even in our very souls "the psychology of separateness" rules.[27] We are, Richard J. Neuhaus protests, trapped in a world of "indifference to normative truth, an agreement to court all opinions about morality as equal . . . because we are all agreed there is no truth. . . . The result is the debasement of our public life by the exclusion of the idea—and consequently of the practice—of virtue."[28]

At issue, Michael Sandel argues, is what is left of us "as situated selves" versus our modern "unencumbered selves."[29] It is not just a matter of religion or of values but also of traditions, culture, and institutions: All of them have been eroded. Richard Merelman in *Making Something of Ourselves: On Culture and Politics in the United States* draws on anthropological images. We are now a "loose-bounded" culture. The "weakness of church, state, and clan leaves the individual alone and adrift in an often alien social and political universe."[30] Bloom describes his students as "The Clean Slate," lacking tradition, guidance, and moral foundations.[31]

Rampant individualism is the favorite theme and the constant complaint among many American political intellectuals. As Herbert Gans observes, the complaint is everywhere, diverse in its basic analysis and assignment of blame but truly axiomatic among contemporary intellectuals.[32] Bloom bemoans the world of students where, he insists, almost everything but individual sovereignty is dismissed.[33] Bellah and his associates confirm the same reality in the middle America they study where the reigning value is the individual and his or her freedom.[34]

Classic expressions of rampant individualism garner the most attention, eliciting relentless criticism. A common charge is that barely checked appetites now govern Americans. Conservatives routinely speak in these terms, lamenting "ungoverned will and appetite," citing statistics on divorce or crime and the like.[35] But conservatives are scarcely alone. Another response is the denunciation of the triumph of consumerism as the economic expression of unrestrained appetite.[36] Its analogue is the popular lust for more benefits from the government, especially the drive for ever-expanding entitlements which plays its role in budget deficits and general overload placed on government.[37] In its harsher versions this concern directs us to the underclass or to the serious drug culture and to their locations in American culture where appetite has overwhelmed all else (for whatever reason) and the human wreckage mounts higher and higher.[38]

While some political intellectuals thunder at the American who has no values, only limitless wants, others worry about the self-absorption, or, let us acknowledge Christopher Lasch, the narcissism of the contemporary American.[39] Robert Bellah's *Habits of the Heart* is already a classic in this genre. It describes American life as a perpetual adolescence, a permanent creation and recreation of oneself, an activity revolving around oneself and often unconcerned about anyone else.[40] Of course, Bellah argues, this journey does not prove entirely satisfactory. We cannot just create ourselves from ourselves; such narcissism fails. Other grounding is required, though it is often missing.[41]

Bellah develops a typology of the kinds of individualism prevailing today as well as in the American past. He acknowledges diversity beneath the concept of individualism, yet he also concludes that there is only modest variation among the species of individualism in the present. They all involve devotion to self and to the freedom of self.[42] A key example is Bellah's discussion of love and marriage, a remarkable chapter, perhaps his most powerful, and one which Allan Bloom's discourse on "Relationships" repeatedly parallels— though neither might want to admit it. Bellah's starting point is different from Bloom's and his judgments far less harsh; still, the two analyses are eerily close, characteristic, in truth, of a number of views today. The gods of the contemporary United States, expressed through the gospels of individual absorption, personal achievement, and faith in personal freedom, challenge lasting love, marriage, and family. It is a tough struggle in such a world to affirm such often quaint ideals as duty, obligation, or family. Much better to rush to a new relationship, to a divorce court, or to a family therapist to learn how to have a family on each member's terms and to fulfill each one's individual needs.[43]

Another common complaint emphasizes how many people seem to be left alone—and not alone just in the sense of lacking given values or real spiritual direction.[44] They are often socially alone even when with people or even when married. One refrain is that we cannot build relationships or make commitments or even keep those we grudgingly say we will.[45] We insist we must be free, though free to be what is much less clear.

In this context the image of the sad, stripped-down American gets (negative) attention. Michael Sandel treats this theme with flair. We find ourselves with the "solitary self" who we urgently affirm has (must have) great dignity. However, Sandel notes this dignity has nothing to do with us as particular persons. Anything specific about us and anything that might bring us together as real persons is banished today. We are formally individuals, devoted to freedom, but not real individuals located in serious lives, communities, and ethical roles, both different and alike. He finds it no surprise, then, that our politics is superficial and that we are as "strangers" in our public life as citizens. Sandel does not dismiss dignity; he admires it, but he insists it must be connected to a stabilized order of value and life to allow it or us to be anything amounting to dignified.[46]

Benjamin Barber sneers at what community we have left in our current situation. The "thin liberal community lacks any semblance of public character." He scoffs that it "might be better called a multilateral bargaining association, a buyer-seller cooperative, or a life insurance society," arrangements whose inherent inferiority Barber takes as a given.[47] Sheldon Wolin is among the most bitter and brilliant critics. For him American democracy is a joke of images and manipulations. We cannot take seriously those who claim we have a community in or out of politics. Instead of the participatory community that Wolin believes is integral to our development as social beings, we have inequality, domination, and too many intellectuals who are more interested in word games than they are in either truth or democratic community.[48]

An alternative here is "character," a word now much in vogue. Daniel Bell observes that our society demands that everyone have "personality," which is all individualism implies now. People seem to want in personality what the concept implies, a superficial individual, one with little depth or inner direction. Bell favors its virtual opposite, character—real people with substantial values.[49] Michael Sandel echoes this concern in *Liberalism and Its Critics* and elsewhere, as does Alasdair MacIntyre in *After Virtue*.[50] There are a number of variations, but the core message is the same.

One hears echoes of the 1950s with its intellectual outcry against mass society and against the mass of conforming Americans. The talk then was of the sad and even dangerous "other-directed" individualism and the extent of unfocused freedom, but today there is less sense of a tyranny of the majority and more concern over the prevalent shallowness and the unrealized potential of too many Americans. Another difference is in the degree of intellectual anxiety, sometimes even desperation, that pervades so many of these discussions today; the word crisis gets a lot of use.

Contemporary political intellectuals find several culprits behind the crises of meaning, morality, and character. None, however, begins to rank with liberalism, repeatedly the targeted enemy. Allan Bloom makes it all sound inevitable: Our addiction to liberalism led to a society without standards or substance. What else could one expect, since liberalism lacks absolutes and legitimates only freedom?[51] From another angle Alasdair MacIntyre berates liberalism as a rather pathetic political theory of process, lacking all substance, clinging to equality since it is unable to make distinctions, and making implausible claims to neutrality. No wonder, he observes, "the lawyers, not the philosophers, are the clergy of liberalism."[52]

In a famous analysis C. B. MacPherson blasts liberalism for its disintegrative image of human beings—possessive and materialistic, power-oriented, relentlessly fixated on what they can get for themselves.[53] Liberalism leaves us, Michael Sandel laments, disconnected in a world without meaning, where each of us has to construct his or her own meaning.[54] MacIntyre observes that liberalism today leads us to the triumph of the individual will or to continued lostness. Both are painfully unsatisfactory and leave liberalism without a defense: "We still, in spite of the efforts of three centuries of moral philosophy and one of sociology, lack any coherent, rationally defensible statement of a liberal individualist point of view."[55] Liberalism, Sandel insists, leaves only "the unencumbered self," which we know does not describe or promote valuable things—"character, self-knowledge, and friendship."[56] Liberalism separates us and abandons us, and in the process we fail to understand that significant moral experience is not about a private, autonomous being, unconnected to goals, to tradition, or to others.[57]

Liberalism not only neglects our need for community, indeed it is often downright hostile to it. It impedes thinking in terms of community. The issue is conceptual: Thus, honest liberals such as Nancy Rosenblum acknowledge "the communitarian failings of liberal thought" as a given.[58] Certainly some political intellectuals take it for granted. William Sullivan notes that liberalism simply does not deal with "social solidarity."[59] Samuel Bowles and Herbert Gintis lament how "impoverished" liberalism is in this realm.[60] Michael Sandel agrees.[61] Bloom joins in, but in his own way, targeting feminism as one of liberalism's most powerful disintegrative forces today.[62] The general theme runs through contemporary American political thought: Liberalism is at fault, particularly in its affection for "the acid of modern natural rights," which denigrates and destroys community and leaves only the individual.[63]

John Diggins affirms the analysis that liberalism has long been in the saddle in our political culture and that the results have not been impressive.[64] It has failed to comprehend what Wilson Carey McWilliams calls "fraternal relations," what William Sullivan defines as "the value of politics as moral cultivation of responsible selves."[65] Liberalism does not deal well with relations among people, especially communal relations. Contemporary judgments more and more interpret this lacuna as its crippling flaw. Liberalism drives "relationships to the model of pure instrumentality."[66] This reality, "with its corollary the subjective and finally arbitrary nature of value, is the deepest motif in liberal thinking."[67] And it is a motif (no matter how characterized) no longer in favor among many political intellectuals. Granted, by no means does every critic dismiss liberalism as hopeless. Even Benjamin Barber concedes that it is unfair to blame liberalism for every drawback of modernity.[68] But Clarke Cochran has a great deal of company in his conclusion that liberalism is "too thin" and lacks that center of community, of a public good, and of a recognized standard of justice.[69] If the problem is not natural rights, it is that "liberal pluralism makes any intelligible notion of the common good impossible."[70]

The inadequacy of liberalism in general is not the only popular explanation for present discontents. Some intellectuals look to the past, having in mind a particular moment in the history of liberalism as the problem. For example, some concentrate on the Founding Era as crucial. One version faults that age for its creation of the "very national purpose that first united America, *liberty defined as economic individualism.*"[71] In other viewpoints, too, this period is identified as the moment when a more communitarian ethic became the path not chosen.[72] Another favorite period for historical discussion is, of course, the brief (and to its critics) inglorious era of the 1960s. Theorists as different as Daniel Bell and Allan Bloom isolate that decade as the period of steep decline in our national community, however mixed the historical liberal legacy up to that time.[73] The disastrous costs of technological imperatives are another popular explanation in reflections on the United States today. For example, Christopher Lasch emphasizes the power of technology and how we are more and more its children at the sacrifice of all else.[74] Other structural problems such as our modern economy, large population, or sprawling geography are also perceived as elements encouraging our alleged formless individualism and indifferent success at community.[75]

Yet nothing besides liberalism attracts the attention that capitalism does as the cause of America's ills or, less directly, as the creator and reinforcer of the real culprit: liberalism. One cannot read American political intellectuals today without recognizing that capitalism receives scant sympathy. Beyond the celebrated names, the Friedmans and the Buckleys, the numbers of the faithful are modest. Even conservatism is by no means totally sympathetic to capitalism, as Russell Kirk's continuing observations on its baleful effects testify. "There is no greater fool than the man who dies for his standard of *living*, except the man who dies for someone else's standard of living."[76] Leftist intellectuals such as Joshua Cohen and Joel Rogers center the problems blocking their ideal of democracy and community on capitalism and elitist "capitalist democracy."[77] Others bemoan how "corporate values define modern American Culture"[78] or deplore the "capitalism which wallows in an eternal, spiritless present."[79] Jeffrey Lustig's *Corporate Liberalism* represents one of the liveliest and most trenchant discussions. Lustig claims capitalism has overwhelmed the United States and snuffed out democracy and conflict, mystified realities of power, and exalted science and technique at the expense of a public good.[80] Community got lost in the process, too, a perspective which Lustig hardly holds alone.

Of course, no single opinion dominates. The economics profession in the United States is overwhelmingly capitalist in orientation. Its practitioners proceed in a number of directions, though most are not in the tradition of the nearly unchecked capitalism promoted by the Chicago School of economists. One can hardly doubt that during and after the eight Reagan years there has been a far less doctrinaire dismissal by all but the most ideological Marxists of everything that might be linked to capitalism. So capitalism has at least some intellectual respectability, if not a great many warm supporters beyond the realm of economics.

Still, even though capitalism and liberalism are deeply intertwined concepts (and not just in many contemporary analyses of the United States), the principal explanations for what has gone wrong today lay the blame on liberalism more than on capitalism. Frequently capitalism is identified as part of the problem, but it is liberalism itself which draws the critics. Marxism is not, therefore, currently the most powerful source of the critique of liberalism. Its star may not have set among political intellectuals, but its light is less bright than it was a few years ago.

A favorite intellectual pastime is to identify liberalism's dubious consequences beyond the thin individualism and routine meaninglessness of modern life, such as the tendency for Americans to compensate for liberalism's failures by grasping for any connection, littering the landscape with false communities which divert people from confronting their situation and building serious community to address it. The charge is that our age is inundated with those who do not know what community is, despite a vague popular affinity for the word.

Bellah and his colleagues describe how individualism grips the profession of psychology, itself largely a response to lost meanings in the modern world. Modern clinical psychology tries to patch up relationships and foster community. However, Bellah asserts it does so by justifying community in terms of self-growth and only to the extent that individualist values are promoted by any community. For Bellah, communities founded on this sand will last only so long as they are convenient to their participants, which too often will not be long.[81]

False communities are everywhere for some contemporary critics. Bellah dismisses the multitude of social groupings in America merely as "Lifestyle Enclaves" having few characteristics of stable and deep community.[82] People floating from group to group and acting on the basis of temporary self-interest do not equal community.[83] And although there has been a major expansion of public interest groups in recent decades, it has been argued that they do not advance democratic community.[84]

The family, of course, draws limitless attention, and analyses stress its failures as community.[85] Some proclaim divorce to be America's most urgent problem—concretely but also symbolically. We are more and more divorced from each other and from what families can transmit: love, tradition, community.[86] The family now reflects society: It is no communal bulwark against fashion or the storms of life; indeed, its weak walls are no more formidable than anything else in the United States.[87]

If community is weak and weakening, authority is in even more disrepute and disrepair. Some critics declare that everywhere in our society our institutions have lost the capacity to stand for anything, to stand up for anything. No wonder Bell claims that authority figures have suffered an incredible "loss of nerve."[88] Christopher Lasch is more ambivalent about the value of many American institutions than is Bell, but he shares Bell's discomfort over the decline of authority—of the superego—and over the result that we find ourselves with only the unpopular government to direct us.[89] Lustig sees us left with abundance, which makes him no happier than the consolation of the state makes Lasch. Authority (not to mention a social teleology) is missing.[90]

Also missing, it is sometimes claimed, is a political means to address the crisis in our postmodern era. This lack is the final gasp, the failure of political capacity. The familiar argument is that we have only a mean politics of competing wants, a politics that yields to powerful greeds or that ends with the whimper of deadlocked interests.[91] The only signs of resolution are unsettling ones: a large public and private bureaucracy reaching out to clasp alienated and disoriented citizens.[92]

One notes the reprise here to themes in the political thought of the 1950s: Wants have triumphed over needs, alienation is rife, politics seems unable to break through. But this is not the 1950s, when the faith in liberalism was still vigorous; it was not yet the culprit. Ours is a far more disillusioned age, and perhaps one in which there is much less confidence in the United States as well. The considerable stir over the work of Paul Kennedy and of other theorists of decline is surely significant. As Kennedy argues, there is nothing inevitable or routine about an intellectual literature of decline in any era. Persian Gulf wars or books, some angry, some sober, undertaking to refute theories of decline hardly dispel the idea that suspicions of decline, of a loss of confidence in the United States, are afloat.[93]

Of course this is not the only story. A good many theorists of political philosophy have tried to refurbish liberalism. These thinkers, we may term them neoliberals perhaps, have occasioned a good deal of deserved discussion at least in circles of political theory. On the whole, intellectuals such as James Fishkin or Amy Gutmann have tried to clean up liberalism, sometimes in theory and often in (American) practice without renouncing it in any fundamental sense. There are more students of reform than of crisis. One common theme has been liberalism and justice; another has been liberalism and value justification; a third has been liberalism, democracy, and democratic education. All are topics long of concern to liberalism and on which critics in the present and in the past have concentrated. Whether one may say that community has been as much a topic for discussion among neoliberals is debatable. Equally so is whether community is a concept which provokes much enthusiasm. What is more certain is that these philosophical liberals simply do not share the widespread sense of crisis in their analyses (though they are hardly complacent) or a zealous drive to make community the philosophical center of their intellectual efforts.[94]

From another angle, it is impossible to ignore the controversy during the last several decades over John Rawls's *A Theory of Justice.* His discussion is self-consciously philosophical and thus meant as much more than an argument regarding the United States. On the other hand, it can be read as a defense of the liberal order of the United States. Either way, Rawls is notably silent on the general subject of community.

Yet Rawls and the controversy that has swirled around his book also serve to illustrate my general interpretive point. The truth is that Rawls, though surely a liberal, is hardly sanguine. Liberalism in his mind has failed to address adequately either problems of justice or questions of justification. In both areas liberalism and (by implication) the U.S. face a serious crisis. All may not be lost according to Rawls, but crisis within liberalism there is, by now a familiar refrain.[95]

One should note other voices with a distinctly more optimistic sound. There are those who insist that recent times have been, on balance, good for a great many Americans and that liberalism has produced some unquestioned glories. In one version, this view beholds a stunning expansion of human liberty in the United States beginning in the late 1960s, especially for women and for blacks. This view also argues ours has been a wonderful time of spiritual liberation and development when many Americans have turned to self-fulfillment in a bewildering, but also exciting, variety of ways. The result of both phenomena has been in practice an unparalleled democratization of society. Although not fully open to all or in all areas, the doors of opportunity have opened wider.[96]

This approach, well articulated by Peter Clecak, is more enthusiastic than that of Richard Reeves, who makes considerably more modest claims. Reeves speaks for those like him who share the mood of criticism and unease. He offers a host of complaints about American policies, especially during the era of Ronald Reagan, and also about some American institutions, while scrupulously avoiding such abstract matters as the metaphysics of American society. Yet Reeves represents those who conclude that things are, on balance, satisfactory in the United States. Reeves claims that ours may be a "selfish democracy" and that we are barely holding our head above water with our great problem and challenge, race relations.[97] Still, he rejoices that the American Dream is quite alive and grants that Clecak is correct: We are a more democratic country than ever.[98]

Much more positive analyses also exist as illustrated in Daniel Boorstin's history in the grand manner and his political role as something of a celebrator of the American experiment. Exemplified by his classic *Genius of American Politics*, if often repeated later, Boorstin's view is distinctly negative toward intellectuals and abstract intellectualism. In his analysis, our culture has produced little political thought and as a result has had little fundamental political conflict. We have been free of the abstraction which often leads to real political division and blessed instead with a practical mindset which has had and can continue to have impressive results in terms of "life, liberty, and the pursuit of happiness."[99] He implies that skepticism should always control our apprehension of intellectuals who shout crisis or rush forth with one or another nostrum. In Boorstin's histories such intellectuals are a nuisance, and the idea that they have much creative energy is laughable.[100]

It is not surprising to learn that the mood of complaint is hardly the only attitude present among political intellectuals. Who would have expected consensus? Such an expectation was perhaps never reasonable despite the brilliance of Louis Hartz; certainly it is not now. My purpose is not to show that all political intellectuals agree, a task beyond both my intentions and my capacities. Yet there is little reason to contest the claim that the mood of complaint is the current reigning disposition and that it represents a major turn in American intellectual thought over the last twenty years.

The breadth of complaint is impressive. Thus we hear from traditionalist Robert Nisbet a dirge for "the present age," where we have degenerated until about all we have left in the United States is the "loose Individual."[101] Or we learn from Alan Wolfe why we must decry the excessive individualist ethic ruining American culture. For him the liberal capitalist market has penetrated and undermined all aspects of our common life, the family, the school, even the ordinary civic and charitable organizations. In his chosen language, market relations have subverted civil society. Moreover, according to both Nisbet and Wolfe liberalism's only solution, the state, has done little good once we get beyond questions of economic survival. It has had nothing positive to offer to resuscitate human lives and human relations. As Wolfe put it, liberalism simply cannot meet communal needs.[102]

What should be done? Over and over the question is asked, "What medicine does one prescribe for a social order that is sick?"[103] The answers, alas, are sometimes disappointingly thin. It is unfortunately true that "too much time has been spent assaulting liberalism, too little articulating and defending an alternative in any detail."[104]

And yet. And yet there is a distinct turn in American political thought that has moved and continues to move beyond the present taste for complaint as almost an end in itself. This shift is toward a broad and various but far from formless response, a shift toward community. The rest of this book is about that turn in contemporary intellectual thought.

Chapter Three

Rummaging through American History

In discussing contemporary America, the friends of community focus on the inadequacies of American culture, philosophy, or institutions. Indeed, at times the banner of community is waved more to express a diverse and almost inexhaustible set of complaints about contemporary America than for any other purpose. Yet the negative mood, the mood of criticism, is far from the entire story. The idea of community in general (and indeed specifically, as we shall see) is pervasive. Its existence as a concept, an ideal, and a possibility represents the standard from which criticism comes—a standard which encourages the mood of substantial dissatisfaction.

What is perhaps curious in this urge toward community is not the varieties the ideal takes but the pronounced interest in exploring both the urge and the failures of alternatives to community in American history. In probing the attraction of community as a normative goal one finds a deep and powerful desire to explore American history, to rummage through history somehow to find what went wrong, to find why we do not have community. Despite all other available explanations, for many intellectuals there is no better way to examine the weakness of community in the United States. Nothing is more revealing than the workings of history and historical factors. A standard assumption is that somehow we lost a vision of and the chance for community during our historical evolution. Rarely is it assumed that community is somehow alien to our story, however much it may seem so at the moment. Thus the recourse to history is also a matter of affirmation, an affirmation that community, however defined, is not

23

something beyond our experience as a nation. Community is a lost, not an alien, ideal.

Some critics express reservations about the romantic images of past community that can afflict contemporary accounts of American history.[1] And there are interpreters who scoff at talk of missing visions or lost community. Samuel Huntington's analysis of the American past, for example, isolates as the central dialectic of our collective experience the tensions between our national ideals and our practice. Concentration on community, especially lost community, is beside the point. At moments we demand that our liberal creed be real and instantiated; and that is when political turbulence explodes, sometimes preventing decay and promoting our vision, sometimes creating false expectations and dangerous dreams.[2]

More often community is viewed from the historical perspective. Some efforts seem forced, merely a fantasy to garner support for a particular conception of community by claiming it once existed or exists now as a minor chord in American political or social history. Some efforts, in short, appear to be no more than strategies to legitimize the argument for community. Much more often, however, communitarians' constant grappling with American history reflects a widespread and sincere belief that community is not a remote idea in our experience. The purpose of turning to history is not only to validate the idea of community but also to search for the reasons why community did not flourish. Thus the historical journey is integral and represents an opportunity for discoveries about the past which may be applied to the present and the future. Seen in this light the engagement with the history of community in the United States is less a curiosity and more a perfectly logical enterprise for many contemporary intellectuals.

Often not explained, though, is the plausibility of the more optimistic turnings toward history. Exactly what is the realistic or practical connection between one or another experience of community in the American past and our present perplexities or dreams? Why does the presence of community in our nation in the past make its revival today more likely? Indeed, why would one necessarily assume that there is any connection at all, especially since most of the communities cited are long past, not even of the twentieth century?[3]

So much taste for history quite apart from the exigencies of intellectual strategy and fashion is no accident. The interest distinctly hints at the relative conservatism of the modern intellectual engagement with community. To be sure, this engagement is the occasion for stinging critiques of the United States and its liberalism as well as for proposals of community that often would impose drastic alterations on our values, institutions, and lifestyles. For all its amazing pluralism the movement toward community is sharply critical of our status quo, and in a progressive fashion. It is rarely overtly reactionary, yearning for a return to some moment in the American past.

Yet it is also conservative and must be understood as such in its common (though not universal) affection for conceptions of community associated with our history and for those our history defines as legitimate. More than strategy is at issue. It is a matter of temper, of many intellectuals not really wanting a radical break with the American past or even considering one necessary in the journey toward community. Of all the judgments common (again, not universal) to the intellectual advocates of community this may be the most controversial, but it is true enough and we should not ignore its implications.

Analyzing community in the American experience is not only a matter of selecting certain periods when community was very much a part of our story but also of considering what kinds of community existed, where they were, and who the participants were. And it means asking whether there are any discernible patterns to the history of community in the United States. Do we learn from such patterns that the reality or the possibility of community has disappeared? Or are there no patterns, only different communities and varying possibilities in changing eras? These are open questions of great importance, especially if one goes to American history to explore community rather than merely to indulge in romantic nostalgia.

In this active intellectual enterprise there is more interest in and controversy over the status of community in the years of the American Revolution and the formation of the Constitution than in any other period. The kernel of the debate is whether liberal values were at the core of the American culture at its birth and Founding as a nation or whether republican norms, far more oriented to community, were at the center. The reason for focusing on the Founding years of American history as the favorite era for intellectuals studying community is less obvious than it appears, or perhaps it should be said, less obvious than it is sometimes alleged to be. It is assumed that this period is self-evidently essential in United States history. Thus to study it is not just to enter another boring scholarly dispute heavy with competing sources and footnotes, but to ask who can claim title to the American Dream, to America itself? Who speaks for the values of America at its birth?

Yet there are definitely other reasons why this period merits so much attention, including those that derive from the perhaps modest of debates over community elsewhere in the American experience. No doubt the effect of the recent bicentennials of both the Revolution and the Constitution is another reason, as is the obsession with the intentions of the Framers in legal argument and jurisprudence, which has spread to our general public life. But the cult of the Framers goes much further. In this skeptical age and diverse culture, turning to the Framers as a source of authority is now everywhere popular. For many thinkers they are the foundation, and as a result we can expect that an intense contest over their teachings will follow. No wonder so many enter the fray convinced that obtaining the approval, so to speak, of the Founders would be a major victory in the wars to legitimize community as an idea in American political thought and especially for one or another particular understanding of community.

Louis Hartz forged a classic position after World War II in his masterwork, *The Liberal Tradition in America*. Hartz argued that John Locke was the dominant intellectual influence on our Founding. What he had in mind was "Lockean liberalism," a set of ideas that many of the late eighteenth-century intellectuals distilled from Locke and others of similar mind in England. Hartz presented these values in simplified form as natural rights, individual liberty (political, economic, religious), and consent of the governed. He did not totally ignore community, the public good, civic virtue, or other catchwords of republicanism. He understood that property was the basis for the United States' particular sense of virtues and he appreciated that liberal values had a distinct historical place in this country. Both realities served to restrain liberalism. Even more, Hartz appreciated that consensus on values was a substitute for community.

Consensus was, however, quite a contrast with the affectively-oriented world of community, rooted in local traditions or transcendent convictions, and it was decidedly political. Consensus was about outer conformity, superficial if powerful, and was hardly particularly political. Middle-class virtues and consensus did serve to restrain American liberalism in some ways even though it was intolerant in others. But the fact was that American political culture was about liberalism, not republicanism.[4]

Hartz's view was hegemonic for decades. As late as the early 1970s a skilled critic of the lack of community in the American political tradition reflected this consensus when he analyzed the status of community among the Founders. With considerable regret, Mason Drukman agreed that Madison was no supporter of a serious public community; no one who acknowledged the insight of Hobbes could be. Jefferson's claims in this area were not worth much either: He offered only "a rather tepid assertion of community," which was duly ignored.[5] Alexander Hamilton simply opted for government and especially for patriotism and nation, but not out of concern for real community among public citizens. Nor would one expect otherwise, given Hamilton's pessimism regarding people's capacities as citizens.[6]

What Hartz noted (and Drukman and others regretted) constituted a consensus that J. G. A. Pocock shattered. The pioneering student of the republican vision of community, Pocock asserted that an appeal to community was integral at the crucial, Founding moment of American nationhood, a thesis developed in his remarkable *Machiavellian Moment* (1975). This claim struck a resonant chord among some historically inclined political intellectuals eager for the news that liberal individualism has not been the only mainstream voice in American history.[7]

The claim that republican community in one form or another was the (or a) dominant political idea in late eighteenth-century America is now the ascendant view among intellectuals and scholars involved in this surprisingly busy corner of American intellectual life.[8] The vast literature invoking the republican model ranges from historian Bernard Bailyn's *Ideological Origins of the American Revolution* to sociologist Robert Bellah's *Habits of the Heart* to philosopher William Sullivan's *Reconstructing Public Philosophy*.[9]

In its usual form republican community is strongly associated with the American Revolution and Revolutionary patriots "who sought to promote civic virtue through an active public life built up through an egalitarian spirit of self-restraint and mutual aid."[10] The main terms associated with republican community are "public," "equal," "virtue," and "resistance to selfish corruption."

One of the major debates over this special image of community is whether the adoption of our Constitution reflected a (partial or substantial) surrender of the dream of republican community by the Founders. One perspective insists the Founders "had not yet abandoned the classical tradition of civic humanism."[11] Although the Constitution hardly promoted the small-state, virtuous community of republicanism, it created a system of government which is an adaptation of the "tradition of civic humanism that dated back more than two millennia."[12] Another view describes the Constitution and its writers as on a journey of transition. Their Constitution was not perhaps the end of our republican spirit but a signal that liberal individualist and indeed capitalist tendencies were marching to the fore. Thus the dualism is drawn: the (good) original republican dream versus the (evil) "disintegrative tendencies of commercial society"—more bluntly, capitalism or liberalism or both.[13]

According to this version, the Founders were republicans but through the Constitution they laid the groundwork for liberal capitalism, preparing the way for a large national state determined to promote economic growth. The Founders "still saw themselves ideally as a leisured, cosmopolitan, liberally educated gentry bound by a classical patrician code of disinterested public leadership." Yet "they prepared the way for the individualistic, egalitarian, and democratic future of America."[14] And the irony was that the resulting "society of acquisitive individualists had neither room for nor need of the kind of virtuous public servants who so abundantly graced the public community during the Founding Era."[15]

This conclusion makes the political point debated in so many current intellectual discussions of the Founding period: how community rose and fell in American public life and how it might rise again. However, the complexity was very real: "The Founders were politically multilingual: They could speak in the language of Bolingbroke, Montesquieu, Locke, the classical Republicans, Hume and many others"—and they did so.[16] Moreover, they were inventive as well as eclectic. They simply cannot be put into any category, including that of being mostly philosophical in their approach.[17]

The most admired historian of republicanism in our Founding Era is Gordon Wood.[18] His understanding is rich and detailed, based on intimidating research, marked by nuance, and reasonably dispassionate. He is careful to disavow any simple liberal versus republican dichotomy in describing the contending political forces of the Revolutionary/Constitutional age. Yet for all his resources and caveats, Wood argues for (or reinforces) the idea that the energy behind the Revolution was, above all, "a utopian effort to reform the character of American society and to establish truly free governments," that is, a revolution for "republican regeneration."[19]

In his detailed discussions Wood provides the best feel for as well as the most reflective discussion of what republicanism is, or was, in the U.S. two hundred years ago. Its essence, Wood suggests, was a self-conscious commitment to a greater good, the good of the whole. This did not involve a rejection of individual liberty. Republicanism's genius as a model of community was that it aspired to combine individual freedoms with a broader public concern. The liberty it honored and encouraged was public liberty, active, democratic participation in deciding on the common good. It was not a liberty which praised privacy, or possessivism, or self-chosen alienation. It had to be on guard against the constant threat of corruption—the triumph of self-interest—which was why virtue, especially virtue as public-spiritedness, was so needed. But the Revolution was, Wood insists, a revolution of hope, made by those who thought a virtuous republican community was achievable.[20]

The age of the Constitution and thereafter was, on the other hand, hardly an affirmation of the republican vision. Wood rejects those who contend that the Federalists, their politics, and their Constitution had no republican side; their taste for limited power and a substantial role for the people demonstrated that they did.[21] Yet the Revolution's dream of republican community was lost by 1787. Liberty was more and more seen in private and personal terms rather than in public and collective ones. Virtue was no longer the answer to corruption.[22]

Like all academic debates which touch an intellectual nerve, the argument over the nature of community at the end of the eighteenth century has become a growth industry feeding on itself. In some settings it draws thoughtful and balanced participants who are less inclined to make a passionate political statement than a careful if rather bloodless scholarly evaluation. An excellent example is the work by James Kloppenberg. He judiciously grants that both Lockean liberalism and Pocockian republicanism were major aspects of late colonial and early national American thought—as were, he notes, explicitly Christian ideas and the notions of the Scottish moral philosophers, in whose views the individual was decidedly accountable to the larger community.[23] Kloppenberg stresses that republicanism was significant in the Revolutionary period in its emphasis on the need for public community to address corruption and excessive selfishness. Its role in influencing the equally prevalent language of active natural rights, or pursuit of happiness, is much more doubtful. Locke, who offered the language of both natural rights and Christianity, was a decisive force, though liberalism if defined in market terms was not.[24]

Another relevant example is the work of Joyce Appleby, who underlines the liberal (and capitalist) side of early national American thought. As she tells the story, republicanism was part of American political thought at the Revolution. Yet by the 1790s it had faded before a kind of Jeffersonian liberalism, which conceived of people as free and independent, socially equal, optimistic, and sympathetic toward economic growth. It proceeded on the assumption that the result would be more beneficial to the people than republicanism with its concern for community, public life, and the public sector.[25]

The struggle over the status of community in American political thought in the years of the Revolution and the Constitution is the biggest single topic of interest for political intellectuals rummaging through American history. But there is no reason to assume this will be permanent. After all, the Founding period is hardly all of our history, though at times in the heat of the currently fashionable discussion, one can forget this. Times change. During the 1940s and 1950s the largest efforts and greatest energies centered on Puritan colonial New England: It had the key to everything—every glory, every failure in American life. Preceding this trend was a tremendous emphasis on the closing of the frontier and the period from 1870 to 1900, the age of immigration, urbanization, industrialization, and its significance for the nation and for political thought. And there will be new foraging in new times. Even so, it is not just the Founding Era which generates current interest. Far from it. For example, Puritanism as a source of community in the American tradition can hardly be ignored. The Puritan community was as real as an ideal and in its time and place (seventeenth-century New England, at the least) more dominant as a practice than republican community ever was. And today there are those observers who acknowledge (once in a while even with a bit of approval) the Puritan tradition of community in our history.[26]

Normally, though, the Puritan age does not prove to be an attractive area of study for intellectuals in search of community in our history, in part because of the frequent suspicion that the Puritans exemplified a narrow and static kind of community which does not fit with the (somehow) free or free-wheeling community that attracts some contemporary advocates of community.[27] Another reason may be that the Puritans do not fit neatly with the secular, egalitarian, and often participatory democratic model of community favored by other communitarians at present. I suspect, however, that the biggest problem some intellectuals have with the Puritans is their religious foundation. For them community was a commandment of God (and also a gift of God's grace). Motive and meaning were clear and followed from metaphysical certainty. It could not be said of them, or even speculated about them, that their urgent reach for community was a substitute for a silent and empty universe.

If the Puritans are a mixed model and republicanism did not last much beyond the first decades of the nineteenth century, where (else) are we to look for role models for community in United States' history? Not much approval falls on the mid- or late-nineteenth century. After all, republican sentiments (however present once) declined (though exactly when is a matter of contention) into the greedy culture of the self-absorbed intellectuals in the pre–Civil War decades. Thoreau rejected social solidarity and had no interest in any recognized forms of human community, certainly not public ones.[28] Emerson was little different; his edges were merely more sanded, his tones loftier.[29] The soul was the concern of the Transcendentalists and community was just another institution ready to paw the soul.[30]

Of course, growing capitalism in American life had great sway over the culture. For some political intellectuals rummaging in our past, the latter half of the nineteenth century stands as an especially long, dark time. The costs of economic individualism to any kind of social community—the family, the local community, the idea of the public good—were too slowly recognized.[31] The warnings of nonliberal eccentrics such as George Fitzhugh won no applause, in part because their alternative notions of community were so remote from the established patterns of American life.[32] And although there is considerable agreement that the force of public community was collapsing by the Jacksonian years, later figures who appreciated community of one sort or another (Lincoln is a popular example) did not prevent its breakdown.[33] The tide of Locke's ideas, of possessive individualism and of capitalism, swept all before it.

The movement on behalf of community in the later nineteenth century was populism. Once scorned as a reactionary, anti-Semitic, and petty capitalist outbreak,[34] populism has made a surprising (if not totally convincing) comeback. Lawrence Goodwyn has been a driving force for revisionism here, a force fueled in part by the desire to ground contemporary political values within the American political tradition. According to his view, the Populists represented hope, and their enemy, the corporate state, represented power.[35] The Populists stood for the hope of democratic promise,[36] democracy understood as community, a life of active, participatory work toward self-government and dynamic change, including the economic sphere where it represented a "cooperative crusade."[37] Indeed, in Texas populism, which is the basis for Goodwyn's particular enthusiasm, cooperatives were central—in practice and as an ideal. They were the living models of economic democracy, of community. The Populist defeat in 1896 was a tremendous setback for the hope that the United States could "be fundamentally democratized," and once that idea was rebuffed, what was left among reforms was called (again, the unacceptable) "liberalism."[38]

The current interest in community and history has not led to much attention to the Progressive Era, 1900–1917, allowing for stimulating exceptions, such as the work of David Price.[39] Yet far more than the Populist outbreak of the 1880s and 1890s, the Progressive Era influenced American intellectual life in the twentieth century as well as the New Deal, the Great Society, and other ventures in social welfare, including government involvement in the economy and reliance on social science experts.

One current fundamental criticism of that era is that Progressives were not truly enlistees in the cause of community, however defined. This defect, it has been argued, is demonstrated by their (at best) mixed concern for democracy. There was, after all, little engagement by Progressives with participatory models of community in either conventional politics or in economic life. Without question, Progressives were a diverse lot, but their attitude was less fraternal than paternal (or maternal) in dealing with people. There was tremendous concern for a common good, but one directed from above, by elites and experts.[40]

And yet the Progressive Era is certainly the age which most closely resembles that of the Founders in intellectual affirmation of community or of a social perspective. Jane Addams's Hull House and John Dewey's "Great Community" were only two of innumerable ideals of community, ideals of a social individual, which became standards of the era for many intellectuals. At the center of that period's intellectual enterprise, as at the core of ours, is the same reach for community. Eric Goldman catches something of this spirit in his *Rendezvous with Destiny*.[41] This spirit was there, surely, but sympathetic attraction to the era is not there now. One reason may be that some contemporary historical treatments describe a Progressive intellectual world of such complexity and paradox that any generalization appears blocked.[42] Perhaps as telling a factor may be the philosophical orientation of Progressive thought; science was its talisman, and such Progressives as John Dewey worshiped at its altar. Today science, however interpreted, lures few worshipers among intellectuals engaged with community.

Another aspect of some Progressives' concentration on community is its sometime abstraction, which clashes with the driving, urgent character of much of modern interest in community. Vague affirmations of the social individual or equally vague discussions of the common good among Progressives did not seem to amount to much. Abstractions linger in books by John Dewey, Charlotte Perkins Gilman, or Herbert Croly.[43] On the other hand, much of Progressive concern, especially among urban Progressives, was the opposite of abstract or ethereal. Community sometimes had very specific referents: needs regarding slums, women's suffrage, education, or industrial working conditions.

It is in the twentieth century, though, that explorers of American history in the service of community find the driest wells. As in the previous century, there are sometimes moments or movements in labor or in immigrant, minority, or popular socialist histories that inspire.[44] Yet they seldom reflect the mainstream enough to provide the hope and the plausible examples from which one could construct a tradition that cannot be too easily dismissed. Self-conscious twentieth-century radicalism also provides some affirmations of community, but one can encounter a good deal of ambivalence among Left-leaning intellectuals about that history. Christopher Lasch is a harsh, but no longer lonely, example of one critical mood. For Lasch, American radicalism does not deserve much attention. It has simply not been serious about community or much else except a certain cultural style of alienation and ritualized radicalism. In terms of disciplined thinking or action it has little to show for itself.[45]

Richard Flacks, in his interesting book *Making History: The Radical Tradition in American Life*, argues that a powerful legacy of radical history is to be found in the story of the United States. But he does not propose that leftist organizations, the parties, and the experiments are a particularly rich vein to mine. They were often too rigid and too far from people's lives to have much influence beyond training activists. Yet Flacks argues that radicalism in the United States has flourished in cultural and intellectual life and from time to time has had great impact. He is right, to some degree, and one of the principles radicalism has sometimes nourished is the idea of (egalitarian) community.[46]

There are other judgments; the trails between the 1960s and the New Left and a good many contemporary intellectuals and community are as numerous as they are tangled and surprising. Yet pre-1960s radicalism in the twentieth century inspires few communitarians. It had little use for traditional communities of family, church, or locality and a great deal of affection for a state which nowhere has turned out to be a community.[47] Broader movements of considerable popular and intellectual appeal such as the New Deal and its latter-day reincarnation, Lyndon Johnson's Great Society, warm few community-oriented hearts either. The Great Society, for example, talked a good deal about participation in community, but there was much more talk than participation, and in the end much of the community-based participation went sour. Neither the Great Society nor the New Deal appears to have inspired community intellectuals. Rarely does either seem to merit mention.[48]

What is the historical record found by the travelers into American history? In terms of the broad picture, little praise is offered. Yet these travelers do find community, especially in the republicanism of the Founding age or the Populist revolt and occasionally elsewhere as well. As a result, few declare America hopeless from a historical perspective.

There are, of course, ways to conceptualize American history other than through the frequent search for the good periods, a point granted all around. A harder (and not self-evidently better) approach assesses the strength of community over the course of the American experience. Its practitioners sometimes follow up with a theory of development or underdevelopment of the civilization on that basis. One interpretation suggests that although community has had its moment in American history, the unfolding of our story has sapped its possibilities. Thus we have undergone a continuing "absorption by the market" complemented in recent decades by an "absorption by the service state."[49] In the process community and the idea of community have all but disappeared. Another and similarly pessimistic view contends that there have been few developmental changes to record. Rather, the truth is that as a nation we have never been very willing "to treat seriously the idea of community."[50]

Of late, however, this pessimism is very much under attack through arguments that a language of community (and to some extent its practice) is definitely part of our historical experience. The influence of Robert Bellah and his associates in *Habits of the Heart* has been striking. Their conversations with contemporary Americans confirmed for them that we have a powerful language of individual freedom and self-absorption.

Beneath that, however, half-articulated and struggling against cultural conventions, is another vocabulary, one of community, of concern for the public good and for each other. This is our second language and it is connected with our second history.[51] It is not so much to be found in one period or another as in all periods, though increasingly it occupies a secondary position in our public discourse.

Bellah and his associates based their interpretation on their interviews, but its theoretical origins in history lie with Alexis de Tocqueville. As they observe, it was de Tocqueville in *Democracy in America* who formulated the thesis that despite their zealous approval of individual freedom, Americans were ambivalent about it. Their uneasiness, as de Tocqueville described it, resulted from the tension between their affection for equality and their enthusiasm for liberty. Less noticed for a time was de Tocqueville's observation of people's evident preference for community over liberty in a number of areas. This was the reality, he suggested, in the private realm of life, of family and religion. Here people were not especially in love with freedom; they were looking for something else, for community. And things tended to work out well in the subsequent interactions of the public and private dimensions of society, as de Tocqueville understood them. In the family and at church Americans learned values that restrained their individualism and disciplined their lives. At home they found the community they needed and the inner restraints required of people in an economic, social, and political existence where unchecked freedom would lead to anarchy and worse. In public economic and political life they enjoyed their freedom; at home they enjoyed their community. De Tocqueville's model was highly gender-specific, of course. For him the second language of community was spoken by women, the first language of liberty by men. Women were essential, then, in the American story, for they measured the restraints, they built the communities. At the same time, they were clearly the voice of the second language, second in the obvious senses of place and power.[52]

As there has been a rediscovery of the social and political significance of the family and other so-called private institutions, de Tocqueville's analysis that community was a major component in the American system of values has gained strength. Louis Hartz's *Liberal Tradition in America,* while influenced by de Tocqueville, often set the tone for cultural interpretation and argument in recent decades and claimed that Lockean liberal, individualist values dominated our culture.[53] De Tocqueville would not challenge that conclusion for our public life, but he was useful in leading observers to note Hartz's limitations. While community was not in American public culture and history, it was very much present in our private places, "places of the heart," places where neither Hartz nor many earlier historical studies ever ventured.

Both the growth of interest in American republicanism and the redirected interest in de Tocqueville's analysis of community in the United States pushed people toward the same conclusion: Community has existed, but today it is in eclipse. The second language of community is overwhelmed and struggling merely to survive. Indeed, community is on the defensive even in its natural place, the home, as marriages falter and families break up—a dreary modern picture. Yet for Bellah and his coauthors the American experience contains hope. The world de Tocqueville describes reminds us of the second language of community that Bellah finds still alive today.[54] Once again history serves to reassure proponents of community that the concept is not alien to the United States. Rather, it is a (weakening) secondary chord in our experience, one which some would transpose to a primary chord.

History, then, is important in the intellectual engagement with community in American political thought today because it is a source of hope. Approaches differ. Some intellectuals concentrate on the presence of community, as they may define it, in one or another historical epoch. Others find it far more widely in the American experience, perhaps as the dominant political language there. But it is the existence of community and hope within the American context that is important. Moreover, the presence of the idea of community in powerful form at our Founding or continuing in our private institutions reassures us that community has been more than a minor theme in our history.

Thus we are not, on the whole, dealing with communitarian intellectuals who are either particularly discouraged or radical. They describe a crisis or rather many crises and agree that community is not a hegemonic idea in American culture and, sometimes, that it has never been. Yet some of them find within the American historical experience both intellectual and experiential resources to advance the idea of community. In that sense they are seeking neither an alien idea nor an alien experience. Their journeys into history are often an affirmation of exactly this optimistic belief.

Part Two

Images of Community: A Brief Preface

A deluge of complaints often dominates present intellectual discussion of community, sometimes interfering with the serious consideration of its theory and practice. Also pervasive is a search through American history for past communities and the tragic missteps which have led the United States away from community. Sometimes this search is a journey toward optimism; other times it is a setting for reflection on community as a challenge. Rarely is it just a nostalgic trip to a lost ideal or the resurrection of the past as a stick for beating the present.

No set of categories can capture the current range of conceptions of community which are part of a large and expanding conversation. The idea of community is now too alluring to be contained any longer within a discrete group of intellectual discussions. Such pluralism is no surprise given the formlessness of contemporary intellectual life. It is both free and uneasy as its political imagination pursues community everywhere and anywhere.

The following chapters will demonstrate this richness and display some of the many portraits of community among contemporary political intellectuals. We can see for ourselves some of the directions taken by community-focused thinkers. These directions are not neatly separable since contemporary intellectual life is too fluid for that, yet they exist nonetheless.

In this journey, I have selected six directions in contemporary thinking about community. Even taken together they do not begin to encompass the multitude of current explorations on the subject. Moreover, each contains generous diversity within its own world. Yet

39

each is a worthy and significant illustration of contemporary patterns of thought about community as an ideal. The basis for selecting each approach varied, though each one's appeal among a number of political intellectuals was essential. In some instances the quality of the argument was crucial; in others, the extent of intellectual controversy swirling around them; and in yet others, the connection with arguments about our historical experience of community. My goal was to consider a mosaic of images of community in contemporary intellectual thought, one faithful to the pluralism that surrounds the topic today.

First, I chose community as participatory democracy, a vision which preceded the era of the New Left. It had its heyday in the late 1960s and has not died since when so many of its youthful adherents have matured into active intellectuals. This notion of community is public and political, affective and altruistic. It affirms decentralized decision making and a participatory experience that seeks to transform politics from a process to a way of life.

Three other forms of community have attained their fullest modern expression in the post-1960s and represent postmodern renderings of ancient themes. One idea, republicanism, attracts the greatest interest in scholarly and academic circles. Known for its historical roots in classical European experience and late eighteenth-century America, the republican ideal of community focuses on public community. Its advocates insist that true community requires a life of shared virtues and shared history. They give serious consideration to the challenge of reconciling liberalism with community and propose in republicanism a version of community which they judge is not alien to American experience. They see a tradition of republicanism in the history of the United States and are anxious that we acknowledge it also.

Another central arena today for the debate about community is what I call the realm of roots, where community is less public, less formal, and less modern somehow than in many ordinary political models. It is a realm where we find our origin and definition, the roots of our lives, the roots of communities in which we live or from which we may escape in order to live. The two examples I explore are roots in the sense of tradition and in the sense of family. Both areas attract many observers interested in community who are eager both to defend and to attack. The lines of debate are complex and community in any form is not always the winner, but the discussions are important and interesting.

What I term globalist images of community are now much in vogue. Survivalism is the pessimistic face, globalism the optimistic, of the same disposition: community defined and justified in terms of the globe as a whole, the earth and its life. The last two decades have accelerated openness toward this conception of community.

Far more familiar in terms of Western political thought are religious understandings of community. After all, the world's great religions have long affirmed community, albeit more sometimes in theory than in practice. And yet a revival of thinking about community in religious language was perhaps unexpected in a supposedly secular age. The growth is strong, however. In many instances it reflects the influence of the 1960s on current political theology. It is also, as we shall see, quite pluralistic in its expressions.

A final perspective is what I might call existential community. Its advocates seek community, but they distinguish themselves by their overwhelming suspicion that it is an ideal beyond actual achievement. For them and them alone in this age of both desperation and optimism, community is an ideal whose social reality (as opposed to private or personal reality) is permanently elusive—and must be understood as such. Perhaps they remind us of themes of the 1950s, and thus that even that decade lives on.

Again, I stress that these directions and the detailed considerations of each are but images of community. Images do not form sharp outlines or have tight boundaries and, indeed, they easily blur into each other. This is, I think, perfectly apt for the fluid world of modern intellectual reflection and argument over community. The lines between participatory democratic models of community and republican ones are not always sharp. Ideas of religious community may seem distinct in the obvious sense but in form are often recognizably participatory, traditionalist, or republican. And this analysis looks at the perspective of the whole image, not at the particular visions of assorted theorists within each image of community. What we face may seem bewildering or overwhelming, but it is not in the least discouraging to my mind. It is, rather, a testament to the richness of intellectual focus on community in contemporary American political thought. The subject is flourishing: developing, wide open, exciting, a major turn.

Chapter Four

Participatory Community

Despite the flourishing interest in community today among American political intellectuals, the appeal of participatory democracy may come as a surprise. Embraced by the New Left in the mid-1960s, this vision of community is easy to dismiss as a relic of more optimistic (or naive) days. From a skeptic's view participatory democracy has had only a modest connection with American history, and an even smaller one with general human experience and deserves scant role in contemporary understandings of democracy or community.

The truth is different, however. Participatory democracy may have won few lasting battles in American life or anywhere else in the 1960s or at any time, but it has won a considerable place in the hopes of some contemporary political intellectuals. The New Left is long over as are many (but by no means all) of the experiments in participatory government it inspired. The idea of participatory democracy, however, lives on. Its proponents have no difficulty in connecting their vision with the dramatic pantheon of predecessors they enshrine from Western history. Originating in classical Athens (albeit excluding slaves and women), the ideal has been reborn in the hands of such theorists as Rousseau, Jefferson, and G. D. H. Cole, among others.[1]

In recent decades, make no mistake, the proximate lineage for the participatory democratic community is the New Left, often members of the New Left grown up or grown old. Contrast the intellectual dismissal of participatory democracy, not to mention community, in the United States in the decades after World War II to the famous (if short-lived) fervor for participatory democracy and community in the late 1960s.[2] No matter how much the realists of the 1970s or 1990s

42

dismiss direct democracy, in a few short years during the 1960s it made enough intellectual converts to last for a generation (or more).

There is no single definition of participatory democracy or of the participatory community. Even in its most substantial modern forms it wears several faces; certain themes, however, are frequently invoked. Of course, one is the importance of face-to-face direct self-governance.[3] Another is the ideal of community as a public group, a group of citizens, each respected and heard, united by common purpose, encouraged by shared human sympathies.[4] Equality receives great emphasis, economic as well as political equality. The rationale is equal respect for the needs of all and the necessity of equality for authentic mutual deliberations.[5] And proponents of every version are confident that the result will be growth in individual self-determination and with it self-esteem. The community and the individual will advance together.[6]

The usual defining elements are also expressed in negative terms. In this case they include pointed complaints about selfish individualism in the modern, noncommunitarian world, where "possessive individualism" or "market rationality" rather than participation are ways of life. These are routinely condemned as a travesty of the goal of a communal "politics of altruism and collective interest."[7] Equally condemned in almost every version is the giantism prevalent in modern business and government, along with any other sign of denial of what Sale calls "politics on a human scale."[8]

Integral to participatory democracy, then, is small-group decision making which respects each person, ensures his or her essential equality, and strives to achieve a deep and intensive relationship among its participants—that is community. In such a vision participation is the very model of community and of political education.[9] The way Benjamin Barber describes the project is especially helpful: "At the heart of strong democracy is talk,"[10] he says, which gives life to "participatory deliberation and ongoing, public" communication.[11] It is a "process of ongoing, proximate self-legislation and the creation of a political community."[12]

The Case for Participatory Democracy

According to its eager proponents, the reasons one should reach for a participatory community are numerous and not necessarily mutually exclusive. A standard reason builds from the claim that direct democracy is integral to what it means to be a person and to live a significant, nontrivial life. It is somehow "natural because it is a necessary condition for, indeed is an essential manifestation of, a dignified human life."[13] It "has intrinsic value . . . because it is necessary for human maturation."[14] Or, it is vital for the central ingredient of life, authentic human freedom.[15]

Another reason supporters advance is their belief that participatory politics is the remedy for the moral and metaphysical drift that liberalism has bequeathed us. Some argue it will address the moral vacuum because participatory discussion is likely to develop community standards. Others argue that although participatory democracy needs no foundation of absolute truth, "it may be the political answer to the question of moral uncertainty."[16] Common decisions will be enough to operate a community well.

Such an analysis annoys some proponents of community because it is thin in its understanding of the needs of people and of community. People are seen as simple, rational discussants whose emotional depths and crosscurrents somehow disappear, and community can become little more than a debating society.[17] This is not a general view, but neither is it entirely mistaken. Perhaps the idea of community has always been something of a substitute (skeptics might say only a postponement) for metaphysics.[18]

A less problematic argument, though surely no less controversial, concentrates on individual development. Participatory democrats are almost invariably attracted to the cause of individual growth and are intrigued by its nature. They are resolutely convinced that a powerful means to its realization would be a participatory community. Carole Pateman is typical, consecrating the activity of citizens in direct self-government because, she contends, it increases their sense of personal competence and self-esteem and thus their participation.[19] Atypical about Pateman is her famous attempt to argue rather than proclaim this crucial linkage by presenting studies of the efforts of employee participation in a number of contexts to sustain her argument.[20]

Note that this popular idea, that direct participatory politics will increase human esteem, assumes the model person is active, energetic, self-confident, articulate, public—rather like the self-image of many intellectuals. This model of the good person is endlessly held up as the correct one. Indeed, at times it is lauded in a ritualistic manner suggesting its acceptance as a self-evident truth.[21]

None of these reasons for direct participatory politics necessarily connects immediately with community, but community is part of the thinking here, just not all of it by any means. For example, the bridge between individual development and community is to be found in what one learns (or, in how one develops as an individual), according to the participatory model. Among other things, one learns to be community-minded. The idea is that "the two terms *participate* and *community* are aspects of one single mode of social being: citizenship."[22] Participation is an education into a public, shared, social life. It transforms "dependent, private individuals into free citizens"— people of a community.[23] As participatory democrats articulate the goal, one can learn about others, their needs, and the broader social good beyond oneself through participation.[24] Meanwhile the increased self-esteem generated will allow one to reach out to these others. Thus participation also promises more social or communal harmony.

The case that participation is indissolubly fused with community is often made by empirical studies. Again, Carol Pateman has been the honored exemplar. She draws on a lengthy series of investigations and interprets them to back her claim that direct political decision making is an agent for community, for "enhanced group harmony and sense of co-operation."[25] Indeed, in general the case for participatory democracy comes armed with facts aiming to establish its empirical possibility and its attractions to a practical world. Although critics are skeptical, many participatory democrats insist that they be taken seriously on empirical grounds. They may be idealists, but they like to think that they are prepared to use the weapons of pragmatic Americans. Bowles and Gintis, for instance, argue at length that worker-run industries "are both more productive and give rise to higher levels of work satisfaction than capitalist-controlled firms." They make their empirical case and in the process underline the familiar approach.[26]

Three Faces of Participatory Community

Community is the goal of participatory democrats in many cases, if not the only objective, but there are really three faces to communi-

tarians who concentrate on this image of democracy. The first is the
visage that participatory democracy often wears today, despite its
flamboyant reputation—measured, chastened, alert to complexity and
argument. For example, community is central to the case for participatory politics in Jane Mansbridge's sophisticated discussion, *Beyond
Adversary Democracy*.[27] Mansbridge is characteristic in her selfcon-
scious sense of limits, her toned-down claims and enthusiasms. She
has, for instance, no expectation that participatory democracy is really
possible at a national level. In that realm it cannot generate a serious
sense of community and "the assumption of a common good"; there
are too many diverse interests.[28] Of course, she is much more hopeful
about possibilities for community (she calls them "unitary" possibilities) in small groups—especially work situations—in our nation. She
is sure that the results would be a marvelous experience as long as
community did not serve, as it would have to at a larger level, to
suppress conflict.[29] Her interesting case study of the young, committed workers at Helpline demonstrates the appeal of the workplace
community.[30] However, her study of the town meeting in "Shelby,"
Vermont, alerts her readers to the imperfect ideal that unitary, participatory politics can become if interests diverge and/or are not
equal.[31]

Consider the extensive and reflective explorations of Benjamin
Barber in *Strong Democracy*; he too invokes many a cautionary nod.
Although granting that any leadership in a participatory setting is
problematic, he confesses that one must simply accept the necessity of
leadership. Protests against this are beside the point to Barber, the
correct issue being simply what kind of leadership. Barber then considers the possible alternatives and concludes, perhaps predictably,
that leadership in its least authoritarian (and least authoritative) form,
what he describes as "facilitating" leadership, is the best. He contends
its great virtue is that it promotes the greatest group involvement and
decision making since its only purpose is to do precisely that. But
leadership it is, and we must frankly realize it.[32]

Or note Barber's retreat from language which a few years ago was
mandatory for those holding his views. He self-consciously distances
himself from a participatory model in the ancient sense of a "way of
life" and is explicitly hostile to the still more extravagant claim that

politics is *the* way of life.[33] Rather, participatory politics is "a way of living."[34] Although this distinction is not exactly self-evident, indeed it is downright murky, Barber's intended expression of chastened expectations is transparent.

Of course the self-restrained motif can end in subversion of the participatory ideal, and occasionally it does. Calls for a tough-minded communitarianism can turn out to be little more than the approval of a large, freely-taxing national government letting local communities have a say in how the money raised is spent.[35] This is not quite the participatory ideal in structure or in spirit. Yet, on the whole, chastened does not mean abandonment of the ideal, nor does use of the communitarian language always imply addiction to statism.

This conclusion, however, is not obvious to the second face of participatory politics today, a version often recalling the 1960s. It does so in its ideas and designs for participatory existence as a way of life and in its proponents' passion for participatory community, which is not as obvious in contemporary voices such as Jane Mansbridge's. Kirkpatrick Sale's *Human Scale*, for example, honors the spirit of this age by avoiding unrestrained architectonic impulses. Sale accepts the proposition that he must offer specific ideas in order to advance his desires. He would build as we all must build on something empirical: "No better guide has been found than the human form, no better means than the human scale."[36] But though this conclusion is coupled with claims that his plan "is far from being utopian" and is "practical and possible," one can hardly doubt that his deepest disposition is to dream.[37] Sale is obviously happiest when he breaks free from the conventional and designs utopias. He has, for example, two model societies, one of about five hundred people, the other of five to ten thousand, on which he has lavished great attention.[38] He is sure they will be practical: Coordination via "networking" with other communities is quite possible, he expects, and community control and democracy will expand production.[39]

Yet the larger point is that Sale is a reminder of the 1960s because he is so passionate a believer in the participatory ideal. In him the dream lives on, and it is by no means always kept hidden. From time to time, it is right there, out in front, not marred by even a trace of self-conscious apology. Thus Sale breaks into almost lyrical affirmations of what participatory politics would resemble and how it would transform us. We would metamorphose into supportive "participants and protagonists," "neighbors and lovers," "makers and creators."[40]

A quite popular genre of essays in support of participatory democracy derives from the small-group communities functioning today, communities sometimes originating in the 1960s, often considerably more recent, sometimes more or less permanent, sometimes not.[41] Authors of these books accent the highly positive: smiling (youthful) faces, tales of success, and announcements that these experiments in community are about "new people," about learning how to change fear, selfishness, and conflict into love, cooperation, and sharing.[42]

The aura of these books radiates excitement as their authors rejoice in all that community can do, can be, and in some cases has become— sometimes in unlikely places and circumstances.[43] Diversity (and comfortableness with that diversity) is a watchword in these experiments in community.[44] Other cited advantages include growth in personal spirituality, psychological strength, freedom, and empowerment. The list is long.[45]

Supporters of participatory community contend that a historical tradition of community (or communities) exists in the United States, though they rarely agree that it has been mainstream. Yet they are confident that modern communitarians need not carve their way out of a strange and totally hostile wilderness[46] and also that we have been learning progressive and positive things about community: that there must be a spiritual dimension or an acceptance of a reexamination of reflexive opposition to leadership under every circumstance.[47] Above all, there is a belief that the future looks good for community, that present seeds promise much fruit.[48]

This zeal for communitarianism is notable because even amidst the optimism are a good many words of caution. They do not cloud the visions or diminish the expectations, but they place them in a certain context, one might say a recognizably contemporary context. Explicit recognition that a tempered mood is appropriate for the community of today abounds. Above all, experience gives them pause. There are warnings that "communities are not utopias where life is always easy and joyful,"[49] and observations that the road to community is hard.[50] One hears explicit discussions of specific problems, dilemmas, conflicts that occur in participatory settings, for example, how to get idealists and realists, or thinkers and doers, to work together; or what to do with those who confuse community with dependence or with liberation from any work; or how to handle the frustration associated with too much work or too many meetings, activities which drove people from mainstream culture in the first place.[51]

A third face of participatory community is not entirely familiar: the face of populism. To locate populism in this context may seem puzzling. As an idea, populism has been associated with majoritarianism, sometimes in the negative sense of an unchecked and unthinking mob. Often connected with the Populist movement of late-nineteenth-century American history, its image as such has not always been good.[52] Contemporary intellectuals sympathetic to populism are sometimes distinguished by their heroes but more often by their emphasis on informal, grass roots, popular movements, regardless of their adherence to the more formal concepts/practices of participatory democracy.

Populism as part of the contemporary enthusiasm for participatory politics comes through two channels. One is historical: Populists often emphasize the people's rediscovery of their own and their nation's story, one which is partly the history of populism.[53] Considerable work on what we might call populist movements has been done. In the process E. P. Thompson, the English social historian, has been quite influential through his explication of popular protest movements in nineteenth-century Britain.[54] Thompson and other social historians sympathetic to popular movements have clearly influenced reinterpretations of the late-nineteenth-century American Populist movement.

As a result, American populists are no longer the mob of ignorant, anti-Semitic, country fanatics that their critics once saw. In some views, they have become concerned, active citizens, expressing "a remarkable democratic spirit," informed by "a broader vision of the common good,"[55] not at all in the service of the narrow, selfish interest of incompetent farmers. Lawrence Goodwyn's work has been especially important in this historical rehabilitation of American populists. His scholarship on Texas populism, detailed in its archival research and celebratory in its assessment, drives home a message about the achievements of Americans devoted to participatory community in our past.[56]

Today populist sympathizers sometimes reach far beyond the

farmers' revolts of the 1880s or 1890s to identify with larger parts of the American experience in the nineteenth century. Loyal to an older American vision, this is the fabled America of rural/small town life, one of community, local institutions, and direct democracy, not flawless but in many ways a participatory society (at least for white males).[57] De Tocqueville also described this world, though he did not think it so self-evidently attractive as its contemporary proponents believe. This is not the point, however, because populists invoke historical images of past Americas more to fault the present and to establish their legitimacy than to indulge in nostalgia. History is, as we have seen, a favorite weapon in the contemporary communitarian strategy.

Populist participatory community reaches American political thought today also through the channel of contemporary analyses. Populists such as the prolific Harry Boyte and his associates glowingly report on the outbreak of popular movements in concrete political situations—"spaces"—quite apart from theories of participatory government or traditional labels. Popular action and popular communities as they happen are their interest and their passion—journeys in the populist cast of participatory community. For some of its advocates ours can be a heady time. They see populism poking its head up everywhere, and so they judge it to be by far the largest movement toward democratic community in the United States today.[58] Wherever they look they can encounter populist activism, in rural communities, in neighborhood organizations, in citizen action groups on the state and local levels.[59] Each evidence underlines for populists their belief that participation must be a dynamic, grass-roots experience rather than a formal philosophy. Thus the interest in observing spontaneous outbursts of popular action and in savoring their potential: "participatory, egalitarian, and open character" for public life, "the heart of democratic movements."[60] Each allows another chance to affirm populist loyalty to the "potential of the ordinary person."[61]

Often less developed is the relationship between society on the local scale—people and experiments that contemporary populists welcome—and society on the larger scale. There is some reluctance, perhaps, to explore such a comparison. Yet the lesson of the populist movement in the late nineteenth century may be sobering in that the decision was made then to go past localism toward national action, a

national program, and a national party. To do so may have been necessary, but the movement did not survive.

It is also important to identify carefully just what populist-
oriented thinkers seek; goals can vary widely. For example, Goodwyn
is in love (it is not too strong to say) with the historic populists he
studied because they lived the kind of decentralized democratic community he favors above all else and because they sought to transform
the world through this model. They were a movement which sought to
be a community.[62]

Some other contemporary populists appear to be concerned first
for popular power, "empowerment" they call it.[63] To be sure, the local
and/or single-issue movements which populists respect have aspects
of community too. These communities, though, are more open and
loose bounded than many communities based on ideas of participatory
democracy and are less models than events, less communities than
sometimes short-lived experiences.[64] There are, in fact, many claim-
ants to populism in American political life, and self-declared populists
often are extremely generous in their use of the term, including almost
everything and every person they like.[65] Even a postmodern populism
now stresses feminism, holism, environmentalism, marching right in
step with the latest trends.[66]

By no means are all populists on the Left. People such as Goodwyn or Boyte belong on the Left because for them populism is not just
grass-roots democracy but egalitarianism in economic and political
terms. For other populists economic egalitarianism is not central, but
popular determinations of cultural practices and values are; and their
judgments, one suspects, would vary widely from those of a Goodwyn
or a Boyte. Both varieties of populism stress popular will, of course, but
the contexts are different. Populism is like existentialism and need
imply no particular agenda on policy, though it does routinely if
vaguely embrace community.

Populists on the left are, not surprisingly, extremely anxious to
discredit other contenders for their sacred word. According to some of
them, the use of "populism" by others, especially conservatives, turns
out to be an exercise in mystification and distortion. It amounts to
being a fraudulent scheme which lauds participatory power but carefully protects rule by the economic elites whom populists on the Left

see everywhere. Nor can it be taken to honor authentic community. More accurately, it is a scam allowing the entrenched economic elites to grab all they can while affirming the interests of community. Conservative populist movements, in short, turn out in practice to encourage "Powerlessness, Tinsel, and Greed."[67] In conservative hands populism represents a "static, narrow, and defensive" world, obsessed with "order and stability," dominated by reactionary impulses which strengthen vested economic elites.[68]

Such analyses raise persistent questions about populism (among other versions of community): What is the ideal that intellectual advocates are pursuing here? Is the goal community (variously conceptualized)? Is it a community which dependably (or conveniently) will generate politically correct policy outcomes? Or, is there any difference between a proper community, populist or otherwise, and one which is reliable as to policy? Indeed, the larger issue is whether populism's supporters seek it for democratic community or as a form of policy advocacy.

Arguments Regarding Participatory Democracy

Supporters of participatory community hardly live in a vacuum. They are part of the conversation, sometimes intense, over the attractions of community, particularly participatory community. No vision of community draws more criticism than participatory democracy today, and no advocates are more zealous in defense of their vision.

Yet participatory democrats can hardly ignore two major reservations. One is both normative and empirical in content, the other empirical alone. First is the query of why a democrat concerned for reflective and egalitarian participation in community decisions should find participatory democracy attractive. Put sharply, does participatory democracy guarantee a community that will be both too authoritarian and generally too tightly bounded?

This question arises often and with good reason. Behind it lies the fear that in participatory settings restraints on the exercise of power by the majority or those manipulating the group are few. Democracy, not to speak of an authentic community, can disappear in popular enthusiasms. Critics insist that individual rights must be guaranteed and

that considerable pluralism in any participatory community is a necessity.[69] They argue that such assurances are needed, moreover, not just
for protection but also for the freedom to develop the existential self.
There is plenty of unease that conformism in small communities can
starve the human spirit and mind, a cost too common in any tightly
bounded group. Thus communities must be open and pluralistic, but
this is not simple to accomplish. How much trust can one maintain
while also celebrating openness and development and pluralism?[70]
Applied to an economic form of participatory community the related
query asks what the limits and costs of egalitarianism will be. Critics
fear the worship of economic equality pursued in the name of community, which leaves less community than conformity and a lifeless,
unproductive economy. They wonder how many people want to have
the community of the poor.[71]

Also inextricably normative and empirical is the dilemma of authority in participatory community. Participatory democrats do not, as
a rule, like to think about authority, except to go on record as being
opposed to it. Authority and duty are concepts which do not capture
the libertarian (or the 1960s) spirit often infusing these discussions. It is
much more popular and characteristic to inveigh against the evils of
power and the concepts of "rule over," "totalism," and "unitary"
order.[72] However, declaring one's opposition to domination does not
really satisfy those who are uneasy about problems of power, much
less of authority, in participatory communities.

Authority and power are not likely to go away; to expect otherwise
is simply not credible in the light of human experience. Thus they have
to be dealt with by proponents of participatory community. Moreover,
they are needed in such a setting in order to promote such allied ideals
as economic equality or even political equality. Only the naive can
expect that sentiments of communal equality will bring everyone
along.

Some thinkers try harder than others to respond,[73] but the discussion of this concern is too modest. It is not enough to take a kind of high
ground and insist that no one except the perverse or mean spirited
could deny the concept of participatory community *as an ideal*.[74] Such
a stance betrays insufficient appreciation that problems of authority
and power may be inherent in the ideal itself.

Yet some able intellectuals do not wish away the challenges, such as Jane Mansbridge in her complex and atypically reserved analysis. True, Mansbridge does not wrestle directly and determinedly with the conundrum of authority in the participatory community, but she is acutely sensitive to related questions on the potential normative drawbacks of participatory politics. Thus although she is highly sympathetic to unitary democracy, she is so only when there is a unity incorporating shared interests. She knows that fraud can be practiced under the name of community or democracy, and she is not sympathetic when such a community masks conflicts, as is inevitable sometimes, or when equal representation is sacrificed.[75] Perhaps this makes Mansbridge no more than a qualified participatory communitarian. It is not her language when she sternly urges "adversary watchfulness" whenever conflicts exist (and always at the national level).[76] But such reservations do not alter where her heart is. They are just a response to normative anxieties about domination which she discovered to be empirically legitimate (if exaggerated) when she went into the field to study participatory democracies. The empirical side of her work fits nicely with the critique of participatory community that its enthusiasts must constantly address. Skeptics on all sides, including some who attach a certain, perhaps romantic, legitimacy to the ideal, have continually dismissed participatory community as impractical. The focus is always on practicality in terms of a large society; the dilemma is that a society small enough to be a community cannot simultaneously be big enough to be effective.

From one angle the practicality of participatory community does not fundamentally matter. Surely its normative status as an ideal can be defended in any case. But for the intellectual advocates of participatory community its viability matters enormously. After all, everything in America must eventually appear able to pass a pragmatic test, even if it obviously cannot, even if it probably should not. Thus these democrats make a major effort to meet objections and to fashion a practical case for participatory community.

The work of Carole Pateman and Benjamin Barber illustrates how legitimate this task is in participatory circles. It is crucial to them and they seize the opportunity.[77] They argue, for example, that participatory politics (incorporating workers' control) can pass tests in the real world because industrial experiments show that it has;[78] because considerable experience in Yugoslavia shows its empirical possibilities;[79]

because the neo-Hobbesian alternative of Western economic life works much less well, mired in waste, inefficiency, popular distaste—ironically all charges hurled at economic democracy.[80] We are offered a barrage of empirical and historical studies, or interpretations of them, to establish that this is a tough-minded and empirical approach strong enough to match any other.

The feasibility of the ideal is also questioned because of other problems in a major economy where coordination and consumer satisfaction will be essential. There is the issue of how to maintain a common defense in a modern age when a people's militia may not be quite enough. Advocates also have to confront those who charge that in practical terms participatory community is impossible because it faces an almost inevitable fate of degeneration into community-denying parochialism and closed-mindedness. In this context the reply that much good will come of "empathetic imagination, common talk, and common action" is debatable.[81]

Yet the range of practical difficulties acknowledged by participatory intellectuals can be broad. To illustrate, Goodwyn notes the challenges posed by race, ethnicity, religion, region, different histories, and the like. Each can derail popular communitarian dreams. Such awareness is of considerable value in Goodwyn's perception of the richness of actual human history. The respect many other participatory democrats have for these dimensions of human definition and history is uncertain. Participatory communities vary in how loose bounded a spirit their authors envisage for them.[82]

Roberto Unger, priest of the leftish critical legal studies movement, has expressed both sides of the participatory mood, first cautiously but now without restraint. He has long been a celebrant of "the experience of empowerment," absolutely sure that it will assist people as they reach for "love, faith, and hope."[83] He is also certain that self-assertion and conflicts will never entirely disappear and is confident that they can provide opportunities for communities to break through the blockade that stands in the way of resolution of differences and dilemmas.[84] His confidence in dialectical possibilities is real and has expanded sharply.

Until recently, Unger was also given to noting that wonderful as it is, community could threaten the individual and conflicts could damage community.[85] He agreed that the goal was to develop a system that brings together in theory and practice democratic community and the empowerment it promises with respect for individuals and their privacy. Although he declared "nothing is beyond" politics "inherently or forever," he considered guarantees for human respect essential.[86] He had to, since he believed that by "its very nature, community is always on the verge of becoming oppressive."[87] He proposed a sober choice, not for utopia, but for taking a risk to advance human fulfillment communally and individually.[88]

Of late, however, Unger has swung toward urging far greater risks. He now favors people's reaching toward freedom or liberation by their actively breaking down institutions and destroying existing contexts. He has turned to a sort of postmodern anarchism, a process which he insists will be a permanent necessity. Everywhere and always boundaries close in on one and perpetual smashing of them is essential.[89]

Though optimism sometimes leads some participatory communitarians to ignore doubts about such community, Unger seems more driven by desperation. He is frightened by the power of context, institutions, traditions, customs, and the like. They haunt him, and his fears suggest he has little confidence in people's ability to sort out their lives and their desires. No wonder Unger's latest direction is attacked as limited in its understanding (and appreciation) of people and their wants. Certainly his demands on people are great, complex, and perhaps contradictory: He wants kind and caring people who are militantly independent and who constantly change and upset the settled order in all things. Who will ever rest in his universe? And how would one fashion community?[90]

Debate and disagreement over conceptions of human nature are always the greatest stumbling block for participatory community. In truth, few advocates of such community do not believe that people are fundamentally sound and cooperative or that they can develop deep capacity for cooperation (and internal checks).[91] Often this judgment is literally a matter of faith for intellectuals who may seem—even to themselves—strangers to the twentieth century. Where others see pride, selfishness, or sin as integral to our century and our being, they stress hope and possibility in the language of psychological optimism, growth, and development.[92]

Neither simple declarations that participatory politics "posits the social nature of human beings in the world"[93] nor calls for "a temperate spirit" or for institutionalized ombudsmen[94] close the gap between the optimists of the participatory ideal and the skeptics; perhaps nothing really can. But as Eric Gorham reminds us the risk and dilemma of hope is to some extent present for most liberals or democrats, just as it was for Adam Smith and John Stuart Mill.[95]

Herbert Gans represents one effort to do the nearly impossible. He concedes the challenge of motivating people to enter politics and political institutions, indeed all institutions today. The goal must be, therefore, to bring political institutions to people if one seeks participatory politics. Gans proposes to make political institutions much more open, to create more lobbying opportunities, more pluralism in the media, more polling, anything and everything which might facilitate participation by lowering its costs.[96]

Still, reservations are appropriate about enthusiasm over the results of participation. "Empowerment does not unfold a magical process that immediately wipes away all human frailties." To say "empowerment," "local," or "decentralized" is not necessarily to say "democratic" or "effective."[97] Many of the doubts about participatory democracy have their historical origins in reactions to Hitler, to Stalin, and to the Holocaust and other events in the twentieth century which cast no good light on group political behavior. Nor have the studies of voting provided some observers with much inspiration.[98] No doubt it is useful to see the intimate connection between participatory communitarians and the optimism of the generation of the 1960s; but it is uncertain whether empirical and historical discussion can answer anything in this realm or whether we are in a world ultimately beyond their reach. Thus it is refreshing to encounter Benjamin Barber. He grants at once that there is inevitably an irreducible element of risk in his participatory goal. "Is it possible that you are wrong, that your vision of a common future omits contingencies or nurtures pathologies that will be *my* undoing? *Our* undoing?. . . There is no answer to this query."[99]

Economic Democracy

There is measurable awareness among participatory enthusiasts today that communities of political equality face structural realities which make their realization daunting.[100] The favorite example is the frustration associated with taming capitalism. This judgment goes hand in hand with the frequent perception that serious participatory democracy must apply directly to the economic institutions which are so much a part of people's lives. Especially for Left-leaning intellectuals a participatory community must include direct involvement in self-government by workers (employees) in decentralized work settings. Indeed, allegiance to such a view is a major article in the catechism of the contemporary American Left and has been since the late 1960s.[101]

As in Joshua Cohen and Joel Rogers's *On Democracy*, most versions of economic democracy endorse the usual features of the participatory ideal of democracy. They affirm civil and political liberties, maximum decentralization of decision making, emphasis on political, social, and economic equality, focus on a public perspective, and the value of common deliberation over goals.[102] What is particular is the extension of participatory democracy to economic (and other) institutions. For us the question is, what reasons are given for moving in this direction? How much is community the motive force here?

The questions are definitely relevant. There are economic democrats for whom economic democracy and decentralization are the means to a community-oriented society.[103] They want people to control all sides of their lives in a collective setting at as local a level as possible.[104] To leave out the workplace would be to split people's lives, not to fashion community.[105] For others community grows in "the revitalization of our mores and our public life."[106] Therefore, to bring economic life and economic institutions into a public forum makes it possible for people to think and act as a broad and encompassing community and to develop the skills for self-governance so necessary for free, democratic life. It speeds both democracy in action and education for democracy.

Some economic democrats argue that there need not be any cost in terms of standard of living.[107] Others suspect there may be real costs, but they are not necessarily upset that their system might—or would—reduce growth or even the GNP. As Michael Harrington remarks, the ultimate goal of (his) economic democracy is not a burgeoning GNP but a flourishing community.[108]

Thus community, though rarely community alone, is often a goal of economic democrats today.[109] Much more rarely, though, do advocates of economic democracy establish community as their principal end. There is no such agreement, a reality which can be obscured by the pleasant exhortations and affirmations some economic democrats offer. In fact, community is often not quite the point for economic democrats. Community may receive praise and, though frequently undefined, be one of the benefits promised. Yet other goals can crowd the picture. It is not at all unusual to hear economic democracy lauded for its eminently practical benefits, for what it can accomplish— increased production, improved working conditions, or smoother labor-management relations.[110] At a philosophical level, many economic democrats are clearly more engaged by something else: justice. Economic justice is what they want, a goal they interpret as the achievement of a highly egalitarian economic and social system. The point is not that such justice-seeking intellectuals reject community, but that its allure is often secondary to them. Problems such as social meaning, relationships, and cohesion do not escape them, but they frequently skirt the psychological, not to say spiritual, analyses that are absolutely central to engagement with the ideal of community. They prefer to summon people to economic justice.

Two rather contrasting examples are the arguments of C. B. MacPherson and Robert Dahl. The late C. B. MacPherson, long associated with economic democracy, was a combative critic of the limitations of Western democracy and an admirer of the putative evidences of democracy in non-Western Marxist regimes. He was not, however, an assertive disciple of community. MacPherson stressed instead issues of equality, especially economic equality. He also had ideas about the kind of citizens he wanted in society, and he knew what kind of spirit he did not want in his citizens. His famous and influential critique of possessive individualism, the rapacious and unconnected individualism which he contended dominates liberal, capitalist societies, is strong testimony here.[111] But nowhere does he really concentrate on community. And MacPherson's assurances to the contrary, merely making a democracy into "an equal human society" does not address those whose major goal is community.[112] What it does do, though, is reaffirm what MacPherson is all about: economic equality.[113]

Thus for MacPherson the standard for democracy was never its success as a community, just as community was not a normative goal.

MacPherson faults Western liberal democracy not because it falls short of his ideal of community but because it is interconnected with the capitalism he hates and the economic inequality he intensely opposes.[114]

MacPherson seriously entertained use of the word "democratic" for Marxist states because he associated democracy with equality. Never mind MacPherson's embarrassing ignorance of the inequality in these nations; the point is his definition of democracy. Of course, he knew that his view met rejection from those whose conceptions of democracy have something to do with popular rule, majority decision, or the like. But even here MacPherson was so anxious to promote the legitimacy of economically egalitarian states that he argued one-party states could still satisfy democratic standards if they had at least some intraparty democracy.[115] MacPherson defended the larger philosophical point that ends are what matter. He then concluded that third-world, one-party states and other forms of authoritarian rule can be democratic, for if governors enact what the people want, all is well—especially if what they want is an anticapitalist economic equality.[116] In any case, there is no invocation to community here.

What is most intriguing about an economic democrat such as Robert Dahl is his openly acknowledged disinterest in community.[117] His brand of economic democracy is unambiguous in its goals: economic equality, and through it, political equality to achieve economic justice and other equalities which permit human development and liberty. Not for Dahl any sentimental affirmations of community as a human teleology or primary social goal.[118]

Dahl is quite explicit that many other democrats are not to be taken seriously in their conceptions of democracy, including the usual participatory democrat and the republicans. For Dahl they are essentially romantics and lack concrete agendas for the realization of their often proclaimed ideals.[119]

Dahl is no socialist or socialist communitarian either. Socialism's record does not impress him, certainly not in the increasingly messy Yugoslavia, once the favorite of earnest participatory democrats. He finds the answer in an affirmation of popular involvement at all levels of government and in the extension of democratic governance to private business. Such a move will not only enable political democracy to be equal but will also bring under the rubric of democracy the enormously important economic realm. The result will not necessarily be community, but it will be democracy as far as Dahl is concerned.[120]

He first developed this understanding of democracy forty years ago. Wondering about workers' control, he concluded that perhaps modern interdependency made the goal elusive and energetically insisted that socialist democracy must be about a good deal more than planning. Now he has come back to the idea that workers' involvement is essential, though not for some soft ideal of community.[121]

Socialism's modern enthusiasts also favor equality, yet they can be equally sympathetic to the language of liberty. This is certainly true, for instance, in the rewarding work of Bowles and Gintis. They reject liberalism, to be sure, but they do so in good part in the name of a full liberty, not in the name of a socialist community. Liberty, as they understand it, requires ending economic dependence to the maximum possible extent. Because capitalism (or any other weakly controlled or mediated economic system) allows such dependence it must be attacked for the liberty-denying agent it is. The same applies to patriarchal authority wherever it still casts its shadow. It breeds dependence, denies liberty, and thus impedes viable community.[122]

Beside liberty marches community. Liberty is, for Bowles and Gintis, a precondition for community, as are economic equality in and popular rule over economic institutions. Liberty will assist people in discovering their essential beings, their social and communal natures, whose fulfillment in turn will expand practical liberty and actual community. The hope and the expectation is that in the end both liberty (though not the liberty to exploit others economically) and community will expand together.[123] With this analysis in mind, one should note the important voices on the American intellectual Left for whom the socialist dream must, finally, usher in community.[124]

Accent on justice also finds expression in Michael Walzer's splendid *Spheres of Justice*,[125] widely discussed and admired in our time. Walzer is something of a pluralist and a liberal, something of a participatory democrat and Jewish communitarian, something of an economic democrat and socialist. His primary emphasis is not the consecration of a society of participatory politics or economic equality or anything else quite so simple. He articulates a far more complicated justice than what he patronizes as "simple equality." What he has in mind is that we honor alternative conceptions of justice depending strictly on the realm of life. In short, he is a pluralist regarding justice. Not that just any view is acceptable; in every instance and in every sphere the case for what would be justice must be argued, and Walzer does so.[126] The pluralistic result, as he molds it, is fascinating and impressive as his discussion roams over education, leisure, welfare, the justice of gifts, citizenship, and much more.[127]

Walzer insists that what is appropriate justice in each arena must depend in part on concrete culture and history (here he skates close to traditionalists). Justice is not an abstract philosophical question that one can pursue outside of a particular culture or history or a specific sphere. Thus grand theorists of justice from Plato to John Rawls are no heroes to him.[128]

He brings the same reservations to the ideal of a participatory democratic community with which he has often been associated. He is sympathetic to the ideal as he conceives it; for him the ideal must be seriously devoted to real politics. Thus he is not vulnerable to the accusation haunting some participatory communitarians, that of being nonpolitical or antipolitical.[129] Walzer's model incorporates conflict, disagreement, dialogue within his community to bring about the realization of politics. And yet for him this ideal, though just, is limited since justice varies by sphere. Participatory community cannot and should not override the plurality of spheres and their particular understanding of justice; that is exactly what tyranny is about. Participatory community must be sensitive to the possibility of casual or arbitrary exercise of power, which for Walzer is a warning most applicable to the populist and to "push-button participation."[130] Neither justice nor democracy nor community is about some superficial majority rule.

The absence of a neat guide as to "where to put the fences; they have no natural [abstract right] location" does not mean there should be no fences; Walzer argues that there should always be many fences.[131] The different spheres, degrees, modulations result not in a cardboard participatory vision but in the modern vision, circumscribed but also very much alive in modern American communitarian thinking. Walzer's ideas may offer a summary of where participatory thinking has arrived today. Certainly he is a peerless articulator of the communitarian ideal.

Chapter Five

The Republican Community

The republican image of community has become a major factor in current discussions among political intellectuals. Proclaimed by some as "a rare and delicate achievement,"[1] its popularity suddenly accelerated in the 1980s. In some scholarly settings it even left behind the once dominant legacy of the 1960s, the participatory model of community. By no means has republicanism seized the entire field in American political thought. But what once began as a somewhat arcane historical study has blossomed into a subject attracting sociologists, philosophers, and other self-conscious political intellectuals.

Although impressions of republican community come in assorted shapes, republicans share a vision of a polity where the common good rules and public concerns triumph over the goals of the self-interested individual. The ideal is a place where citizens are united in public action and public spiritedness, reinforced by a rough equality, common respect, and basic human virtues, above all where "disinterested regard for the welfare of the whole . . . *civil virtue*," holds sway.[2] The threat to achieving and sustaining this kind of community in republican eyes is ever present. Forces of human and social corruption, most of all self-interest grown out of control, loom over the good community permanently. Good government means in large part defeating corruption so that the common good may reign.

Republicans also share a sense that this sort of community once flourished in our country (or now has a chance to do so) and sometimes see their work as an effort to recreate conditions in which our good past could be reborn. Thus they do not visualize their project as utopian (yet practical) so much as a movement toward rebirth in the American context. "If American society is to weather the . . . remainder of the present century, shared meanings and ideals must be rearticulated and reassessed. . . . The reconstitution of a genuine national political society requires widespread participation in working out a more explicit moral understanding of citizenship . . . that is embodied in the life of the citizen . . . reforging a language of political discourse that can articulate the . . . common good."[3]

The classicus locus of republicanism is the Founding age of the United States, the moment of glory, not to say nostalgia, for republicans. The central historical questions are, first, how much did republican themes influence the Founders and thus the decisive moment in American political thought? And second, where did these republican themes come from?[4] Are they traceable to the civic republicanism of Machiavelli, the Greek classics, the eighteenth-century Scottish Enlightenment, or to the ideas of commonwealth dissent in English thought in the seventeenth and eighteenth centuries?[5]

The answers are contested and controversial, but even observers who acknowledge that the Framers had many vocabularies and drew on a multitude of traditions can agree that republican themes were powerful and evocative in America's origins as a nation.[6] Michael Lienesch, who has studied the political thought of the Founding period in detail, is a good case in point. He argues that unquestionably there were complex views among political actors of the time which cannot be categorized simply. Yet he claims that a good part of the diversity was represented by republicans. He understands that they had their own disagreements about how to deal with America in the 1780s as it faced crisis and corruption, but that does not alter the fact that republicanism was a major factor in the intellectual setting of both that age and subsequently.[7]

Part of the consideration of republicanism consistently involves reflecting on its pre-American roots. The connections among republican ideas in eighteenth-century America, the tradition of the West, and the contemporary United States become an important matter for investigation. The result usually is the perception that our Constitution is a dramatic point in a long history, the history of "the tradition of civic humanism," which in some forms "dates back more than two millennia."[8]

Within the context of the study of republicanism in the intellectual history of the West, J. G. A. Pocock has been the chief pioneer of the revival of interest in republican community. Pocock's leadership in studying republicanism and the interconnections between its European past and American practice has proceeded largely through the medium of rather esoteric academic scholarship, debates, and conferences, above all through his masterpiece, *The Machiavellian Moment: Florentine Political Thought and the Atlantic Republican Tradition* (1975). He insists that his approach is not meant as advocacy; he is the scholar only.[9]

Pocock's analysis of Western thought escapes easy summary or quick synthesis; *The Machiavellian Moment* is too dazzling a book for that. It is in good part a study of Machiavelli's and others' ideas about the good community in sixteenth-century Italy. But Pocock, anchored as he is in scholarship, has a normative message for us that is far more straightforward than one might expect, given his disclaimers. Pocock leaves his readers with the unmistakable impression that if we were wise the United States would select (aspects of) Machiavelli over Locke, that we would select the goal of political community by a citizenry committed to public participation and a common good—to public virtue. Such a community would be vigilant in detecting the corruptions of self-interest that are in constant dialectic with public virtue in every society and every person.[10] Indeed, "the confrontation of virtue with corruption" is the essential "Machiavellian moment." For the republican it constitutes the supreme challenge to any living political community.[11]

The republican view is committed to the primacy of politics as opposed to nature, the more characteristic standard, perhaps, in Anglo-American political thought. Citizenship, politics, and rational interaction are the esteemed basis for a vigorous community, one which nature does not really afford. The alternative is traditional American liberalism, which in Pocock's view wrestled away the promise of American community from the republican ideal as early as the adoption of our Constitution. The fatal move came in the substitution of interest for virtue in society, a surrender of any serious political community to selfishness and self-interested groups. To be sure, the shift was never complete in our historical journey; Locke did not totally abolish Machiavelli. Concern with virtue and its counterpart, corruption, continued through American political life, but the shift was substantial and decisive.[12]

Pocock, of course, is hardly the sole participant in the conversation about republicanism today. There are a host of students and/or advocates of republicanism currently engaged in vigorous interpretation (and reinterpretation) of American history in the light of this lost ideal. It is clearly true that "historians now are falling over themselves in their attempts to discover republicanism in American history."[13] Other thinkers concentrate on arguing for republican community without much historical fuss. An avalanche of literature on republicanism is generating a busy counterindustry of criticism against the new republican orthodoxy.[14]

The list of prophets who went before Pocock but met only wilderness is long. For example, Gordon Wood identifies the followers of Leo Strauss as a worthy example of early discoverers of the republican strain in the Founding Era. Wood faults Straussians for tending to banish or reduce self-interest, historical circumstances, and chance from the Founding story in the process, but their insight was real—and their contribution might have been influential.[15] More to the point, it is Wood himself who has produced in his magisterial *Creation of the American Republic 1776–1787* the unsurpassed substantive historical achievement, the great work on republicanism within our own history. Chapter three of this work considered his book, but we need to understand that debate continues to swirl around his work as it remains a kind of center for the entire discussion about republicanism, community, the Founders, and our era.[16]

Wood is fully convinced that there were no clear-cut choices in our early national period (e.g., liberalism over republicanism); matters were hardly that simple. Alternative ideas were definitely present and frequently mixed together in different people, places, and times in a complex, not to say bewildering, manner. And if perhaps varieties of republicanism were the dominant intellectual tradition, there was also plenty of evidence of liberal, enterprising, self-interested behavior. This is far from any neat picture regarding the Founding Era, but it is what Wood finds.[17] Yet he concludes that republicanism suffered a major defeat in the writing and adoption of the United States Constitution. That act was something of a swan song, in fact, for this disposition in American political thought. The Constitution's authors abandoned belief in the possibility of the disinterested community, and the Anti-Federalists, who held on to more of the republican ideal, did not win in the struggle over the Constitution or later on in American history.[18]

Wood lets the proverbial chips fall where they may and is consistently dispassionate in his approach. Still, no reader can doubt his republican sympathies or that many other laborers in the republican vineyard are advocates as well as analysts. In some cases, their normative biases do not show, though certainly in others they do, for better or for worse. And there is little pretension to disinterestedness in other realms where republican community is on the agenda. Doubtless, a considerable part of the impetus for reexamining the Founders is political, to attack liberalism and encourage republican values.[19] For now, though, I wish simply to demonstrate the considerable interest in studying republicanism at the time of the Founders.

Lance Banning, for example, in his measured assessment of the evidence of the Founding Era, finds a substantial presence of republican ideas. Republicanism, he argues, was a part of the perspective of the authors of the Constitution, not just of their Anti-Federalist opponents. Certainly it was a significant part of Madison's view, despite his reputation as one who spurned republicanism as unrealistic when he composed much of the Constitution. Not surprisingly, Banning discovers a Madison who was far from the national centrist he is sometimes portrayed to be and who was much more sensitive to local and state communities or governments than even his contemporary critics imagined.[20]

An example of more open and ardent republican sympathies may be found in Russell Hanson's compendious and yet trenchant *Democratic Imagination*. Hanson deftly courses through American political thought in search of a community-focused democracy. In his treatment of the Founders he assertively seeks to corral them for the cause of republicanism. In his analysis they were republicans, including James Madison, whom Hanson renders as far from being a liberal pluralist. Hanson's study is sophisticated, and it also appears to be in the service of recognizably republican goals.[21]

Recent work suggests that republican ideas have even more legitimacy in the American story than might derive only from association with (or against) the Founders. Republican ideas are now found extending far beyond the formulation and adoption of the Constitution. Drew McCoy has drawn the picture of a republicanism much alive in the Jeffersonian period of American life, and Lance Banning has focused quite specifically on the continuing presence of republican ideas into this era.

Banning appreciates that republicanism was hardly triumphant in the early nineteenth century. There were recognizably liberal values at work then; individualism and private property were integral along with considerable enthusiasm for commerce and industry. Nonetheless, plentiful republican sentiment existed also, especially fear of greed, of financial corruption, and an uneasiness and tension about public versus private communities.[22] Wood's view as to where the break with republican community came is perhaps correct, but it is incorrect to think that it was a total break. Republican ideas lasted well beyond the Constitutional debates.[23]

There are also critical readings of republican history, usually by those who are not known for their own republican inclinations. Nineteenth-century republicans, for instance, can emerge as a predictably mixed lot. According to their critics, some of them can quite fairly be associated with ugly outbursts of nativism, racial and ethnic discrimination, and assorted crusades to promote a narrow American homogeneity. The republican concern for the common good often veered in a nonpluralist direction.[24]

It has also been noted that republicanism was often silent or at least underdeveloped in its political economy; what little there was though revealed no particular interest in egalitarian or social democratic concerns. Moreover, the same critical argument contends that models of classical republican community offer nothing which should satisfy social democrats. Classical community was very much about economic master and workers or master and slaves, not just in Athens but also in eighteenth-century America and thus not a desirable community at all.[25]

Republicanism, however, has now moved beyond its limited and limiting borders of the politics of history. Perhaps the most discussed example is *Habits of the Heart* by sociologist Robert Bellah and his associates. For Bellah republicanism is not only the approved category from the American past; it is also frankly his aspiration for public community for the present—participatory, public, committed. With this objective in mind he writes not on history but on contemporary American society.[26]

Bellah edges close to but does not quite embrace the dominant mood among the republicans, what I would call "Left republicanism." As with other conceptions of community, Left republicanism is in good measure a safe harbor from which critics venture to try to sink modern liberalism. Characteristic complaints include liberalism's alleged antipathy to the reality of social life: "Civic republicanism denies the liberal notion that individuality exists outside of or prior to social relationships";[27] liberalism is ambivalent regarding citizen participation as reflected in elitist liberal democratic theory and institutions;[28] and, of course, there is the discontent over liberalism's inability to promote a public consciousness.[29]

Indeed, it is public consciousness that a republican such as William Sullivan cares most about, and it must be a public community with a certain Burkean touch. Unlike many participatory democrats, Sullivan emphasizes that community must be rooted in time, in place, and in shared values. Community must be woven with specifics of actual lives; only then is it valuable and viable. There "can thus be no public philosophy in general but only specific, historically conditioned public philosophies."[30] In fancier language what is needed, Sullivan argues, is "a framework of institutionalized norms establishing and sanctioning the conditions of reciprocity."[31]

As Jeffrey Lustig outlines what looks like the republican goal, such connections must involve the supremacy of public concern, perceived mutuality, and interdependency, a notion both moral and psychological and substantiated by human and institutional experience.[32] More straightforwardly, community rests on publicly demonstrated commitment to one's fellows: "As citizens we make an unlimited promise to show care and concern to each other."[33] For Left republicans this commitment requires a repudiation of capitalism, at least in spirit. The need for a democratic economy is almost always taken for granted, though this does not mean any warmth toward state socialism. Minimally the objective often includes support for increased worker participation and a national economic policy oriented to the public interest rather than toward profit or private property.

The case is made in republican language rather than in the language of nineteenth-century European socialists. American republicans do not appear to identify with European socialist tradition; they prefer to speak of matters of political economy (insofar as they refer to it at all) in terms of public community and the common good. Concepts such as "justice" or "equality" or "worker control," the familiar vocabulary of the socialist tradition, are not so often heard. The difference is substantial. It appears among Left republicans in their emphasis on the community spirit of the democratic economic order they seek and on control rather than on ownership in that order. Their objective is an economic order for the common good and in expression of the common community as they undertake to break the selfish bonds of liberalism. More often than not, it is seen as a vital, practical task which has nothing to do with a giant crusade for an abstract socialism.[34]

If republicans seek rooted, historical people in local political communities, they also try to promote a national public philosophy. Its heart is really an attitude of inclusive public caring. Achieving such a national disposition would not be quite the same thing as the realization of a national community, an elusive possibility for a republican such as William Sullivan. The best communities will never be national, as the Anti-Federalists long ago warned the nation builders who wrote our Constitution. Other hopes are too abstractly idealist for the many republican intellectuals who visualize themselves as rather practical souls, historical by temperament and political by instinct. Platonism and republicanism have little in common.[35]

On the whole, intellectuals attracted to republicanism, including those I have called Left republicans, are not notably radical. They possess neither a theory of historical revolution nor, on the other hand, the philosophical alienation from history which might encourage radicalism. Thus, although they frequently think we are far from our republican roots in the United States, they doggedly insist we are not hopelessly lost.[36] We do not, after all, have to journey to new intellectual or historical worlds to encounter the republican example; we need merely travel back to our own best traditions.

Problems

Of course, the enthusiasm for republicanism as a rallying point among community-oriented intellectuals runs into some problems rather quickly. The question arises of how accurate their readings of American political history are. No one can ignore the clear republican influences present, especially in our Revolutionary age. However, critics are inclined to point out the exaggerations present in many sweeping republican analyses.

It is hard to evaluate the extensive debate over the republicanism of the Founders in that a good portion of the discourse is offered as technical historical argument. The issues turn frequently on different readings of the same evidence or on varying methodologies or concepts. At the same time in the background lies the larger issue, the relevance of republican values. If the discoverers of these values in the Founding Era are by no means always simply neutral analysts, the same may be even truer of skeptics. Concerns about values and political agendas hover over much of this argument without a doubt.

In chapter three I noted the work of historian Joyce Appleby and her argument that liberal values which considerably encouraged economic development in a capitalist mode were very much a part of the Founders' framework. She resists, for example, the claim that Madison was a familiar republican. In doing so, she joins a debate where much is at stake, since Madison, as the principal author of the Constitution, is the crucial real and symbolic figure in the discussion about community and our Founding. To Appleby, Madison may have been a republican, but not in any recognizably classical form. The truth is he wanted a society far more in the developmental mode, directed toward economic growth, economic enterprise, and the promotion of science and invention, and the encouragement of great personal freedom.[37]

Appleby is by no means alone in her conclusions. Wood, for example, has attracted critics who are distinctly hostile to capitalism. For them the Constitution was a disaster since it allegedly facilitated the triumph of capitalism. From this angle Wood should have been much more critical of the Founders than he is. The Constitution lost the dream of the proper community, and Wood is too admiring of those who took this fateful step.[38]

Everyone has an assessment. Some take the opposite tack and fault Wood for underrating the republican influence on the Constitution.[39] Others hold the more common view, though, and see the Constitution as the defeat of republicanism (and are often unhappy

about it), an analysis that receives sweeping support in a rather different mode in the work of Robert Webking. He pushes matters much
further by denying that republican ideas were dominant even at the
Revolution. He finds that the Revolution was about liberty and individual rights, not about republican community or the development of
republican character.[40]

Some mount an all-out attack on the republican history (and
ideal), as does John Patrick Diggins in *The Lost Soul of American
Politics*. Although Diggins's argument is somewhat scattershot, his
intention is to convince us that the republican version of our history is
wrong because it always exaggerates the sway of republicanism in the
United States at any given time. The reality has been the cultural power
of Locke and the belief in self-interested individualism. America was,
as Louis Hartz long ago claimed, born liberal. Diggins acknowledges
the Founders used the language of virtue and other republicans words,
but it was all talk (though selectively used talk—no republican language is in the Declaration of Independence). Thus we never developed a real definition of virtue or the public good. Republicanism
in our story has been lost rhetoric.[41] Moreover, according to Diggins,
all signs of republicanism were in steep decline by the era of the
Constitution—and thereafter. Even the rhetoric disappeared as issues
of authority, faction, interest, and control came explicitly to the fore.
Questions of self-interest, its promotion, and the checks to preserve it
became central in word as they had long been in deed.[42]

Diggins also protests that republican-inclined intellectuals do not
help their cause by these too imaginative historical recreations. They
dangerously mislead Americans about our historical background,
which has little to offer in terms of republican community or of any
model of community. He demands that his readers face this fact and
not try a romantic reification of a nonexistent American tradition of
community.

Diggins prefers to reiterate how liberal a culture we are and have
been. His reason is not out of sympathy for some socialist or other left
view, nor is he a defender of liberalism. Diggins wants us to see our
Locke-ness, not to celebrate it or to replace it with Marx. Instead, he
wants us to understand how great the chasm is that we must leap in
order for our society to reach what Diggins considers the only secure

place: religion—Christian religion and values—the foundation Diggins favors. In his mind, American political thought has lacked these values, despite occasional countermoments. They alone could be the source for the forgiveness and compassion that might enable community to flower in America.[43]

From a different perspective and in a more tempered mood, Forrest McDonald shares Diggins's doubts about our republican tradition. He acknowledges the republican side of our Founding, though he admonishes us that republicanism came in several forms which reflected significant intellectual, regional, social, and economic variations. He argues that we must resist broad generalizations about republicanism. McDonald insists we must also recognize the influence in the Founding period of the Scottish Enlightenment, of Locke, of assorted British legal traditions, and of those men such as George Washington whose minds were moved less by ideas than by practical considerations. Republicanism was hardly the whole story of the Founding Era.[44]

Another determined critique, and a sharp one, comes from Thomas Pangle, a self-conscious student of the classical tradition in the tradition of Leo Strauss. His approach is an all-out assault on the theses of the republicans. To Pangle modern republicans are intellectuals "captivated by a romantic longing to discover, somewhere in the past" a "prebourgeois and non-Lockean" American.[45] Their favorite hunting ground, the Founding period, presents far leaner game than they would imagine. Their republicanism is a hodgepodge of ideas, really notions, which fit together far more coherently in the hands of their skilled intellectual weavers now than they did at the time of the Revolution or the Constitution. Ideas from Machiavelli, Aristotle, Sparta, and numerous other thinkers and places do not constitute a coherent view and can be made to do so only by major distortions.[46] There simply was no distinct republican tradition two hundred years ago, certainly not one resembling the aspirations of its contemporary advocates.

Machiavelli was not a distinct source for republicanism, despite the assertions of Pocock and his admirers. Machiavelli's views had much in common with the Lockean values in the Declaration of Independence; no wonder nobody then thought he represented a distinct tradition. There is and was much "harmony between the new Machiavellian republicanism and the liberal economic and political thought of Locke," a fact then "well understood."[47]

Efforts to equate the republicanism of the Founding with the classical philosophy of ancient Greece, the world of Plato and Aristotle, did not work either; matters were too complicated for this kind of simple-minded equation. The Founders did follow in classical footsteps in emphasizing virtue, but they saw virtue as a means to all sorts of ends, including personal happiness, security, prosperity. Classical conceptions are a study in contrast. Virtue was an end in itself, one associated with the soul, justice, and the search for truth. One era stressed means, the other ends; one honored the mundane and the material, the other the intellectual and the philosophical.[48] And, after all, Pangle insists, when we think of the Founders we remember properly natural rights, hardly a perspective known in classical thought.[49]

In short, Pangle dismisses claims that the Founders had a coherent republican outlook and denies that the republican strands of their thought can be tied to Machiavelli or the classical understandings of community. On the other hand, he is not persuaded by Diggins's effort to resuscitate the Christian or Calvinist roots of the Founders; another dead end. Diggins's skepticism about republicanism at the Founding is well taken, but his alternative flies in the face of the scant Calvinist/Christian side of many Founders.[50]

One might assume the same fate would befall the famous interpretation argued by Louis Hartz in his formidable *Liberal Tradition in America*.[51] Certainly, Pangle is alternately contemptuous of and exasperated with Hartz. He faults Hartz in part because he misunderstands Locke. Hartz correctly drew the Founders as Lockean liberals focused on natural rights, individual liberty, and consent of the governed, not as republican advocates of community, but he did not discuss Locke's religious side or his views on community, which are necessarily part of a richer picture of Locke. This limitation is part of Hartz's persistent blindness to the dimension of community in American political thought, in Locke, in the Founders, or in general. Still, Pangle does not propose to reject Hartz, far from it. How could he? After all, Hartz may not have gotten Locke fully right, but this does not vitiate Hartz's basic insight: America is more about Locke than anything else.[52]

Pangle's complaint, when all is said and done, is that republicanism is a species of intellectual nostalgia fed by a make-believe version of our nation's political origins. He joins with other skeptics who are tired of those who conveniently find republican moments in American experience. Pangle joins Diggins, among others, in concluding that these discoveries are mostly exercises in nostalgia, distant from more sober and less romantic historical judgments.[53]

One may ask how relevant such historical considerations are. After all, the basic issue is the normative attractiveness today of republican community, not its role in the American past. This is a fair query, though it overlooks the republican desire to show their ideal's historicity as part of their argument for republican community. Perhaps other reservations are more to the point. Finding, fostering, and maintaining common ground is a much more formidable enterprise than denouncing capitalism or ridiculing liberalism.[54] Given human selfishness, it will be a challenge to instill this ethic of citizenship in people through education. Yet republicans sometimes neglect the problems of civic education and the plan to nurture a republican mentality within the citizenry. The challenge is to fashion a broader sense of a common good in a resistant culture, a challenge that cannot be met by reflections on the republican elements in Machiavelli or in the United States Founding.

Appreciation of that challenge lies behind the interest in a reconstitution of youth national service, perhaps a means to a more public-regarding citizenry.[55] Others express interest in leadership and what sort of positive role it might play in the process.[56] Its civic potential might be great as long as it is distinguished from the bane of republicanism, the politics of competition among interest groups, pathological in its teaching of self-interest and the wrong kind of civic norms.[57]

Even if advocates of republicanism succeeded at some point in advancing their attitudes among the larger populace, national (or international) public attitudes must fit with the localist and even participatory side of republicanism. It is not for a minute obvious that citizens with a public orientation in one local area will or necessarily could agree with their counterparts in another place. Yet to weed out such local republicanism would be to strip away much of the democratic side and, in a substantive sense, much of the dimension of community in republicanism.

On the other hand, fiercely localist republicans might become, as Jean Elshtain warns, dangerous.[58] Decentralized, community-oriented republicanism may encourage excessive conformity in local settings, which should give us pause. Benjamin Barber is fond of participatory democracy, as we know, but he dislikes what he calls "the republic nostalgia," sometimes motivated by the inclination toward a unitary politics that lays claim to the human soul and pretends to express men's "higher nature."[59] Barber might easily have identified this approach with more than a few advocates of republicanism who are very much alive; he discreetly links it with the safely dead—Hannah Arendt and Leo Strauss.[60]

Another objection contends that modern republicanism is more a method or a mindset than a substantive outlook about the good community or anything else. It always involves invocations to the public good and supports open, public deliberation from which its proponents hope a public good will (somewhat mysteriously) emerge. Yet John Diggins argues that republicanism "remains morally empty." It affirms no truths beyond those needed for its operation, what we might call process virtues.[61] Lacking a definition of the public good in general and in particular, it is thus impoverished at its center. Though it often comes in the garments of ancient Greece, Renaissance Italy, or Revolutionary America, it has the look of a modernist doctrine which appeals to (and is the creature of) skeptical modern intellectuals.

Efforts to delineate what substantive values republicanism implies are overdue. Patriotism, for example, is intimately connected with historical republicanism. What does this concept mean in late twentieth-century republicanism? John Schaar led the way here some years ago in his reflections on patriotism as a basic concept.[62] Recent endeavors such as those by Mary Dietz to explore what a republican theory of patriotism might encompass or what republican citizenship and feminism might offer each other are welcome steps in this direction.[63] Though the journey may be a long one, through it we should be able to discover what republicans are all about, what they share. We also need to know whether as an idea republicanism contains any serious doctrine of mutual obligation or if it is just loose sympathy for community.[64]

One might also ask whether republican community is a bloodless version of community. It honors political relationships, but it has been weak in addressing the more personal communities of the heart (home, family, religion) that people have placed first everywhere and at all times. In this view the republican vision with its stress on public community is curious in that it sometimes neglects (or is hostile to) many citizens' deepest yearnings (an irony which is not at all just a product of a liberal culture). Republicans proudly claim to be realistic, practical, and historical. Yet the demand they face most immediately is to develop and defend a conception of human beings which coincides with both republican hopes and human practices.

Fraternity

It is with these considerations in mind that we examine Wilson Carey McWilliams's achievement in *The Idea of Fraternity in America*. [65] McWilliams is very much a part of the republican tradition, yet he is so from a distance, not one of the advancing phalanx, not quite a member in good standing in the current phase. He proceeds in his own impressive way.

As with other republicans, McWilliams's analysis is richly grounded in historical discourse and reflection. His book is a cornucopia of (not necessarily brief) essays on all sorts of thinkers, ideas, and eras in American history. It sprawls; it wanders; it enlightens; it argues. What holds the enterprise together is McWilliams's search in our history for a tradition of community he favors and which he chooses to call "the idea of fraternity." For him "fraternity" is a sense of trust, of common purpose, of common respect, a sense of connection among the citizenry.

For McWilliams this ideal is not only about localism, or public institutions, or a public philosophy, or anything so specific or focused. It is a matter of the spirit, of feelings, above all. Thus he seeks it everywhere, especially in our nation as a whole. Fraternity cannot be stuck in one corner or on one level of government but should reign in the culture and system. Perhaps surprisingly, he concludes that sometimes it actually has. McWilliams supports fraternity as an ideal not because of its occasional presence during the American historical journey; rather, he is convinced that fraternity is a fixed need of human beings, part of our nature, of our very being or soul. Therefore, although people are not guaranteed fraternity, they will reach out for it. Even in a resistant culture such as he judges the United States to be, they will seek it, and McWilliams desires that fraternity be found among Americans as a whole, in the public realm.[66]

McWilliams worries as much as other modern communitarians about our unsatisfactory liberal society. He describes us as adrift in a situation where solidarity must struggle to exist before the force of a privatist individualism whose temper has little use for fraternity or community.[67] Even though self-consciously a member of the party of hope, McWilliams is pessimistic enough that he shares the reaction of Bellah and others who are skeptical of chit-chat about subcultures and alternative lifestyles as authentic manifestations of community: They are no such thing and they will never be. Community is far harder to achieve than that.[68] And real community has to be based on unpleasant facts and paying careful attention to human limitations and incorporating their consequences in efforts to encourage fraternity.[69]

Christopher Lasch, also intrigued by fraternity, makes this point even more bluntly. The danger lies in the ruthless individualism and the extravagances of the participatory model, especially its sometime fantasy (attractive neither to McWilliams or Lasch) of the disappearance of the self into community. Neither American individualism nor community in some romantic, decentralized model appeals to them.[70] The search for their fraternal community must navigate between these alternatives, which means no gentle voyage.

Spirit of the Age

Ours is a time of vigorous health for the republican vision. It is somewhat astounding how true this is, when ten and certainly fifteen years ago there simply was no discussion of this model of community. And yet should there be much surprise at this development? The language of republicanism fits, one might say, in the 1980s and 1990s, a language of restrained and chastened communitarianism. No wild ecstasy is associated with the idea; rather, it offers a sober and modulated image of community, promoted by chastened, responsible, public-spirited men and women. Moreover, much of its impetus is practical, if sometimes urgent, energy—the need to have a focused, surviving nation. It is self-consciously less about utopia than about an enduring, sensible public community.

Critics of republicanism, as we have seen, assert that it does not always have a core, a moral center. Others have worried that it avoids political economy and much reflection on justice.[71] Republicanism does often come today in postmodern clothes. Not self-evidently about metaphysical truth or economic justice, their existence, definition, or revival, it can appear to be a substitute for such things in the spirit of the last decades of our century. Although it is for community as the public good, the crucial choices about what that means are often vague or postponed. Moreover, though republicanism has a theory of community, it is less clear in its interest in real people or in its sympathy for them. It is often true that the republican psychology of the human person is as underdeveloped as its concentration on the age of the American Founding is overdeveloped.

Whether this distance from people is related to and yet also a recognizable artifact of the age one might wonder. Expressiveness is hardly dead, as Bellah and his associates show so well.[72] Yet ours is an age of minimalism, as Lasch acutely describes it.[73] And republicanism is community in the minimalist style, community stripped to an uncertain minimum of truth, common values, and psychological analysis. It is a powerful vision for just this reason; it can appeal not only to the American past but also to the American present.

Chapter Six

Community and Roots

Perhaps the search for community is particularly a search for roots, for a place where one is or has been connected. In contemporary intellectual thought there is much interest in what I would call the communities of roots. This interest crosses conventional political lines and includes enthusiastic participatory democrats, hierarchical conservatives, path-breaking feminists.

This chapter considers perhaps the two most discussed examples of communities linked with the idea of roots: communities of tradition and the family as community. I examine several examples of the former to give a sense of the kinds of advocates of tradition one may find in contemporary intellectual life. Turning to the latter, I explore the debate over the family as a proper community, considering different images of the family and of the family as community. In particular my subject is feminist thought about community and family.

Communities of Tradition

Integral to discussions about communities of roots seen as communities of tradition is the idea that community flourishes best when securely tied to familiar practices of the recognizable past. Equally central is the view that community does not live as an idea, much less as a dream, but only when it is conceived practically and takes on material reality. It must be something of the present and past which one can touch. One might say this is a Burkean conception of community even though proponents do not always recognize, or acknowledge, this ancestry. It is Burkean in that the goal of preservation is at its core. It is about preservation (not necessarily of what exists) of community grounded in practical or historical reality/possibility. It is not about a community to be discovered or imagined, but about one to be reinforced or reachieved.

A logical starting point with communities of tradition might be to look within American conservative thought to see if this version of community of roots plays a major role in conservative intellectual thinking. One might think so, given the conservatives' often loud celebration of patriotism or family or other traditional values. Yet the expected is not all there is to report.

In fact, the history of American conservatism in recent decades is hardly a story of the exaltation of community. In the years after World War II American conservatism began the long journey out of the cold shadow cast by Franklin Roosevelt. Its most popular and most urgent themes were individual liberty, especially economic liberty for capitalism and capitalists, and the fight against communism and the Soviet Union. On these matters conservative intellectuals could and did agree.

They did not agree on either their definitions of community or its relative importance. In most cases this did not matter much because community was usually only a minor theme in American conservatism.[1] It was deemphasized (and still is) as a subject of lengthy and formal intellectual consideration. Even, or especially, procommunity conservatives resisted abstract discussions of a concept they assumed to be rooted in specific traditions, practices, and ways of life. Thus there was little talk of something called "community" in most conservative intellectual circles. The exception was the work of Russell Kirk. Indeed, Kirk still is the leading proponent of traditional values in the conservative movement, values which honor community in traditional terms, family, neighborhood, region, church, nation.[2]

In the 1960s tensions boiled over between the libertarian, procapitalist wing of American conservatism and the smaller, more traditionalist wing (sympathetic to community). Perhaps this was fortunate for conservatism because in the long run it hastened a sort of compromise. Under the guidance of Frank Meyer, especially, conservatism as a political theory emerged with an uneasy unity, an intellectual compromise devoted to the free market and liberty in the public realm and to traditional values and community in the private realms such as the family and church.[3]

Although most self-declared conservative intellectuals respect this compromise, beneath the surface are unresolved, perhaps unresolvable, tensions, well illustrated by William F. Buckley, Jr., and his *National Review*, after thirty years still a focal point for conservative intellectuals. Buckley explicitly supports the public freedom/private community distinction. Community does garner his attention and at times the subject appears in *National Review* articles, especially in connection with religion and the resolution of personal spiritual crisis. But Buckley's heart is elsewhere; and community usually gets lost, albeit unintentionally, in the crusade against the state and for capitalist liberties.[4]

Currently this situation is most clearly indicated in that virtually every issue of the *National Review* contains another article calling for abolishing the laws against (illegal) drugs and drug use. Such libertarianism does not sit well with conservative traditionalists, among others. No wonder Kirk and other conservative advocates of community have long complained that some conservatives are not really interested in any form of community, unless defenses of the traditional family count as everything.[5]

The process of drawing boundaries is interesting. Russell Kirk, for instance, explicitly rejects Ayn Rand and the cult that grew up around her and her objectivism. Like Buckley, Kirk wants nothing to do with such a militant atheist. Yet Kirk also spurns her for her doctrinaire individualism, which classifies every ideal of community as appalling.[6] Though most conservatives agree that her ideas are an extremist embarrassment, traditionalists fault libertarians as a group. Many libertarians may not be as insistent as Rand was or as uncritical of the exercise of the human will in service of objectivism, but a traditionalist critic such as Russell Kirk sees and dislikes their cult of individual freedom (especially in economic affairs) as the answer to all moral conundrums.[7] This notion amounts to the endorsement of moral isolation, the very problem Kirk finds so appallingly pervasive in American thought and life as well as in the precincts of American conservatism.[8] Put another way, Kirk argues that American "conservatism has its vice, and that vice is 'selfishness.'"[9]

John Adams receives Russell Kirk's highest approval as "the

founder of true conservatism" in the United States. In Kirk's view, Adams was no laissez-faire capitalist and no romantic about the glories of unchecked human freedom (selfishness). Nor did he gush about a conservatism in love with acquisitive principles. Rather, he was a sober, restrained, cautious defender of human freedom set in a context of community.[10]

Of course, Kirk does not blame his conservative allies for the weakness of community in the United States. Community is undernourished here, but the fault lies with liberalism and liberal culture (which has infected too many so-called conservatives). Liberalism has made the individual everything, affirmed the illusion of sweet reasonableness, ignored sin, and produced an alienated, drifting population, thirsty for communal connections.[11] Yet the nature of the community a traditional conservative such as Kirk seeks is unclear. He is strong on criticizing individual self-indulgence in the United States but that is quite different from formulating an image of the good community.

As with other traditional conservatives, Kirk insists that deep, communal connections among people are possible only when we are welded together in union with Truth, commonly religious truth. As Kirk proclaims, "society is a spiritual reality, possessing an eternal life." It "cannot be scrapped and recast as if it were a machine."[12] A proper community is grounded in God and his will, which has unfolded throughout past human experience.[13] From this perspective most human problems, including faltering community, originate in spiritual imperfections, lack of belief, connection, or focus, and can be seriously addressed only by spiritual regeneration in a spiritual community.[14]

For Kirk a more inclusive concept of community points toward tradition, a disposition more than anything else. It translates as the Burkean concept of an invisible bond between the present, the past, and the future. At its best, tradition in this spirit provides a kind of special perspective which tempers the present and the future with an appreciation of practices and ideas from the past.[15] In another incarnation traditionalists promote familiar American institutions and practices from the traditional family to patriotism.[16] Kirk makes these concerns central, far more so than the condition of the GNP.[17] A frequent parallel theme is the traditionalist defense of community as a necessary grounding to help each individual control himself (as they normally express it), "something more difficult than chastening Russia: he must chasten himself."[18] This focus, with its powerful undertone of fear of human appetite and lack of discipline, suggests why conservative community so often circles around order. There is a near obsession with the alleged collapse of authority in ordinary American life along with the conviction that an ordered community is essential for what one can only term the most obvious of utilitarian reasons.[19]

Concern about authority, order, and community is also important to another strand of conservatism, the so-called neoconservatives who came to public consciousness in the 1970s and 1980s. Among its leading lights are Peter Berger, Midge Dector, Irving Kristol, Richard Neuhaus, and Michael Novak.[20] Neoconservatives are sometimes very interested in spiritual problems, both personal and cultural, as Peter Berger and Richard Neuhaus illustrate. Yet neoconservatives as a whole do not concentrate on tradition defined in metaphysical terms or, indeed, in any terms which might seem abstract.[21] The tradition of neoconservatives is specific, covering the basic political and economic institutions and associated practices of the United States. It is a tradition of form and practice developed over time, which neoconservatives honor and seek to preserve. They defend our overall system, "democratic capitalism,"[22] in good part because it is a product of American experience. It is of our tradition.

Many neoconservatives are former liberals who during the 1960s or later became disillusioned with liberal/leftist politics. Indeed they cannot be understood without appreciating the decisive impact the 1960s had on them. They are as much children of the 1960s as the leftists whom they fault as excessively critical of American institutions and values and who are unable to appreciate the existent cultural and political compromises that are the American tradition. Neoconservatives complain that this approach dominates current intellectual opinion, encouraging an adversarial, negative mood which undermines American traditions. Naturally each neoconservative (while normally denying the label) has his or her individual perspective. Some favor more change than others, some are reluctant Republicans, others conservative Democrats, and so on. They are alike, though, in their determination to thread their way between the traditionalist conservatives, whom they judge to romanticize the past, and those liberal and leftist intellectuals who, they feel, abhor the present and do not respect the past of the United States.[23]

A good illustration may be found in Irving Kristol's defense of capitalism; he argues that capitalism and its institutions deserve qualified support. They have produced material prosperity and simultaneously sustained a generous range of political, religious, and personal freedoms. Kristol freely acknowledges that capitalism has features which pose problems for him, such as its enervating bureaucracies and limited spiritual dimension, but for him the balance is positive. Capitalism (checked by government) is the realistic best alternative ("two cheers") in our tradition/experience.

Kristol does not propose the creation of some elaborate myth to sustain limited capitalism in the United States. He is an uncritical traditionalist no more than other neoconservatives. Tradition is connected with empirical reality and not a mystical substitute for it. Our traditions are good not because they are traditions but because of the record of our institutions over time; just as with capitalism, they have worked. Kristol grants that his defense of capitalism is a relative judgment, not the proclamation of a Platonic form. Yet it has force once one considers that its "alternatives . . . range from the hideous to the merely squalid."[24] What bothers him is the flabby response from leaders of capitalist institutions to the relentlessly hostile assaults on capitalism and other American institutions by American intellectuals and doyens of culture.[25] Like Daniel Bell,[26] Kristol is disturbed by the passivity he observes, and he forgives neither the perpetrators nor the passive victims.[27]

Neoconservatives are sympathetic to community in terms of local institutions, often those at least somewhat private—the home, the church, the voluntary association. They are quite like other conservatives in this affinity (and also like Alexis de Tocqueville), but they favor the rooted varieties of such institutions, traditional ones, not utopian adventures in community somehow situated at the local level. The latter often remind neoconservatives of the communities of the New Left, which they hate. That movement created innumerable artificial communities which soon failed, though not until they had helped to erode American traditions.[28]

Michael Novak, a good representative of the neo-conservative disposition, argues that local traditions of community serve as the vital groundwork for our society and our valuable national institutions. Our traditions of liberty, respect, and patriotism can be and often are secured and strengthened at the local level. There community must live and thus enable the national society (community?) to flourish.[29]

At most, though, neoconservative discussion of local tradition constitutes a quiet defense of a modest theme in a larger agenda. And yet one may argue it plays a greater part there than it does among typical conservatives' voices where Russell Kirk is an exception, more respected than followed. After all, capitalism and undiluted (if sometimes rather abstract) enthusiasm for liberty are not self-evidently congruent with tradition or any other model of community. No wonder most American conservative thought shows almost as little interest in tradition as it does in community in the public spheres of economics and politics.

The Community of the Ancients

One stream of conservative intellectual thought, however, is very much about community. Developed by Leo Strauss and those influenced by him ("Straussians"), this view holds that the good life can be realized only if experienced in community, indeed only in the true community. Such a community must exist under the aegis of what Strauss called classical "natural right," which he distinguished from modern conceptions of natural right based in a fictional state of nature and crowning the selfish individual as sovereign. Strauss's natural right emphasized a human telos, which he conceived to be a life of virtue and duty defined in a community ruled by the wise. The model (and the tradition derived from it) has its origin in elements of classical Greek thought, a world and a tradition Strauss saw as far from our own.[30]

Strauss believed and many of his followers agree that for our age liberal democracy is the best practical form of government. They honor Aristotle's distinction between the best state and that which is the best possible. Their view seems informed by the sense that liberal democratic regimes will secure freedom for philosophers and will also need them as the source of truth and virtue, given the example of the classical tradition, without which liberal democracy founders in license and confusion.

The Straussians are controversial, without doubt. To their critics they are sort of a cult who are delighted (in cultlike fashion) when they bog down in questions about the correct interpretation of Strauss himself or of their near sacred masters, Plato or Aristotle.[31] They also annoy many other conservatives who consider them irrelevant, prickly, and precious. Into this context fell Allan Bloom's remarkable polemic of the late 1980s, *The Closing of the American Mind*.[32] Bloom is a self-declared student of Leo Strauss, and Bloom's book quickly became a subject of intense debate among contemporary intellectuals. As with any really challenging work, *The Closing of the American Mind* (a book whose best-seller status cast doubt on its title's premise) transcends any neat categorization or pedigree. The book and its author have become symbols less of the small Straussian movement than of the broad interest in traditionalism in American intellectual life today. Neither should be misunderstood, however, as comfortable allies of American conservatives as a whole.

Bloom is upset about the neglect of tradition in the United States today, almost regardless of its substance. He aims his arrows, for example, at the decline of tradition in general in the United States. There is simply no commitment to preserving tradition, neither by the failing family nor by any other means in our country. And it does not surprise Bloom because the United States does not operate as a community with a tradition. "America is experienced not as a common project but as a framework within which people are only individuals, where they are left alone."[33]

In fact, Bloom is ambivalent about America. Despite our absence of tradition and community, he is not ready to abandon the United States. We lack tradition, but at least we have not built on false tradition or a false community. If we are about Locke and liberalism that is lamentable, but it is also minimally acceptable. At least we have not built on Marx or on Rousseau, far worse models. We may not deserve praise, yet we are more than nothing; we have "built on low but solid ground."[34]

For Bloom, perhaps the major proximate reason for the crisis in America is our declining family community. He diagnoses the family's condition as pathetic and desperate; its present fate is predictable, given the "decay of the family's traditional role as the transmitter of tradition."[35] Stripped from a context of tradition, the family cannot perpetuate itself effectively and the less it does, of course, the more it speeds its own death. Only families—of which there are too few—which exist in a stable, traditional fashion can fight the trend, and even these are trapped in a culture which has lost any sense of norms they might seek to enforce.[36] When divorce comes, as it does too often, and the family's walls fall down, more children are left rootless. They are not just the usual products of our society, people without much sense of socially shared values or traditions, but much worse. According to Bloom, they are seriously damaged kids who can never grow in wisdom or tradition, who will be always angry, scared, desperate.[37]

Bloom's withering assault on modern education, especially education in tradition and community, has earned him his special notoriety, however. He wonders if education can help fill the emptiness of the modern American soul to develop a sense of tradition and connection. Expecting little from what he judges to be the hopeless public elementary and secondary schools, he is more concerned about the college education of American elites of the future. Here he would aspire to make an impact if he thought it were at all possible, but he does not. To Bloom our colleges are a miserable failure. In the classroom he finds neither the traditional liberal arts nor the search for truth. Outside the classroom superficial fun and games dominate. Colleges are at best relentlessly thin, like America; at worst (and they are often at their worst), positively dangerous and destructive. The ugly fact is, Bloom says, traditional wisdom and learning are rarely respected or practiced today. Thus modern students are simply cut off from the intellectual tradition and insights of their civilization, of all civilization.[38]

Bloom reserves his principal educational enthusiasm for a Great Books approach, a project which some other Straussian thinkers assertively share.[39] The objective is to stimulate serious thinking about great issues of life through the medium of works from the past which do exactly that. Its proponents see no alternative, arguing that because modern philosophy departments do everything but this kind of thing and literature departments have sunk into deconstruction and Marxism, there are few places where serious thinking can be done anymore.

The intention is not to substitute one form of propaganda for another. They want to develop genuine openness to wisdom; and it comes, they are convinced, from reading the works of great minds which have never agreed about politics, either in the past or now.[40] The Straussian Harvey Mansfield, Jr., asks how such activity can hurt democracy. He is convinced it can only stimulate democracy's intellectual health and at times lead us to the exploration of what might lie beyond it.[41]

The rejection of the Great Books approach pains traditionalists like Bloom. He finds it terribly sad that "nobody believes that the old books do, or even could, contain the truth."[42] Even when great books do get attention, they are "deconstructed," "relationized," "situated." By whatever method, the great tradition of Western intellectual thought is removed from the place that matters, the arena where one searches for truth or wisdom. No wonder, Bloom laments, there are simply no standards anymore in the university or in the United States as a whole.[43] We have only war between various empty contemporary ideologies, while the real ideology among college students and most Americans—vague openness and tolerance—drives out all else.

In Bloom's harsh vision, a vacuum exists in the typical head, with little present but the flicker of immediate experience.[44] Music, for example, pounds into the college student, but it is a music which taps into no cultural traditions of the West or anywhere else; it does not expand student horizons. Rock is basically no more than "the beat of sexual intercourse."[45] Moreover, "as long as they have their Walkman on, students cannot hear what tradition has to say. And, after its prolonged use, when they take it off, they will find they are deaf."[46]

The point of Bloom's provocative chapter on music is to emphasize his conclusion that an empty openness to little more than the immediately pleasurable ironically results in closed minds unable to take in tradition and truth. The paradox of modern liberal society is that its alleged openness and its clichéd and pious invocations to "celebrate differences" block openness to great insights of the minds and spirits that have gone before us.[47] One remembers Marcuse's analysis of more than two decades ago on how repressive a vague and vapid tolerance can be.[48]

Bloom's disadvantaged modern students have no inkling of what a noble life might be.[49] Thus they see sex as nothing remarkable: Their erotic existence is lame with not even a faint glimpse of awareness of the divine madness Socrates praised.[50] Their lives are without passion, *closed* to deep passion; they favor peace and conflict resolution and little more.[51] Out of touch with tradition and with examples of people who lived nobly in allegiance to truth, they descend into ever narrower and flatter lives.[52] They are necessarily vulnerable to the dull conformity which is so much their current fate and their unrecognized crisis.[53]

In Bloom's analysis, the damage from the absence of attention to tradition affects our nation as well as individual students. The greatest loss goes beyond a lack of an appreciation of community or tradition in our society and in our souls. This loss has nothing to do with tradition or community in any conventional senses but with the disappearance of motivation to search for the truth (the good), the highest human pursuit. Traditions, great books, ultimately serve, not as channels toward conventional community or personal identity (though they lead there too), but as the way to the passionate quest for truth, which alone finally matters. Thus the greatest fault of relativism is that it crushes the proper motive of education, the search for the good.[54]

Such a search, of course, leads Bloom and all Straussians back to Socrates and the classical Greek intellectual tradition. When they get there, they find a model of a community of those who are searching for truth. One must accept this ideal, so well illustrated by its ancient exemplars Socrates, Plato, Aristotle, and others in the Greek tradition. Their search is to be our goal. Strauss, Bloom, and others celebrate this classic tradition and insist we answer its call. If we do so we will find ourselves in tension with ordinary communities just as Plato, Socrates, and eventually Aristotle did with Athens. Of course, everyone needs the ordinary society to exist and thus one must be very, very careful in dealing with it. Prudence becomes a crucial value and for the philosopher it may be necessary to deliver one's message in guarded or esoteric language.

To be sure, we need not abolish democracy in politics. As Bloom's ally Mansfield puts it, the issue is whether a democracy allows people to pursue something greater. If, as he believes, ours does, then we can live with it.[55] Bloom agrees. Indeed, the community of seekers, even the community of the wise, need not be a small group. It could be large, though Bloom concludes our educational and other institutions ensure it will be small. "The real community of man . . . is the community of those who seek the truth; of the potential knowers, that is, in principle of all men to the extent they desire to know. But in fact this includes only a few."[56]

It does not follow directly for Bloom that to support the elite of the seekers after wisdom implies support for rule by a political elite. What is required is a society such as fifth-century Athens sometimes was, a relatively open society tolerating those determined to love the search for truth. Mansfield agrees as he explicitly denies that elitist political implications are implicit.[57] Still, one need not be a hardened cynic to wonder how such intellectual elitism could fit comfortably with any version of democracy and vice versa.[58]

The list of other conceptions of the proper tradition is endless. For instance Eric Voegelin's understanding, religious, historical, and challenging, has its own following.[59] The larger observation must be that traditionalists abound today, rejecting the modernist present and sometimes defending American institutions. They are repulsed by what they describe as our rootless culture and politics, an empty liberalism, cursed by a barely unchecked individualism; and they often bewail the transformation of the American into a sadly stripped-down and quite lost creature.

Perhaps more than anyone else, Alasdair MacIntyre, through his stimulating books *After Virtue* and *Whose Justice? Which Rationality?* has brought the subject of roots and tradition to the fore of contemporary intellectual discussion.[60] His reflections have won him the kind of broad attention that is uncommon, even if the mood is sometimes grudging.[61] MacIntyre's argument at its baldest is that America and the West as a whole have cheerfully swept away tradition, roots, and community. He locates the crucial originating point of decline in the Enlightenment. In the eighteenth century intellectuals began to jettison both the conviction of a Godly universe and of a human telos, a historical process which has accelerated in more recent times.[62] Now we are left with little other than empty emotivist and relativist approaches to truth and to values which provide no authority and flagrantly repudiate reason.[63] Thus to him it is no wonder that "our society cannot hope to achieve moral consensus."[64]

In political terms we have another legacy, liberalism. To MacIntyre it is bereft of any defense except by its own assumptions.[65] Con-

sequently, modern people are trapped in a world where meaning is
missing, life is lonely, and existence is disastrously compartmental-
ized.[66] Civilization has cracked and "the barbarians are not waiting
beyond the frontiers; they have already been governing us for quite
some time."[67] Now we have to confront the lonely and declining remains with escalating horror.

The answer for MacIntyre is community, recognizing that community has only one source, local and particular traditions and understandings. Its roots will vary enormously from place to place and from
time to time because each of us is different and will bring our own
story, experience, and circumstance. We are story tellers, narrative-
offering souls, who have stories to tell, stories of our lives, and communities will necessarily reflect this fact.[68] No other road to community is possible, certainly not from philosophical abstraction or the
yearnings of intellectuals. There is, thus, no one true community,
tradition, or rationality which is the path we must follow. Bloom is
wrong, but this inclination is also in good part the problem with
liberalism and with modernism in general. They push us to think in
universal terms, though they turn around and tell us that our search is
in vain. We are left with self-interest or despair.[69] "The notion of the
political community as a common project is alien to the modern liberal
individualist world."[70] No wonder present-day "politics is a civil war
carried on by other means."[71]

MacIntyre proposes we pay attention to another mode of thinking
about social life and community, that of restated Aristotle and MacIntyre's reading of the classical Greek era.[72] Here, he claims, one encounters respect for local communities, for settings in which people can
advance in self-respect for each other and nurture shared norms,
customs, traditions, and goals, for MacIntyre the heart of any community. In such a life we develop toward our possibility as people, renew-
ing or rebuilding our connections with others. We develop as integrated people, citizens in touch with each other in comprehensible
settings of community, no longer so alone, so lost, so unfulfilled.[73]

The kind of education we require honors our traditions, practices,
and ways of life. It promotes whatever virtues are integral to every
tradition and to seeking our telos[74] and is quite different from Bloom's
traditionalism. To MacIntyre, Bloom's Great Books theory is one more
example, well intentioned as it is, of an abstract, universalist approach

to education. Studying the great books would make sense only if they are studied in context: exploring where the traditions came from and what they express.[75]

One may puzzle about conflicting traditions, indeed conflicting communities in MacIntyre's world. How does one achieve reconciliation or practical coordination? In trying to confront this dilemma he separates himself from what he believes are the ideologies of (one) tradition (or another) and from uncritical traditionalist communitarians of any variety.[76] MacIntyre's loyalty is to reason, never to simple assent. Where there are divisions, he declares, our hope toward resolution must depend on dialogue, conversation, debate, reason, in a context of one or several traditions.[77] Although such a view may seem a statement of faith more than of reason, MacIntyre insists that community can be achieved only through human reason.[78] After all, he asks, what is a tradition anyway? It "is an argument extended through time in which certain fundamental agreements are defined and redefined . . . in terms of external/internal debates."[79] And every community and tradition will be strengthened in the ongoing, rational dialogue that is so integral to the process. We learn from engaging other traditions, and they learn from us too. Ironically, MacIntyre depends finally on the credo of the liberal John Stuart Mill.[80]

MacIntyre's vision is richly expounded, moving from detailed and articulate analyses of classical Greece to directed and sometimes uncautious characterizations of our era. Yet the acclaim for his view of tradition as an ideal of community (as opposed to those arguing for one or another particular tradition) naturally stimulates reflection about his claims. Some ask why he gives so much authority to community as an ideal.[81] Others may object to his blistering critique of our age and his characterization of liberalism as a decisive influence in the decline of the West as more stated than argued. His denunciation of universals and his praise for localism and community are not self-evidently convincing either. And in this very context matters are complicated by MacIntyre's affirmation of Christianity and his comment at the close of *After Virtue*: "We are waiting not for Godot but for another—doubtless a very different—St. Benedict."[82]

Moreover, MacIntyre does not illustrate what he has in mind in concrete, modern, political terms. His work is distanced from the conflicts and trials of ordinary life in our era. This is no surprise since he appears to loathe much of modernity; but it does not help us in practical terms. Thus in the end we are left somewhat stranded without any particular path or tradition or much else to follow. Affirmations of something called dialogue only get us so far.[83] In a curious way MacIntyre is very much a creature of the modernity he spurns. After all, he does not offer Aristotle as the answer. Even his Christian inclinations are indicated obliquely, and they are not integrated with the rest of his thought. He reminds me a great deal of the postmoderns he scorns. They do not honor reason, to be sure, but MacIntyre is like them in his refusal to affirm any truth, his profound skepticism, his lack of interest in politics, his devotion to the particular narrative. Thus he reminds us again that much of the search for roots in modern thought is about philosophical homelessness above all else.

The Family and Roots

More of intellectual thought today circles around the celebration of roots and traditions than is suspected by those who think of it simply as a product of American conservatism and little more than cheerleading for capitalism. Moreover, traditionalists in some self-conscious sense are hardly the only contemporary intellectuals engaged with roots. Some argue that our culture, however lightly brushed with a tone of diversity, remains homogeneous. By this perspective, we are children of a conformity that does not provide us with either a deep or a specific grounding.

In Charles Taylor's analysis, we desperately need "geographical, or cultural, or occupational" communities to help us to form our personal identity, to become what I describe as being a rooted person.[84] Richard Merelman has a similar appreciation of the centrality of roots—of codes of clan, family, religion, and the like—for character formation and identity. Roots allow us to become integrated persons (as opposed, apparently, to free-floating intellectuals) and provide us with an identity from which to proceed to the public realm.[85]

Of course no institution is more closely associated with roots or with community than the family, nor is there any institution (including capitalism) which so engages contemporary American intellectual analysis and debate. The engagement is itself a sign of the rediscovery of the ideal of community in our age. Family attracts attention not just for its current real and alleged pathologies but also because talk of community is so widely present. We can predict that where such talk flourishes, so will discussion of family.

Some urge family as the community, others as an essential one. Still other voices condemn all family in the name of community (of other forms) or else defend it, once it is strengthened or changed in either minor or integral ways. The directions are multiple and endless. But family is very much on our agenda today, in good part because community is the goal many seek and the question keeps occurring: What is the good community? This in turn has led to the query, what is the good family, if indeed there is such a thing. As we all know, current discussion teems with lament over the alleged decline of family and related pathologies, divorce, child abuse, juvenile delinquency, infidelity.[86] And yet the family remains for many intellectuals the central community for human beings, one with much to teach us about achieving and failing to achieve community. One thinks at once of Daniel Bell's "public household," his idea of public community drawn from the family as community.[87]

Christopher Lasch's discussion of the decay of family life recounts how the breakup of the family has proven disappointing as a means to realize human liberation, contrary to the expectations of its more eager visionaries. The weakening of the family has instead left too many individuals without the grounding (psychological, ontological, and institutional) which strong families are uniquely able to offer to "resist new forms of domination."[88] Lasch bemoans the new dominance of psychology over the family: Modern psychology propagates a model of family which stresses individual happiness. If one does not focus first on one's self in the family one risks being proclaimed "unhealthy."[89] The goal as Bellah and his associates grant is to sustain the family. But the family community that modern psychology seems to respect demands each member first and foremost address the question, "What is in it for me?" Bellah also believes that such an approach will do little for the family or for the family as community.[90]

Yet Bellah and Lasch do not for a moment want to be identified with the so-called traditional family. The family's importance in providing for roots is one thing, but the old patriarchal family is another; it is rejected almost everywhere in modern American political argument. There are those who disagree. Antifeminists such as Phyllis Schlafly emphasize that family survival and strength depend on women. Without their traditional service in the home, family will fail and, indeed, does fail; the wreckage of modern families all over our society is the dramatic testimony.[91] It follows for antifeminists that family (and through it community) is possible only if feminism is rejected. Feminism is bad not solely because as a movement it has often scorned family, as Schlafly would define it, but because behind that rejection lies its disastrous central motivation, selfishness.[92] The exaltation of selfishness by feminists in a world already too cursed with selfish people threatens civilization itself, not just the family. In building the family women can offer another model and thus can serve the larger community as no one else can: "It is on woman that a civilization depends . . . on the moral fabric they weave . . . on the new generation that they breathe life into and educate."[93]

Community and roots go together then for antifeminists such as Schlafly in the form of family, defined in a traditional, patriarchal sense. This is God's model, we are told, and the only way; husbands must rule.[94] The alternative is the absent or defeated or new liberal man and a morality of self-indulgence which has left women free sexually but unprotected and too often exploited or abandoned.[95] George Gilder has also advanced this argument in his provocative works, such as *Naked Nomads*.[96]

Allan Bloom attacks feminism as basic to the collapse of the family as community. For Bloom family decay is too overwhelming to ignore. He finds that the family rarely bonds in the first place and often does not endure. Sex occurs, marriages take place, children are born, but the result is something very different from the community that family ought to represent.

People are in love with sex as a form of self-love, not as a means to the creation of family as a community,[97] which would require serious, other-directed commitment. Youth, Bloom's main subject, resists the commitment integral to community and thus cannot forge successful families. "Young people today are afraid of making commitments, and the point is that love *is* commitment, and much more."[98] Of course, as always youth has its dreams, but they are not of long-term human commitments: "as to dreams about the future with a partner, they have none."[99]

Bloom hardly blames everything on feminism. It is a puny force in comparison with what Bloom believes to be the near deterministic powers of the ideas of wrongheaded German metaphysicians. Still, feminism is a proximate cause of what plagues the family. It voraciously eats up family (and all traditional) roots in its fanatic devotion to self-absorption. Thus feminism is the ultimate victory over the family community. Moreover, in addition to striking at patriarchy and the idea of commitment, it tries to make the male himself almost irrelevant, guaranteeing all but the most unconventional families will also be irrelevant. Women, Bloom's radical feminists teach, do not need men; they have no role beyond the morally ambiguous provision of sperm, should that be desired. All the rest women can handle—and handle better than men.[100]

Feminism and Community

Perhaps nothing illustrates the complexity of contemporary American political thought more than feminist intellectual reflections on the family— and on community. The diversity of modern feminist thought is itself contested, but there can be no doubt that it brims with myriad attitudes toward community and the individual and on how family should fit as a decisive community in women's lives.[101] But there is consensus that what Barbara Ehrenreich calls the "authoritarian" and "punitive" notions of community today, including traditional images of family, are wholly unacceptable.[102]

Some feminists have carefully articulated the historicity of models of the family and of women's role in the family. Yet such an approach does not command great attention except as it validates contemporary feminism's antagonism toward the traditional family.[103] Part of the reason lies in the arguments of those feminists who have no good words for family, ancient or modern. Though often the specific focus of this antipathy is the current American family (or traditional ideal of family), one does not have to be a clairvoyant to perceive a more sweeping antipathy. Such views were dominant in the feminist thought of the 1960s and early 1970s, but they still linger.[104] Zillah Eisenstein, for example, is angry about family as she observes it in the world around her. The family is not about community but about male hierarchy, suppression of women and children, and the reinforcement of attitudes and divisions which encourage the capitalism she hates.[105] Jane Flax identifies this strain in feminist writing, now as in the past, and declares the family is "a primary source of the maintenance and replication of both gender identity and the pain and suffering endemic to being female."[106]

This account, however, is hardly the full story today. Perhaps since Adrienne Rich's *Of Woman Born* (1976), a steady shift has occurred toward motherhood as a valuable, if not defining, experience for women.[107] There has been a concurrent rise of enthusiasm for women as women expressed in terms of psychological development, personal values, and warmth toward women in a (properly constituted) family. This trend involves a celebration of the female and a movement away from what just a few years ago was a rather uncritical openness to androgyny. The shift is, as Jean Grimshaw observes, often loose in its conceptualizations, data, and generalizations, but its popularity among feminist intellectuals is strong.[108] This view has not resurrected the family as a problem-free institution and certainly has nothing good to say about the patriarchal family, but the door is now open to discuss community in terms of family, and the argument swirls on.

A favorite target of those who remain angry over the family in any recognizable form has been Jean Elshtain. She has come under fire even though her model is an egalitarian, role-sharing family. Elshtain has drawn criticism, among other reasons, as an alleged proponent of one type of natural gender differentiation—women as maternal—that some feminists accept but that many others reject.[109] This view of women alarms feminists who suspect its consequence could be women's subordination and exploitation in patriarchal family communities once more.

Still, radical feminists who continue to look with frank hostility at models of family as community have shifted away from the 1960s emphasis on radical autonomy and individualism exemplified in the "profoundly Nietzschean" work of Mary Daly.[110] In some cases, the argument is that women are, indeed, more community-oriented than men, for whatever reasons, though feminist critics insist that interdependence—both individual and community orientations among women and men—is a better analysis of the reality.[111]

However, it is always obvious how substantial the radical feminist commitment is to ideas of community as an alternative to family. Some radical feminists are interested in community only if it is socialist and egalitarian;[112] others appear supportive only in the sense of gender, community visualized as solidarity among women. Still others refine that definition to community as lesbian women or women separatists.[113] Other feminists exalt public community as the ideal, implicitly or explicitly dismissing the family. Mary Dietz, for example, argues for what I have called republican community. She faults Elshtain for trying to have it both ways, supporting both public community and maternalism. The form of republicanism Dietz defends, feminist republicanism, holds that women can be a crucial contributing factor in the formulation of a republican ethos but only if they rally to the cause. They can hardly be committed as political and communitarian beings if they are mostly doing the dishes or raising kids.[114]

Jean Elshtain vigorously replies to the assorted critics of family and community and defends the (egalitarian) family as an essential human expression of community. Elshtain gives as good as she gets. She insists radical feminists have an excessively negative image of men as an "implacable enemy, an incorrigible and dangerous beast who has as his chief aim in life the oppression and domination of women."[115]

Such an unaffectionate analysis of men is not likely to encourage family or most visions of community. It is, Elshtain argues, part of an overall belief about relations between the sexes, very much including family life, a belief which deliberately sets out to repudiate all "private life by construing it as a power-riddled battleground, thus encouraging a crudely politicized approach toward coitus, marriage, child-rearing."[116] Routine radical feminist "expressions of contempt for . . . pregnancy, childbirth, and child-rearing"[117] are, by Elshtain's reading, "a rather bleak Hobbesianism in feminist guise,"[118] hardly suitable grounds for building family or any kind of community. Such expressions also represent, albeit unintentionally, "contempt for the female body."[119] Moreover, all feminism suffers from the resulting negative stereotyping as "anti- familial feminist ideology . . . has become linked up in the popular mind with efforts to erode or destroy . . . family life."[120]

This perception hurts feminist causes now that the movement's pace has slowed and when social and political struggle are needed more urgently than ever.[121] Fights over the worth of family divert energy from what should be another important goal for those in support of increasing community, public citizenship which provides a "collective identity for males and females alike."[122] It follows that Elshtain describes herself as a "social feminist" determined to further both public and private communities on every side and to provide a social equality among all citizens. She is no more interested in a liberal feminism of equal rights than she is in radical feminism. Neither has much to do with community as she perceives it.[123]

Elshtain certainly does not travel alone among feminists. Betty Friedan, for example, has strenuously denounced "female machismo" and its consequences for the family.[124] She contends that radical feminism would separate women from their sexual selves, from children, even from family. This is simply unacceptable, Friedan declares, and especially so to almost all women.[125] Women want families—and aspire to realize community in them. We ought to stop fighting over the family and get busy finding means to remold and support it.[126]

Elshtain and Friedan do not invariably agree with each other, nor is either an obvious ally of another defender of family as community, Sylvia Ann Hewlett. Hewlett's *A Lesser Life* appeared in 1986 and generated a storm of feminist criticism because her disgust with what she perceived as feminist antagonism toward the family led her to attack official feminism. Hewlett even repudiated the E.R.A. Yet her argument is in many ways in concert with Elshtain and others within feminist intellectual circles who seek to help working, family women and to strengthen the family (if not the patriarchal family).[127]

While Hewlett is angry over feminists who scorn the family, her main complaint is about the failure to act concretely to bolster the family, whatever the rhetoric. Women trying to make a go of family need specific help, laws designed to provide leave, health care, day care, and other forms of practical affirmation. After all, community does not just happen. To ignore such projects is to repudiate most women—as Hewlett learned in the positive response she received from women.[128]

When feminist thought struggles with the relationship of community and the family, a widespread assumption prevails that community is important and that family (if reconstituted) could be a valuable community. Even when the hostility is permanent toward family, the assessment is often made in terms of (its failure as) community. What distinguishes some self-consciously liberal feminists is their negativity toward community in general and their interest in family (again reconstituted) as a fitting locus for goals other than community. Only among some liberal feminists does family viewed in terms of community receive pale interest, exactly as so many intellectual critics of liberalism might anticipate.

The most explicit and extensive recent discussion is Susan Okin's *Justice, Gender, and the Family,* a book which is unmistakably liberal, ambivalent about family, and disdainful toward community. Okin delights in being tough minded and in speaking out on what she understands to be the truth with little varnish. Here as in an earlier work in which she dispatched most of the (male) greats of Western political philosophy her favored mode is blunt critique. Okin attacks one modern (male) political thinker/intellectual after another. Her test is quite straightforward: whether they adhere to her conception of feminist political philosophy. Few do. In the process she makes clear that no one who approaches modern life with traditional values of any sort is acceptable. She is always the good liberal, in this instance opposing traditional thinking because it denies freedom and is patriarchal and unsympathetic toward feminism. The old liberal mission of Locke, Voltaire, and Jefferson is applied to new enemies.[129]

Throughout Okin's evaluations, her distaste for community in general emerges in sharp perspective. Tradition, she reminds her readers, has often been communitarian in focus. She then declares that the problem is much broader, in fact: "the implication of most communitarian arguments" is bad, "reactionary and inegalitarian."[130] Community's record in her mind is oppressive to women, and she intends to cut through any romantic illusions to the contrary.[131]

The alternative family which she favors is the just family, i.e., the modern family properly understood "As A School of Justice."[132] Feminists or others who resist and would rather conceive it as a place where values of love or an ethic of care flourish get no appreciation from Okin. They do not understand the family as it is, very much a world where issues of distribution are central. Nor do they realize, Okin reassures them, that justice and love can be present together in a family.[133] Okin wants neither an all-out rejection of the family as do some radical feminists nor an egalitarian family as community as do Elshtain and others committed to community. Currently the family must be described as unjust since women in families are not equal and do not have equal opportunities there or in larger life because of it. But if we work to maximize the goal of justice for women (justice as equal opportunity, liberal justice), we will be where we should be. This world will be one step closer to liberal universalism. "A just future would be one without gender."[134]

Barbara Rowland and Peregrine Schwartz-Shea are well aware that critics of liberal feminism see such a view as another example of liberalism promoting an impoverished individualism, in this case for all women. As liberal feminists they fight back in a tight argument recalling what too many celebrators of community in all arenas neglect, that community has often "been oppressive to women." [135] In an interesting analysis, they place the blame not merely on relationships of authority likely to be present in such communities as the family but also on the fact that in such settings women lack space to get a needed rational and distanced perspective. Again, the liberal Enlightenment appears, this time in affirmation of reason and perspective.

Rowland and Schwartz-Shea as liberal feminists are far more interested in self-hood and empowerment than they are in community for women.[136] Talk in the language of Carol Gilligan about women and a natural ethic of caring concerns them. They worry about the subjection of women that can follow from taking such an ethic into families or elsewhere.[137] The objective is the sophisticated liberal individual: women who are rational, responsible, autonomous individuals, modern liberals at their best. Community is understood as a secondary concern, possible sometimes perhaps but to be viewed with suspicion, just as the family as community is viewed.

This discussion reminds us that roots and tradition and family are certainly on the contemporary intellectual agenda as examples of the assorted directions which thinking about community takes. Yet they also illustrate the intense disagreements over community today. No one view presents the outline of the good community or the value of community as an urgent human ideal. What we have, instead, is dispute and debate over the central concerns of community.

Chapter Seven

Survival and Community

Contemporary intellectual life in the United States abounds with thinkers for whom the crises of our modern situation reduce to the question of global survival, survival of humanity, of nature, of the earth itself. They are hardly the first to address the possibilities of human extinction, yet the extent of this anxiety today is rare in human history and may never have been more appropriate, given the ominous trends of world conditions. What is perhaps surprising about these thinkers is their engagement with the idea of community. Rarely are they included in most standard or, one might say, fashionable discussions of community in American intellectual life. Yet for no disposition is community a more compelling matter.

In most instances those who sound the alarm about our collective future—I call them globalists—are very American in scorning mere worry; they hurry to urge action. Proposals range over a host of (not always congruent) specific policies for the environment or world peace. Yet beyond these often lies another idea, that in the end only our collective transformation into a suitable community will save us. Globalists depict survival as the proximate issue, but to survive, we must learn to turn our minds—and modes of living—inside out. Community is the way, not as some abstract good life but as the only basis for the continuation of life at all.

There are exceptions, as we shall see, writers whose goal is an exclusive, egalitarian community of nature as a proper end in itself, but they are far from numerous in the present overwhelming atmosphere of crisis. Turning toward community in this setting does offend some advocates and students of community. Something about the globalists' engagement with the notion seems sometimes to be a bit of a reach, somehow not exactly legitimate. Yet this is exactly opposite from the way the people we shall study in this chapter perceive things. For them the point is not historical traditions of community from the republican Founding to images of classical Athens; nor are philosophical discussions of community among schooled academics significant. They find little relevance in cultural wars over definitions of family as community or in searches for a responsible form of liberalism. All that seems esoteric or worse. Community has many advantages, but survival of the planet and of all its species is the most powerful and practical reason behind its imperative.

Literature of crisis is everywhere today, especially the kind that beseeches us to fear for the survival of all existence on our globe. Numerous authors beg us to understand that "the crisis of the contemporary world is *real*" and before us lies "a series of crises beyond any yet experienced in the procession of Western Civilization."[1] On all sides lie the threats, and globalists take it for granted in this synergistic age that it is hard, indeed impossible, to disentangle one threat from another. Moreover, since human existence is invariably global and multidimensional, they warn that there can be no recourse to quick fixes.[2]

The familiarity of their crises is a measure of the determined commitment of globalist intellectuals to alert us to present dangers. The spiral of global population invariably receives extensive attention in the litany.[3] So do concerns over the expanding use of energy and our shrinking energy resources;[4] extensive environmental deterioration;[5] exploding economic development which draws dangerously on dwindling resources and leaves disturbing costs in its often ugly wake;[6] disastrous signs of physical and biological decline—species threatened, cropland lost, climate warmed, the upper atmosphere menaced.[7]

A favorite metaphor, of course, is Garrett Hardin's "the tragedy of the commons," the belief that people as individuals are abusing the earth and all that sustains life on it when they should be rallying together to protect and nourish our globe as they would were it their own immediate property. People mistreat the earth because it is everyone's and thus no one's—very much like a classic village green where everybody felt free to graze their cows with no thought of the consequences until the green died from overgrazing.[8] The very popularity of the metaphor underlines the communal mode of analysis so common among survivalists and, in turn, what they hold to be necessary for our endurance. Globalists really are united with the many contemporary patrons of community. It is their goal, but what often distinguishes their vision is their unromantic, survival-oriented attitude. They see themselves as theorists of the fact and of the practical, not of the ideal or of the dreamy.

Closely related to the other tribulations which globalists fear is the ever present possibility (probability) of nuclear accident or, perhaps receding a bit now, nuclear war. Jonathan Schell's *Fate of the Earth* was the most dramatic (and best-selling) articulation of this potential terror and of its consequences for our planet. His task, however, has hardly been a lonely one.[9] The theme of nuclear annihilation of the planet is a gripping and, yes, popular one. Schell's assertion that the modern world has been "largely dead" regarding the danger[10] is incorrect and confuses lack of awareness of a danger with disagreement as to what should be done. In this literature, if one disagrees, one can be quickly condemned as unaware, insensitive, or worse.

Schell's conviction that no one is really aware or cares is not uncommon, the frustration being that too few people seriously acknowledge the crises at hand. They will not rethink or develop new conceptual frameworks: for example, we cannot divide the world between the developed versus the underdeveloped any more. We have to get beyond such categories and see that both are "confronted with the grim and very real prospect of drowning together."[11]

The world must end its collective denial of the "reality and gravity" of the challenges at hand.[12] The constant theme is that things must change drastically, and for them to do so we must look directly to the United States. We have failed; we are not the leader we should be in the fight for planetary survival. We are, indeed, a large segment of the problem, which has its origins in "rich and wasteful countries such as the United States."[13] We play at the problems even though "merely reformist policies" go nowhere.[14] We are told to get serious. We must recognize that startling changes will be required: "American political values and institutions are grossly maladapted" to the new world we now encounter.[15]

What new values do we need? What new world do we face? The

answer to the first query sometimes is quite old and very American. Values of efficiency and conservation, practical means and ends related to survival and then a flourishing nature are at stake, altogether a rather economic approach. As for the new world, in most instances it derives from an old world of worry, the enduring Malthusian fear about survival. But beyond these judgments there is much more; the answer is less economic and more democratic and communal.[16] Yet we cannot examine this side of globalist thinking without first fully exploring the gloom that ordinarily settles over globalists. A classic expression in this mode, the joint work of a number of voices, is *The Global 2000 Report to the President* (1981).[17] It details the bases for a pessimistic mood about almost every conceivable global trend in 721 pages of alarms and worries, unrelieved until one pinches oneself to see if one is still alive.

The *Report to the President* speaks in the characteristic voice of the globalist community and depends heavily on a curious methodological mixture, equally standard fare in this literature. The apparatus of modern science is everywhere. Numbers abound: The results of much use of computers are on full display; all the latest scientific theories are there. The analysis depends on elaborate projections of the future, frequently the product of computer modeling necessarily based on present data.[18]

Such analyses of the future have little to do with science, of course, since they are in no way falsifiable—except by time. Neither do they deserve to be dismissed as merely random guesses, but they hint accurately that data or science is hardly the only engine driving some globalists. Indeed, another engine is the conviction that we cannot escape our crises by technology. No matter how comfortable globalist writing often seems to be with the language and metaphors of science, and no matter how much its more scientific aspects depend on computer technology in its analyses, it scoffs at the promise of technology for resolution of our present dangers.

The assumption is broad that technology will not save us, and a corresponding impatience with those who hope otherwise is evident. Many globalists, in a quite familiar community-oriented vision, have confidence only in solutions which are social, having lost faith in science or technology as our savior (though not as a means to warn us of our danger). Thus we are repeatedly told sternly not to dream of a technological guide or a (slow) fix. The limits to what technology can do for us are just too formidable. Perhaps more to their point, emphasis on technology is a kind of narcotic that can only hurt us by luring us away from the overwhelming and likely cataclysmic crises ahead. We need a brutally honest confrontation with our situation instead, an unclouded acceptance of our perilous reality.[19]

What to Do

The gloom that must settle over the readers of these often frightening jeremiads may be much like an immobilizing gas, but this is not its effect on globalist writers. Inaction could not be further from their general mood or their intentions. Gloom may be pervasive but globalist thinkers insist it must not give license to resignation. Quite the contrary, the globalist disposition is always for "vigorous, determined new initiatives."[20] Our future is far from over if we appreciate that things can be done, important, earth-maintaining, and community enhancing things.

Globalists/survivalists are not the pessimists their analyses can lead one to believe. Hope has a legitimate place; what we have to do is get busy practically. Indeed, globalist thinkers show a surprising contrast between their often grim analyses and their considerable confidence that rational, committed citizens and leaders can grapple with the problems. The music of the future need not be funereal.

Exactly what direction to take is, however, another matter. Here opinion is far from consensual, but two models dominate the landscape. One well-known impulse is to look to government (which is not necessarily to say politics) as part of the answer, though there are some signs among the globalists that skepticism about government is alive and well.[21] Often the master concept is planning or, if that offends the prevailing unease about government, the concept of "design" is invoked.[22] But the idea is consistent: Government must act in a disciplined (not to say rigid) fashion to meet the global challenges. We are assured that government efforts to date have been too little and generally inept and ineffective.[23] Stronger stuff is required to address our assorted, but interrelated, crises on earth. What to do in each case will vary, but the active role of a strong, plan-oriented, interventionist state will not.[24] Indeed, as Robert Heilbroner declared in his famous *Human Prospect*, its action may have to extend beyond disciplining citizen practices to sanctioning discordant values,[25] a reality also entertained by others such as William Ophuls in his *Ecology and the Politics of Scarcity*.[26]

But even those who demand that our thinking turn toward a large government to meet global challenges routinely argue they are not lovers of the state; few globalist (or, for that matter, any other) intellectuals in the United States admit to such a sentiment. Their turning to the state comes not from affection; indeed they see themselves driven by the necessities of time (too little) and scale (too great) into what is sometimes an awkward embrace.

Many globalist thinkers have doubts about government. Enthusiasm for the New Deal is modest among globalists, especially as a pure model. A more favored concept is the goal of community. To achieve survival, the argument goes, the United States will have to undertake a new mission and forge a new identity. We will have to stand for community because only this perspective will get us to think globally, to expand the horizons of our rapidly disappearing future, to preserve our children's future, or to acknowledge the underlying, sovereign community of nature. The varieties of communities vary; the recourse to community does not.

Two images of community predominate. One is the local community, which flows from the considerable body of intellectual opinion for whom a small (is beautiful) perspective, local action, and self-help carry the proper luster. Not all celebrants of localist approaches toward global problems renounce a concurrent affection for the big state or agree with each other on anything. Yet for a number of these globalists, in order to address the urgent difficulties before us we must repudiate big state liberalism which, at best, has gotten us nowhere toward solutions so far and (at worst) is, in fact, one of the major causes of our present mess.

There is a somewhat determined 1960s flavor in localists' certainty that only when we get back to a human scale, decentralized power and control, can we transform our global emergency into opportunities for communal human development.[27] Part of the argument is practical, that only individuals working in local contexts will know how to reduce or eliminate the specific causes of excessive consumer waste, tragic misuse of the environment, and the like.[28] Localists are similarly confident that a decentralized orientation will get people involved to help themselves as individuals and as a community. In the process they will develop individual and collective competence.[29] The resulting gains will not be just environmental but will also expand the democratic community. We will begin "empowering ourselves."[30]

Bruce Stokes's *Helping Ourselves: Local Solutions to Global Problems* suggests programs as diverse as home and community gardens, local energy creation, even breast feeding to illustrate what local people can do for themselves.[31] Kirkpatrick Sale is entranced with the promise of small-scale technology, which he expects to flower only in a local setting.[32] Murray Bookchin is convinced that "municipal" operation of the economy will make a tremendous environmental difference.[33] In these and other examples proponents argue that decentralized institutions and local solutions will be more practical, more creative, and more community-oriented, better for the globe and better for real people in specific circumstances.

The high level of conviction of those who advocate the localist approach to global crisis equals the level of urgency common to the writings of those who would have recourse to the central government. In each case the support can run thin surprisingly soon in sometimes very long arguments; one senses a poverty of new ideas. Calling on national government or celebrating localist communities may be the answer(s), but stale air hovers around these proposals.

A second prevailing image is the ideal of the earth as community, an ideal popular not just among globalists.[34] It is favored in self-conscious distinction from nationalism, destructive or wasteful competition among nations, and, of course, war. Less clear are the integral definitional connotations of global community. Also undeveloped is the case for global community in many of the discussions of the topic. Almost ritualistic invocation of the concept of global thinking does not help us; if anything, it impedes the reflection that is essential if the concept is meant seriously.

However, some boundaries may be discerned. Central to the idea of the global community at first glance is one basic empirical belief: the conviction that all people on the planet are increasingly interdependent in everything from economics to the environment. The conclusion follows that a global community is inexorably unfolding (even if often unrecognized) around us. Our first job, we are told, is to recognize this reality and (it is taken for granted) respect it.[35]

Thus on second glance global community is not merely a fact to be accommodated but a normative good. Respect means approve, support, sustain. The urgent necessity is not just to achieve a consciousness of global community as a reality; the present imperative for "world consciousness is also an urgent normative value."[36] One should not misperceive the plethora of computer analyses and statistical projections pervading globalist literature. Whatever else they are about, they are as much or more a cry for global thinking, for global community, as studies on the bomb, mineral depletion, ozone layers, or water pollution.

In the language of jargon, the idea of interrelatedness goes with the core concept of sustainability. Survival is our goal and only by appreciating the reality and necessity of the interconnectedness of the natural world can we survive.[37] The choice is starkly drawn. We must have "planetary government or the war of all against all."[38] From another angle, global planning based on a kind of planetary bargain among the human race to ensure survival constitutes the essence of the community these globalists seek.[39] Another emphasis is on cooperation among nations, a rather vague but clearly more modest goal.[40]

The first step toward a global community is attitudinal change. The hope is that such a transformation will facilitate a similar shift in behavior and lead us to appreciate our global, interconnected community as fact and ideal, spurring us on to preserve what we are so quickly destroying.

Our Survival

The global model of community often complements the theme of survival. Not every globalist speaks the language of survivalism, but survivalists can be counted on to be globalists, concerned with community, conscious of planetary limitations and vulnerabilities, and impatient with human inertia and disunity.[41] A premier spokesman is Jonathan Schell, whose polemic against nuclear weapons takes for granted an obligation to the future of our species as the basis of his communal ethic. In his rendering of our future, a disarmed world free from nuclear weapons gives us the chance to choose to have a future for the planetary community. It does not guarantee survival, to be sure, but without such conditions the chances for survival are bleak.[42]

Schell's commitment appears to derive from his judgment about the possibilities of nuclear Armageddon. This threat to our survival creates an obligation which serves as the foundation for both Schell's community and his politics. Much, then, turns on Schell's estimate of the potential for nuclear cataclysm. What this would look like Schell draws in painful and lengthy detail. He concludes, of course, that extinction is the likely result of a nuclear war; from this conclusion, the rest of his argument follows.[43]

For William Ophuls survival is also the fundamental challenge to politics today, indeed to all human activity. There will be no global community in any sense unless we are able to appreciate what we have to do to advance both the chances of survival and the quality of the human community.[44] Robert Heilbroner's widely read *Inquiry into the Human Prospect* also pursues community almost exclusively in a survivalist context. A self-conscious globalist, he has a genuine affection for a global sense of community and global governing institutions. But his primary concern is survival, and his axis rarely spins away from that point. Thus Heilbroner is not given to effusions on behalf of community as the place for participatory politics, republican virtue, or a religious revival. Rather, he sternly admonishes us that if the first and third worlds do not get beyond politics as usual and unite, they are going to destroy each other and all of us in a war over dwindling resources. Survival is at stake and ordinary politics may have to take a back seat.[45]

Such a perspective is a good deal less unique than one might think. Politics is suspect throughout this literature, for better or for worse. The sense of crisis overwhelms all. Complex, countervailing, and wide open political systems garner little praise. Few of these intellectuals openly repudiate democracy in the manner of such activists as "Earth First!" Indeed, the Greens argue that they are among its most ardent supporters. But whether the goal is national planning, small scale community, or global community, disenchantment has spread to much more than technology. The messiness of mundane politics, interpreted as conflicting interests and passions, draws equal skepticism. The question asked is simple: Do we have time for that?[46]

Still, in Heilbroner and others there is a curious serenity. Amidst alarms over the extinction of planetary life, confidence reappears. Survival may be on the line and we are solemnly informed that we must respond by fashioning an approach to world community. Yet in the long run, with or without proper action from us, fitting responses will emerge; they are inevitable because adaptation is the process in nature and in the universe.[47] There is, however, no reason to believe that humans, much less human community in any form, will still exist then.

Survivalism has its critics to be sure, most acutely Christopher Lasch in his underread book, *The Minimal Self*.[48] Lasch's scathing analysis focuses on Americans who just try to get by or survive, with its implicit corollary that most people have low hopes and few dreams. But Lasch discovers the same phenomena elsewhere too. Our current tendencies to become obsessed with environmental dilemmas or nuclear disaster are emblems of survivalism. For him they are not a sign of commitment to community or to any other major change in the United States or the world (much to his regret) but a language of retreat, stripped of dreams and from which we can expect little authentic community to emerge.

This is not exactly a congenial view for many globalists. They can hardly fail to recognize those who have retreated to the mountains or others who are concerned only with basic survival. In general, though, globalists are activists, determined to fight for a future where community figures prominently; they are not at all in retreat. Yet Lasch is really asking how life-affirming many globalists are who dwell on survival (of the globe or just their own). He points out that more and more, some are proclaiming the necessity of personal and societal asceticism and denial almost as a religion. He sees a kind of minimalism whose only connection with community may be the model of the monastery.[49]

Nature

Walter Anderson in his book *To Govern Evolution* warns his public to watch for a certain type of environmentalist, the kind who adore, even worship, nature and undertake to keep it in a treasured place far from ugly human hands.[50] To Anderson, such souls are not realistic either about nature or the interactions between humans and nature that must be part of any strategy to save the global community.

Nature is at the center of all discussions among globalists. It is routine now to perceive nature as interdependent, with humans as parts of the whole: a seamless web of nature as fact and value. A frequent analysis is that our crises originate quite directly in human separation from the rest of nature (with never a hint of the opposite, which might suggest stunningly different problems). The goal is a return to true nature, a transformation of the human species into a community not just of itself but above all with the rest of nature. This is the real global community.[51]

Urgent invocations to end the war with the rest of nature are frequent and ardent. Sometimes they come with an aura of mysticism; concepts suggesting community such as harmony[52] and holism[53] take on near sacred qualities. But there are also more sober admonitions to construct a communal life for humans that is "compatible with ecological imperatives and other natural laws";[54] at other junctures accommodation is the more modest proposal.[55] Always the analysis is that man and nature are on a collision course and their reconciliation is the only way.[56]

The cause for the failure to achieve this model of community is often found in the tradition of human domination over the rest of nature. In short, humans get most of the blame for our current mess, our deep lack of global community. Schell articulates the opinion: Far from enhancing our lives, "the rising tide of human mastery over nature has brought about a categorical increase in the power of death on earth."[57]

Christianity in particular attracts harsh judgment on the issue of human domination. Lynn White's classic 1967 article "The Historic Roots of Our Ecologic Crisis" laid down a disturbing challenge which has hardly diminished in force.[58] He charges that the West has been too influenced by the Judeo-Christian conception of nature, which he interprets as a belief that God gave humans dominion over nature. The results of such a belief have been little short of disastrous. The case is usually formulated on selected passages drawn from the Old Testament rather than by a serious analysis of either Jewish or Christian scriptures as a whole or of the overall conceptions and role of Christian ideas of nature in Western history. But without question chapter and verse are available in Genesis and elsewhere that affirm a view of human domination over the rest of nature.[59]

That nature is not especially beneficent, or that union with it is a dubious good are, of course, conceivable positions. Among globalists who look to nature such ideas are appalling, in fact dangerous, and deny the proper basis for community. Globalists dismiss any other basis, including faith in that curious creature of nature called man. In an age of intellectual skepticism and, among globalists, overwhelming anxiety, close interrelatedness with nature represents community.

The foundations for such a connection with nature take several forms. Sometimes they appear in religious garb, despite the considerable tension between established religion and a movement which is often secular. As Roderick Nash establishes, there are signs of a "Greening of Religion."[60] What he and others term "ecotheology" has definitely burgeoned.[61] Moreover, tremendous interest in the subject now has grown from within Christianity. Some globalists, such as Paul Santmire, have creatively carved out a notion of the sacred right of nature within God's kingdom. Along with others of a more radical persuasion, he explicitly confronts the concept of domination in Christian teaching and denies its Christian truth or at least its centrality in Christianity. For him God is about all of nature conceived as one community.[62] Other Christian thinkers, more numerous at present, accent the interpretation of stewardship, which they correctly note is an ancient Christian perspective. Within a range of attitudes about human domination over the rest of nature, theologians of stewardship share the conviction that nature is a gift of God and all of it must be held and used in that spirit alone. None of nature exists for human plundering or environmental desecration. Nature is a trust from God and thus is sacred. God sees the planet earth and all on it as a whole, a gift which must be lovingly cared for. Humans in particular have a major responsibility to honor this trust and to preserve God's natural community.[63] Evangelical Christians in particular have made a vigorous case for a biblical basis for a theology of stewardship or community. They often grant the plain teaching of the Bible, that God made all living things for humans, while accenting God's expectations that humans protect God's creation. This perspective has support in numerous passages in

Genesis, in the story of the ancient Hebrews, and in the example of Jesus. Christ is portrayed in the Bible as one who used and loved animals and who saw his relationship to his people on earth as one of love, just as humans were to see their relationship with the rest of God's creation.[64]

These perspectives hardly satisfy those who argue that Christianity in particular has a false and dangerous conception of the natural community. Such critics dismiss it as fundamentally uninterested in the community of nature and as committed to nature's exploitation by human beings (patriarchal or just simply anthropomorphic).[65]

Some other religious traditions are also explored and plumbed by ecotheologians looking for a religious ground for nature and the community of nature. The approach is often rather eclectic and includes celebrating a bit of one religion here and a part of another there.[66] Among the preferred spiritual alternatives are Taoism, feminist spirituality, and Buddhism. The objective is a religion devoted to worship of nature perceived as holistic and holy, nature as sacred community.[67] Views which, however admirable otherwise, do not display proper ecopiety correspondingly can expect harsh censure.[68]

In fact it is not yet clear how many globalists care about spiritual concerns or even want to think this way. One recent survey of the American Green movement concludes that religious perspectives are held only by a distinct minority.[69] Probably this story remains to be developed. The interconnections of religion, nature, and community are only now beginning to receive much attention.

Another approach to nature sees it as morally sovereign in itself, the foundation for its own community, for its own self. This view is most frequently presented in the current claims that nonhumans, as part of nature, have rights. The first sophisticated articulation of the moral authority of the community of nature was in Christopher Stone's essay of 1971, "Should Trees Have Standing?"[70] Advocates of animal rights such as Peter Singer and Tom Regan are also participants in these expanding conversations.[71]

Two dilemmas are particularly significant in this approach. The first raises several questions: Where does one draw the line? Who or what does or does not have rights? How do we decide? Is consciousness required? Will needs serve instead of rights as a criterion? and, to get right to the hard cases, does a stone have rights, does a cancer cell, does a dog with rabies?[72] Second is the issue of relevancy: What does all this discussion about animals or stones having natural rights have to do with community? We know many intellectuals object to modern liberalism because it is too in love with rights, hardly a concept directed to community. The concept of rights points us to the individual as opposed to and often in opposition to others. How does the claim that animals or material objects have natural rights then foster or reflect community?

One may reply that by recognizing the rights of more than humans one is affirming a greater community in nature than simply the human one. But this is as yet a contested and underdeveloped claim. It is, for example, not apparent what the ultimate ground is for these claims. Above all, much more argument and explication is needed.[73]

This perspective has gained a good deal of ground lately through the zealous work of animal rights activists, yet it is mild stuff in comparison to a final model of community as within nature. "Deep ecology" or "biocentric" ethics has among its enthusiasts the radical Earth First! organization and serious thinkers such as J. Baird Callicott and John Rodman.[74] They are explicit communitarians of nature, placing all parts of nature together as a whole, each aspect on an equal footing with every other. For them nature is, in fact, greater than any of its parts and we must therefore not allow any privilege for the human being. Since their vision is self-consciously holistic, ecosystems are what they respect within nature; the essence of their politics is to liberate nature from human domination. Along the way, they are confident that the consequence can be a rebirth of their concept of the natural community.[75]

In contrast to these modes of thinking is quite another perception of nature and its dynamics, the "steady state" thesis, invariably articulated in restrained, minimalist, modern language. Words such as community, interrelatedness with nature, and the like disappear, replaced by words and phrases such as steady state, equilibrium, or homeostatic stability.[76] In each instance the model is nature visualized as a stable, ordered community. Evolution and change take place, of course, but they do so within nature and by its timetable. The accompanying message is that growth at our headlong pace is destructive and must be disciplined within nature, properly understood by humans. We are, in effect, urged to enter the community of nature.

Problems

Amid the arguments over nature and the global community, arguments which head off in innumerable directions, some voices still raise doubts: Some critics just don't see much crisis to get terribly upset about and suspect that we will do just fine at muddling through.[77] The issue often centers on the evidence of whether ours is still a "resourceful earth." Skeptics of the globalist approach read the environmental signs as mixed rather than as unidimensionally alarming,[78] denying that we lack adequate sources of energy,[79] maintaining that we have enough food, forests, minerals, and so on.[80] At their most positive, their dissent is all but total: "The world in 2000 will be *less crowded . . . less polluted, more stable ecologically,* and *less vulnerable* to *resource-supply disruption* than the world we live in now."[81]

Some skeptics defend the value of technology in the struggle to meet global problems, even daring to assert that "the necessary technology to live comfortably on renewable resources exists."[82] Such optimists admit that survival will not be easy—or automatic.[83] They insist, though, that the globalist mood—somber, even desperate—is exaggerated at best. To them its real ground may lie in pessimistic judgments about human nature.

Clearly, some skeptics maintain, it does not lie in the findings of science. Indeed, they charge that many globalists have left science embarrassingly far behind. "The dire talk of impending doom has little place in a scientific analysis."[84] Skeptics insist that the future cannot be easily, much less dogmatically, predicted, no matter how much science teaches us today. Assertions to the contrary blithely ignore the long record of failed past scientific predictions.[85] The truth often is, as dissenters remarked of *Global 2000,* that "the principal findings and conclusions . . . reflect the . . . beliefs and concerns of the sponsors and authors. These preceded the project."[86]

Such predilections may be there or not, but the question is what do these objections and others have to do with the engagement of global community and/or nature and community so prevalent today? The quality of science, the judgment about environmental pollution, and the sometimes flamboyant predictions of some globalists do not affect their orientation toward community. They do affect their sense of urgency and the alarms they raise to the rest of us in the name of the earth or nature as communities. Otherwise, the perspective of community remains very much intact.

More relevant to the matter of community is the need to define and defend claims that nature is a community with normative weight, indeed with supreme normative weight. The same applies to the globe or to the universe. More pressing also is the need to articulate what nature means, what it includes, why there should be no hierarchies in it. Similarly, globalist thinkers need to address exactly what political implications follow from their survivalist analysis and from their aspirations to community. Indeed, their ideas of community in general are vague and underdeveloped, often empty. Some globalists could not agree more, but they are sometimes more patient. Pessimists in some ways, they can also be optimists, confident that the whole earth in nature can be a successful community. Sometimes they have "a vision rooted in attunement to the creative life processes of the earth/universe as primary healer, inventor, and the human as a continuation of those processes."[87] But for right now survival of the global community is essential and nitpickers must face this unpleasant reality. The lesson of community will have to be learned and lived—or else no one will learn or live anymore.

Chapter Eight

Varieties of Religious Community

The greatest nineteenth- and early twentieth-century students of Western society expected religion to disappear within the modern age. Marx and Weber had few doubts about religion's fate; Freud was less sure, but like Marx took it for granted that religion was an anachronism that could and should be abolished.[1] And yet, of course, religion has not quietly gone away. This is obviously true not only in Africa or India or Israel or Iran but also in the United States, where religion in many forms remains securely established in the culture and among the population at large.

Its standing among political intellectuals has been something else again. To say the least, religious themes have not been dominant or even much discussed in the ordinary intellectual discourse of most political intellectuals. Certainly this was true to the 1970s and, one may argue, for far longer than that. It was not so much that religion was denied, in the manner of nineteenth-century combatants such as Freud or Nietzsche, but that it seemed to disappear from the discourse. It appeared to be dying from neglect.

Of late, though, religion has enjoyed a renaissance. Though it has charged off in a grand variety of sometimes conflicting directions, reflecting diverse theologies, denominations, and political agendas, its presence in the public world is evident in noisy debates, determined religious-political movements, and presidential campaigns. This fact has compelled a good many political intellectuals to admit it to their universe—not their universe of faith necessarily, but their world of political realities. And for others it has gone beyond this point, given the revival of interest in religion in a normative sense even (or perhaps especially) outside the confines of elite divinity schools and the like.[2]

My concern in this chapter is not with the revival of interest in religion in one sense or another but with how this connects with and spurs on involvement with community; thus I examine those thinkers and activists who draw a tight connection between religion and community in the United States. In this process my reach will be intentionally broad, in order to embrace the diverse expressions of the interconnections of religion and community in current thinking, and I shall explore specific examples which illustrate this range.

One expression of that revived interest is the current contest over the place of religion in our history and within our political institutions, a debate over religion's place in our national community and in every community in our nation. I concentrate on the era of our Revolution and Constitution as the context for the debate between those who emphasize the centrality of religion in the Founding of our national community and the separatists who have dominated historical interpretation for the past thirty years. Others argue in broader fields. Some theories consider religion's importance in terms of community over the full course of American history. Always the debate is only partly a matter of alternative readings of history. It also includes the struggle over the legitimacy of religious community and sometimes of any perspective on community within our national experience.[3]

Others approach the subject more directly than by arguing from a historical perspective. Proceeding from pragmatism or faith, they contend that religion may be or sometimes must be the only way to encourage the community in the United States that they often ardently seek. These voices, though often tentative and cautious, are very much heard today. They are represented in the conclusions of political intellectuals as disparate as Daniel Bell and Robert Bellah.[4]

Also considered here are those for whom religion is inescapably tied in practice to community. They are less well known perhaps, but their impact is increasing. For them participation and practice, actually connecting religion and community, are essential. They are not prepared to operate only at the level of theory or theoretical speculation about history or current culture, and they do not. Perhaps we may see them as heralds of religious communitarianism in its fullest form, unapologetic and active in presenting their convictions to a country they see as sadly misdirected.[5]

This chapter explores these approaches to community through religion and examines intellectuals who consider religion and community in our history, in our present situation, and in practical living. This arena of political thought is a fractured, sometimes cautious, sometimes zealous, often contentious realm in American intellectual discourse. But it is a fascinating one, not least because so many previous social theorists expected no such discourse to exist in our day.

The Fight for American History

Some intellectuals consider a religious conception of community through arguments over its role in American history. By now we know to expect this contest everywhere. All of American history today is a plain where contestants for the soul of the United States quite openly wage war. Sometimes this is a scholarly dispute which may seem, but is not, distant from the larger struggle. At other points, values and motives of religion/community are directly up front as the fight over our history goes on. Either way the contest demonstrates that religion and community are now significant matters of dispute among some intellectuals in the context of our history.

One central arena for disagreement has been the role and significance of religion in the establishment of the United States as a nation. Put another way, the issue concerns the role religion played in the conceptions of political community in our Founding. Some conservative evangelical intellectuals insist that the United States has a political tradition historically grounded in (Protestant) Christian religious values and founded on a particular religious tradition. Moreover, for them the establishment of our political community from a Christian tradition is an event of central significance which we should not ignore now. They see us as sadly lacking community and call us to look at our past and what it can offer us. Those who reject this reading of our Founding experience as religious or particularly as Christian are equally fervent. For them there is little in the model of religious community in our Founding period or, often, in any case, that has much to offer us in our current age. The contest over religion, community, and the Founding of our nation is often intense, a dialectic serious on its own historical terms but made more so by the concerns of our age.

The argument has its sober, scholarly side. Of late standard interpretations that for the most part ignored or downplayed the role of religion and religious conceptions of community in the Revolutionary and Constitutional periods of American history are under fire. The revisionism often notes not only a more religious history but also the bias implicit in previous versions and is rarely willing to accept it meekly. No doubt, the times are changing in this arena of research. Even such nearly untouchable authorities as Gordon Wood have drawn scholarly fire for their virtual neglect of the powerful and omnipresent role of religion and religious ideas in the Founding Era and before in colonial America.[6]

The argument goes forward one way by considering how religious American political culture was in the late eighteenth century and how religious its principal political influentials were, especially Madison and Jefferson. What were their goals regarding the place of religion and religious models of community in the American political community? Put more narrowly, though always closely connected, the issue sometimes is framed as a dispute over the original intent of the First Amendment of the Constitution and its provisions for no establishment and for free exercise of religion. How important was religion and religious community supposed to be in our national existence?

There is absolutely no consensus among intellectuals concerned with late-eighteenth-century America on these questions. Those advancing the thesis that the United States can be understood only as a nation born religious (Protestant Christian) have an easy time of marshaling evidence for signs of widely accepted Christian culture and its assumptions about community. Their claims are no fantasy.[7] Nor can there be much doubt that it was common for states to have established religions and religious communities at the time of the Constitution (and in some cases long afterward). Indeed, even states often identified as representing an alternative tradition are not effective examples. Such no establishment states as Delaware, New Jersey, and Pennsylvania all routinely required public officials to be Christians.[8]

On the other hand, it is equally easy and quite common to portray another image. Some argue that the late eighteenth century was not exactly a time of religious vigor in American life, public or private. Moreover, it is well known that many of the Founders were not noted for their Christian faith or piety.[9] Their views ran in a number of directions, but more than a few of them were less Christians than vague deists, believers in the rational religion of God's benevolence, a perspective which did not include faith in the resurrection of Jesus or a fundamentally religious view of community.[10]

All of this applies doubly to those central architects of a free United States, Jefferson (of the Declaration of Independence) and Madison (of the Constitution). Given their importance, it is no wonder their attitudes toward church and state and religion and community in American public life have generated such dispute. Critics of claims that Jefferson and Madison explicitly rejected a foundation of religious community for our nation and did so by founding the principles of separation of church and state, separation even of religion and political communities, have opted for one of two approaches: Some dismiss the importance of Jefferson's and Madison's judgments in our historical story; others insist their separatist views have been exaggerated by those hostile to religion and models of religious community in American public life. A third option that assumes casually that Jefferson, Madison, and the other Founders favored an explicit Christian foundation for our government is now recognized as simply false.

William Lee Miller, a caring and yet detached analyst of the subject, concludes that Jefferson and Madison were separatists. They were not hostile to (private) religion necessarily, but they were antagonistic to its use as a binding thread or as the standard for community for an American political community.[11] Miller touches most of the sensitive points and recognizes as much as anyone can the contemporary stakes behind so much of the current intellectual argument.

One of the pleasures of Miller's high-spirited discussion is that he does not replace one piety with another. Jefferson becomes no secular saint fighting religious communities at every point as he advances modern conceptions of freedom. Miller recalls Jefferson's affirmation of separating churches and religion from politics in the name of freedom while he self-consciously promoted his own version of the good community, that is, his own political orthodoxy, eager to use the University of Virginia to serve his goals.[12]

Miller is a weak temporizer in comparison with more militant separatists such as Leo Pfeffer or those who write in *The Journal of Church and State*. They are far more ardently committed to unqualified separation of church and state and the rejection of any connection between religious communities and our nation's overall political order as well as to the argument that Jefferson and Madison were prophets of this separatist view.[13] Still others, such as Richard Cord, argue that the policy record of Jefferson and Madison was more mixed than modern separatists like to suggest.[14] Cord's Madison was hardly reluctant to acknowledge our nation's grounding in religious conceptions of our national community. He allowed government chaplains, for example, and also issued Thanksgiving proclamations. Cord concedes Jefferson is the more fitting exemplar for those who want to claim our Founding was secular and separatist, though even Jefferson used the government to finance evangelism for the Indians. But Cord reminds us that Jefferson was in France during the Constitutional Convention. He was not a central figure in the Founding of the United States as a nation, however great his role in the struggle for independence.[15]

Cord is explicit in his awareness that distant history is not exactly the decisive matter at issue here. He insists that this fight over the Founders is in good part a contest over whether there is a legitimate tradition of America conceived as a religious community and whether there is authority in the American past which can be used in proposing visions of community today. Cord laments the 1960s and 1970s when he claims liberal intellectuals fostered an image of the United States as a public community with religion kept strictly private, thus rewriting the Founding Era for their modern objectives.[16]

The issue today of course concerns how much religion should be involved in public life and to what extent it should serve as the foundation for community in the United States. At times this issue arises most explicitly in legal controversies over how to interpret the First Amendment's prohibition of establishment of religion. Does it mean no government aid to any religious groups except unintentionally, when in pursuit of other legitimate goals? Or does the First Amendment only prohibit assistance to a single religious group? If religious groups in general may receive aid, then the door is wide open for public/religious partnerships in the pluralistic mode of contemporary America where one religion is as good as another—almost. Looming in the background is the matter of how relevant religious communities and religious understandings may be in fashioning our polity and our culture. The stakes are large and everybody knows it.

More and more this debate centers on not just understandings of religion and religious communities in our history but also on attitudes toward religion in general. There is an unsurprising correlation between many of those who believe the Framers were sympathetic to religion and intended to prohibit establishment only when defined as supporting a single church or religion and the interest in a religiously influenced national community today, just as there is between those who see the Framers as opposed to establishment of any sort and the support for contemporary secular politics. This observation does not always apply nor does it ignore the worthwhile work of dispassionate scholars. Yet it does report things as they are.[17]

Leonard Levy's recent argument—that Founders could not have meant to accept multiple establishment at the national level because state establishments were in fact multiple establishments and that the First Amendment was a self-conscious repudiation of state practice for the national government—is a good example of the dominant temper. His argument is a stimulating variation on the separatist reading of foundational history that is valuable in itself. It is also very much a part of Levy's continuing political effort to keep religious (i.e., Christian) elements far away from American political life.[18]

Perhaps the best single meditation on the entire subject is Thomas Curry's *First Freedoms*.[19] Curry makes the case that Americans, including the Founders, were congenial to and connected with religion. Along with evangelical intellectuals such as Whitehead and Schaeffer, he believes that religion provided a supportive setting for the success of the American republic.[20] But Curry interprets much of the current controversy over original intent as miscast. The argument forces us into the debate over whether single establishment or all religious involvement was prohibited. There was little thinking of this sort, he maintains.

The Founders wanted to help religion, without doubt. They approved of it and thought our public community would need its sustaining strengths. At the same time, there was a countervailing anxiety that religion could nourish political and intellectual tyranny, and they wanted none of that in the United States. No establishment was really about checking tyranny, not about eliminating establishment whose

American forms at that moment in our history were hardly tyranny in action. The First Amendment prohibited establishment in the national government on the one hand, while states were busily practicing it on the other. Yet there was no contradiction; people wanted to help religion and expected it to be vital for the American political experience even as they were leery of too direct a connection between government and religion.[21]

Mark Tushnet offers a variation on this analysis, less about detailed state practices, but one which involves a reflective reconceptualization of the debate over original intent in light of the Framers' community-oriented republicanism. Tushnet suggests that the Framers were republicans who were interested in an overall common good and who were procommunity. At the same time they did not have a rigid definition of the common good or community and spurned single-minded and legalistic positions regarding the First Amendment or anything else. That we at times have turned to bitter legalistic hairsplitting, leading to a law of church and state that is in utter confusion, testifies to our current affinity for the stripped-down, rights-oriented legalism which is our sad substitute for (republican) community.[22]

Arguments about the role of religion and religious-based conceptions of community in our history head out into many different corners of American history. There has been a good deal of work, for example, on this dimension in the political thought and action of the early nineteenth century, and Nathan Hatch is a significant contributor.[23] Also present these days are interpretations which assess the centrality of religion for the experience of community over our full history.

Such broad, and sometimes one may say theoretical, analyses have their own history. No doubt the most influential model is de Tocqueville's argument for religion's inestimable importance in America, especially in maximizing community. De Tocqueville saw and expected little in the way of national community or even local community defined as deep, explicitly shared values or ways of life. We were, in his now proverbial image, too restless and competitive a people for that. We were not inclined to go beyond our propensity for associations except in our private lives and private feelings.

In this private realm lay our communities and the foundation for what public community we had—the citadels of family, religion, and patriotism. Here in this private world the public world was made possible. Specifically, religion was the instrument that enabled America to operate. It secured the home, the basic community, and provided the communal values taught there, values which made possible a larger social life: "Men cannot be cured of the love of riches, but they may be persuaded to enrich themselves by none but honest means."[24] That lesson and others were learned through religion, with its ethic of community. Women in the home were specific agents of religion and community, almost as a modern reader of Carol Gilligan would predict. No wonder de Tocqueville concluded of the (male) American: "I am inclined to think that if faith be wanting in him, he must be subject, and if he be free, he must believe."[25] Religion was the cornerstone of all community or of what passed for it in civil society and flourished in the home.

De Tocqueville's perspective on the connection of religion and community is, to say the least, intriguing when approached from our rather contrasting time. Although no analysis today of the intertwining of religion and community in our history matches his in his time, there are a good many others. Consider the hypothesis of civic religion and Robert Bellah's work in this area which dominated in recent years.[26] The thesis itself is simple, though the dynamics it describes as they operate over time are distinctly neither simple nor free of controversy. The thesis is that American political culture, and thus the nation as a national community, has had an intimate connection with religion of a special kind, a civic religion. This has served the immensely important tasks of legitimizing the nation and of guiding its political values. In our country's instance this civic religion has drawn deeply from Christianity, though it is distinct from it. It shows its roots in its ordinary coupling of America and God, God's grace, God's blessing, and in some versions, God's judgment. It also reveals its roots and its sway in the American culture's belief in progress, moralism, and individualism, among other suggested connections.[27]

Theories differ, but there is considerable agreement on the idea that our society and, it is often proposed, all societies require a civic religion in order to exist and that such a religion will grow in good part from what religion is in its culture and then cast its own net of influence into that culture.[28] Thus there is considerable agreement that religion and our national community are necessarily intertwined in the United States.

It may be, as Victor Ferkiss suggests, that our civic religion—our vague association of God and the United States, if you will—may be read as an index of the weakness of community in the United States. Perhaps it is no more than a puny substitute for vigorous community— political or religious or whatever. Even so, this does not diminish the significance of a putative civic religion. It becomes all the more vital for a nation which, by this analysis, may be starved for serious community.[29]

Lately interest in the idea of civic religion has waned somewhat, perhaps a quiet confession of the indefatigable march of secularism into our public life, but other theories associating religion and American community have sprung to life. They testify to the endurance in contemporary intellectual life of the idea that community and religion are inseparable in understanding the American story.[30]

Richard Neuhaus offers the analysis in his *Naked Public Square* that religion has been the strong underpinning of the American democratic community for at least one hundred fifty years. According to Neuhaus, religion furnished American democracy its ideology and its common values—respect for the community, above all. At the same time the nation has kept apart from the dangers of an established religion or the drift guaranteed by a society bereft of religion. It has been a beautiful arrangement, one in which our public community has prospered.[31]

Richard Reeves argues that de Tocqueville's description of the power of private religion in molding public community no longer applies for our era.[32] Neuhaus echoes this conclusion and also remarks on what he sees as the declining energy of religion in the public sphere. His reasons have to do with the secularization of American political and cultural elites, a familiar neoconservative unease.

For Neuhaus the public square (the national community) has been emptied of our historic religiously formed values. But it has not stayed naked for long. Into the space have come the liberal and secular elites who have captured the centers of American culture, intellect, and communication since the late 1960s. Through their strategic locations, these disciples of the ideology of secularism promote the triumph of self-interested and secular society, speeding a predictable collapse of public community. And Neuhaus charges that the consequences are all too obvious in our politics of organized selfishness and in the alienated citizen.[33]

William Lee Miller's engaging work calls attention to another version of the argument that religion has left a decisive imprint on community in America. Miller sees the idea and practice of community in America most enhanced by social religion, by those dimensions of American religion that most honor social reform: care for the suffering, weak, or despised elements of our larger society. Thus Miller follows H. Richard Niebuhr and the tradition of Social Gospel. Religion should be a force for the kingdom on earth, for the community here, for those left out of the whole, calling the whole to servanthood for those left out. His interest in the American contest is in how much it has served this role.[34]

Miller is not especially concerned with religion and the public sector. If anything, his bias lies toward a disconnection between religion, community, and government. Though hardly obsessive on the subject,[35] Miller is distinctly cool to those who care about religion as a grounding for community and are prepared to bring the state to bear as the means to that end. Miller's hero is Roger Williams, who sought to build community through religion but did so outside government and its coercive mechanisms.[36]

Obviously, there are many significant students of the American experience who do not see religion as a significant variable in discussing community. But Bellah, Neuhaus, and Miller, among others, illustrate those who in recent years have begun to do so. Nor is the point some inaccurate claim that their perspectives are the same. On the contrary, they are interesting because they read our history variously. Significantly, however, they all assign a major place for religion in the life and struggles of the idea(s) of community in our historical journey. Moreover, their enterprise proceeds always with one eye focused squarely on our own age.

Religiously Informed Community

We know that the characteristic method for contemporary intellectuals to approach community is through investigating American history. It is a more indirect and a safer route, perhaps, than any other. Yet such an attempt is not the entire story. One can hardly ignore the current and much more direct intellectual engagement with questions of religion and community. Indeed, a good portion of even the historical work today explicitly addresses the issue of the association of religion and community and their interactive needs if one or both are to thrive.[37]

Intellectuals who approach the issue of community directly from contemporary conclusions about what religion may have to offer often start with the familiar mood of crisis. They assume that community, as they respectively define it, has collapsed in the United States with ugly and disturbing consequences and that a need for community is a given. So is the conviction that a properly conceived religious or religiously influenced community represents a possible solution for an atomized and wayward America.

One problem that frequently arises, however, is the (not so little) matter of the tenability of religion. It is particularly troublesome for those such as Daniel Bell who wish they could believe but cannot and who project their existential situation onto the American culture as a whole. For Bell religion could help us fashion a desperately needed public community (what he calls a "public household") and along the way provide both limits and direction for the already swollen numbers of Americans who are lost. It could do these things, Bell reasons, but it will not because religious faith is not alive—in Bell, or in the culture— and we cannot restore that faith by wishing it were vibrant or by affirming its necessity.[38]

For others, of course, faith is very much alive and utilitarian urgencies are not the decisive aspects of religion. In American political thought today one encounters quite a number who, although generally tactful in encouraging religion, leave no doubt as to their stance. Some are direct, as are Bellah and his associates in *Habits of the Heart;* some make the point through marshaling the past for contemporary service, as does John Patrick Diggins and his *Lost Soul of American Politics;*[39] others, such as Alasdair MacIntyre, are more oblique in a setting that covers the philosophical history of Western civilization;[40] still others focus on the present and are direct, while urging historical awareness.[41]

For these predominantly Christian thinkers, religion does not promise an end to conflict or some perfect, cooperative community. Thinkers such as John Diggins or Glenn Tinder refer quite comfortably to sin and the unending barriers it forms to such dreamy hopes for community.[42] Indeed, one of the notable strengths they identify in a religious community, as they would have it, is that it will likely foster "modesty," "magnanimity," and the spurning of "killing in order to reform the earth from all evil."[43]

The persuasion that religion goes with community and that the former must have a rebirth if America is to grasp the latter is a prominent theme in the literature of community. Robert Bellah and his coauthors in *Habits of the Heart* argue this claim even as they admit that nothing is guaranteed, especially in our country where religion has so often taken individualist forms or offered an individualist morality.[44] Still, the hope, their only hope, is religion. For Diggins, the alternatives such as republican community are empty; they offer no "ethic of ultimate convictions,"[45] and in Tinder's view, they cannot carve out the path to human dignity, the absolute requisite for any community if it is to endure. Only God can do that. Without divine grounding we are wounded beings who will never create, much less experience, community.[46]

Stanley Hauerwas is an impressive exemplar of the intellectual as religious proponent of community. A Methodist, an associate of Catholicism, a self-declared admirer of the Mennonites,[47] Hauerwas cannot be typed religiously—or, for that matter, politically. His vision of community is also too textured to fit into any neat category, though it proceeds from his Christian commitment. Hauerwas concentrates on creating the Christian church, the Christian community, as the true community. He insists that Christians are summoned to reach for this goal rather than for a transformation of the United States government or society or whatever. Such is the faithful politics of a religious people, working to be the "kind of community the church must be to be faithful to the narratives central to Christian convictions."[48] Thus Christians as individuals and in their life together must struggle to live their faith. Without this effort and some success at it, without character and community, any broader reach into society fails. Hauerwas thus warns against "the liberal assumption that a just polity is possible without the people being just."[49] The church and its people, then, must start the process. They must be a community of nonviolence, of "acts of kindness, friendship, and the formation of families,"[50] who must care for the poor and the hurt and promote trust and reconciliation, acts so often neglected or left undone.[51]

The objective is a living community of sharing believers, witnessing to each other and to the larger society; it must not be a rigid, fixed community of faith. Hauerwas is too much of a modernist to welcome a religion/community erected on an absolutist or "foundation account" of faith. Such absolutes, he confidently assures his readers, need to be "recognized as illusory."[52] Faith, like community, must rest instead on its practice, on believers' lives or, as Hauerwas puts it in currently fashionable theological language, on their stories, their narratives in their experiences of life, both individually and collectively.[53]

Faith, it would seem, must necessarily bend to the specific context just as community must. And this is precisely why Hauerwas faults liberalism. It "presupposes that society can be organized without any narrative . . . it tempts us to believe . . . we are free to the extent that we have no story."[54] Liberalism strips away the story of each of us and, in a specific context, of what people have in common. It denies humanity and prevents community. Liberalism is also blatantly unsatisfactory for Hauerwas because in his view it is obsessed with freedom and happiness, innocent, so to say, of evil and of tragedy and unaware that freedom and happiness cannot be achieved apart from our history or from a common history—that is, apart from the community of tradition.[55]

Such sentiments unite Hauerwas with others attracted by local traditions and individual narratives in our age—Alasdair MacIntyre, for example. The similarities are there, but the unavoidable distinction is the emphasis on a religious context. It pervades all that Hauerwas says, every word he writes about community. He does laud traditions, cite Aristotle, and discuss the family at length,[56] but the setting is not an affirmation of a certain rationalism or the classical tradition; it is a context-specific Christianity. Thus in lamenting our present infatuation with liberty and diversity (of a sort), Hauerwas affirms that one's liberty can be authentic "only by participation in a truthful polity capable of forming a virtuous people."[57] Such a view would be equally congenial to Bloom or MacIntyre. Hauerwas differs, though, on what is a "truthful polity"; for him it is religious above all.

It is important to return to his insistence that it is in the church, in religious community—not a public community nor a gathering of scholars/students—that virtue is nurtured and community created. The religious is crucial even as it is open to change and growth in every particular context that defines it.[58] The same applies to every society. "Good societies enable . . . argument to continue so that the possibilities and limits of the tradition can be exposed. The great danger, however, is that the success of a tradition will stop its growth."[59]

To be sure, a skeptic, and I do not mean a religious skeptic, might ponder how far Hauerwas really is from the liberalism that he so resolutely rejects. It is true that emphasis on tradition or the reality of a complicated life as the heart of everyone's life story is not exactly standard liberal fare. Yet Hauerwas is the modern pragmatic liberal in his nonfoundational conception of truth, his horror of an unchanging society and religion, his affinity for the test of experience, narrative, and life story. The objective that comes into focus looks distinctly modernist: an open, fluid, flexible society. Yet this is not really quite so and its other face is less so. It is about a religious community of faith, far from the aspiration of modernist liberals of any stripe.

The examples might go on. Whether they foreshadow a dramatic expansion of the numbers of political intellectuals serious about religion in the search for community one cannot be sure; it is hard to tell or to measure such things. There is, however, no longer any doubt of a major presence among American political intellectuals of those who look to religion for nurturance of community. Twenty or thirty years ago their prominence and numbers were unexpected; a closed door appears to be inching open.

Religious Community and Practice

Another locale where religion forms a bridge to community is found in the movement toward religious community, whose origins (as opposed to justifications) lie in the 1960s and the so-called 1960s generation. This turning to community in practice has had as its steady companion serious intellectual interest and commitment expressed in numerous paeans and defenses in print. Several examples of these movements have garnered some intellectual enthusiasm. Few are in the mainstream of contemporary fashion, perhaps, but they are now too substantial an intellectual subculture to ignore. The most conspicuous example is the Christian community movement; the most action-oriented the Alinsky-influenced, direct-action religious groups; and the most intriguing the New Age religious orientations. We shall look at all three.

There are many Christian communities in the United States—partial communities, full communities. *Sojourners* magazine, perhaps the favorite publication of religious communitarians, provides an ongoing window to this world and encourages networking within it through its regular feature, "Connections." "Connections" is in part a publicity, a volunteer, and an employment service to enable Christians and assorted Christian communities and ministries to meet each other. In the process, it also serves as a display case for the dense variety of Christian groups which are at work. [60]

Two influential American intellectual proponents of the model of Christian community are Parker Palmer and Jim Wallis. Parker Palmer, associated with several experiments in community, among them Pendle Hill, the Quaker community outside Philadelphia, and the St. Benedict's Center, Madison, Wisconsin, is best known for his book, *The Company of Strangers: Christians and the Renewal of America's Public Life.* [61] Wallis, associated with the Sojourners Fellowship in a poor black neighborhood in Washington, D.C., is the author of innumerable essays in *Sojourners* magazine and several major works directed at Christian community, including *Agenda for a Biblical People* and *The Call to Conversion.* [62]

Wallis's Sojourners community grew out of the 1960s, the civil rights and Vietnam conflicts in particular, and a desire for engagement with a more communal life stimulated by biblical injunctions. As Wallis tells the story, Vietnam was "the historical occasion for a revival of biblical faith." [63] The fruit was not only the community itself but also its publication, *Sojourners* (at first, *The Post-American*) in 1971. *Sojourners* has come a long way since then and is now something of a modern bible for its Christian radicals, still faithful to its credo: "We require radical transformation, a new understanding of society and ourselves. As the analysis must be radical, so must our solutions." [64] Readership now has expanded far beyond its Protestant evangelical roots.

Wallis and others in the Christian community movement are predictably critical of the United States. *Sojourners* stands out in the intensity of its critique of what it declares to be the United States' vapid liberalism, flaccid institutions, and wrongheaded policy. Its editor, Wallis, has flatly declared "America is a fallen nation,"[65] agreeing with the late William Stringfellow that our "nation *is* fallen . . . America is a demonic principality."[66] Wallis, however, does not mean his judgment of this country to be exclusive, for the entire "world appears to be falling apart" and "the value of human life . . . to be steadily diminishing."[67]

Liberalism's failure to address community is for Wallis and his associates its greatest drawback. They see the problem as very real, demonstrated by the liberal culture in the United States in the existence of the homeless, our engagement with poverty and war, and the failure of Washington to act to change things.[68]

Parker Palmer is less inclined than Wallis and *Sojourners* to argue policy or institutions and more disposed to explore how to build community, how to move on from complaint to community. He insists that first of all people must nurture community and make a commitment to it in their congregation, church, and otherwise in their private lives. Such a mission is important in itself because we need the time and space in our private lives that communities can provide us. Moreover, they can allow us to go out of that world renewed and less "obsessive and fearful" to erect a more communal public life.[69]

The general feeling among all these people is that community building is a tough business. Dave and Neta Jackson have suggested that community is like a household: hard to achieve and harder to sustain. This judgment is, in fact, a frequent, sobering theme.[70] Graham Pulkingham agrees and has suggested that a great deal of luck will be needed along with determination, discipline, and love.[71] In an attractive and regular feature, *Sojourners* has recounted the joys and sorrows of Sojourners' own community.

Of course, Christian communicators like Wallis or Palmer have a passion to extend community far beyond the borders of any particular, local community or communities with which they are associated. They are believers not just in religion but in the religion of community. Much of Palmer's reflective theory, for example, concentrates on how to encourage "common vision, common effort, and common sharing of the fruits" of existence.[72] How to do this constantly fuels the *Sojourn-*

ers' rhetorical attack and leads Wallis and others toward concrete actions, to match deeds with words. Picketing, sit-ins, tax withholding, and symbolic assaults on defense facilities have served as witness.[73]

Palmer is eager to concentrate on teaching and learning, specifically about how to make public community and public spaces more communal and more open to the communal teachings of his religion. He has many detailed suggestions, confident that as involvement in public life helps people, they will appreciate both the expanding community and the individual spiritual growth that will follow.[74] But Palmer shares the view that the building of public community will be tough.[75] Among other reasons, it will mandate a painstakingly difficult interaction between the public and the private both in the larger public and smaller private worlds.[76] That it can be done is at the heart of the Christian communalists' confidence in a God in and through whom all things are possible.[77]

These Christian communitarians will never be satisfied, obviously, until community infuses everyone's private and public world. Community will involve sharing God's values as they interpret them, above all concern for a common good and for every person. Such a community must proceed, they believe, from local communities and local experience in communal living, sharing, and governing. Nothing else will—or should—succeed.

This definition of community is, obviously, close to the participatory democratic vision. Yet it is also a study in contrast. Advocates of religious community are preoccupied with the spirit and the spiritual; their goals and their relationships are ultimately of the soul and (in most instances) in imitation of Christ. Often they reassure us that there will be many rooms in their world, not just room for their kind of Christianity. They are not caught up in denominationalism; *Sojourners* is no longer a voice for evangelicals only, and Palmer as a Protestant lived in a Catholic center. Yet their definition is fundamentally Christian and perhaps inevitably so in this culture.

The Christian groups who have followed in the steps of Saul Alinsky and other grass-roots activists operate at a less theoretical level, in fact and in temperament.[78] Alinsky operated in many contexts and was indeed nondoctrinaire about tactics and strategy, including religious institutions and religious people in his movements for change without being religious himself.[79] In more and more locations those influenced by Alinsky, among others, are taking to the streets, acting to build and express community. Present in such places as New York, San Antonio, Chicago, and Milwaukee, this approach has reached notoriety in Pittsburgh where a group of Lutheran pastors and their supporters clashed with their opponents, including assorted business interests and the Lutheran church hierarchy. The conflict became ugly enough in the mid-1980s to qualify for coverage on CBS's "60 Minutes" and elsewhere.[80]

The Pittsburgh activities first focused on the costs to communities of steelworkers that result from the weak domestic steel industry in that area; they have involved charges that steel companies were irresponsible toward their workers and their families. The entire dispute began, then, with an argument about community. Fights over whose side the Lutheran church was on were also disputes over community, its direction, and its leadership. Such is the approach of the umbrella group in Pittsburgh, the Confessing Synod Ministries. Their newsletter details continuing concerns, such as the steel situation, and more recent ones, especially the family and how it can be strengthened as a community in the face of such potent foes as steel tycoons or television trash.[81]

Rarely does this movement so dedicated to community hesitate over causing conflict. The rationale is that community is not an empty goal; it must be authentic community in service of God's caring and tough love. Thus the newsletters of the group report not only their biblical teachings—"Devotions"—but also their witness for direct action month after month.[82]

Although this movement has spawned bitter and angry divisions, it has generated some eloquent intellectual defenses. Consider, for example, Gregory Pierce's discussion in *Activism That Makes Sense*, his report on the Queens Citizen Organization which operated out of a Roman Catholic church in Queens, New York.[83] Pierce's argument is that religious group activism works: It gets practical results by addressing the desires of the local people/participants and also promotes participants' development of self-confidence and political savvy. Consequently people are not only more effective in politics but they also come to experience public group life and thus grow into a community.[84]

It is characteristic of this approach that little attention goes to such grand objectives as transcendence of self-interest or reaching the common good. The prevailing opinion is that such goals beguile only intellectuals. Most people want mundane objectives which they are sure are in their self-interest. Only if and when they gain these and develop experience through action will larger goals such as community come into play. The same attitude applies toward the means to change. Although many communitarians and definitely most religious ones do not like to discuss or face issues of power (except that of their enemies), these activists take it for granted that they dwell in a world of power and powers. Their model has a no-nonsense political realism and their objectives include getting and exercising power.[85]

At every turn, the focus is on what can make things happen. Thus proponents of this kind of activist community brush aside other alternatives, the usual political options of our liberal age. Social service and social agencies effect little change: above all, they change few people. National religious groups such as the National Council of Churches are too busy on such pointless missions as denouncing Christopher Columbus as an imperialist to do anything concrete. Individual action is hopeless. One must join together with others and get one's hands dirty by organizing and taking whatever steps are necessary. This is the only way to help people in their lives now and to water the seeds of community.[86]

At first it may seem a long stretch from these activists and their intellectual admirers to the world of the New Age. Yet it is an appropriate extension, in part because my intention is to illuminate how wide the net of religious-based thinking about community is in our era. It reaches all the way from Berkeley intellectuals such as Robert Bellah to New Age writers and intellectuals, catching much in between. Granted, it is too early to identify voices from the New Age movement as major intellectuals in the larger culture. Yet we may not dismiss New Age thinking as the expression of a collection of oddballs and cultists. Appreciated or not, it is a serious set of ideas and beliefs, appealing to many intellectual people. And it is becoming a significant example of the involvement of religion with community, one of the most intriguing today in the United States.

No one knows how many Americans consider themselves New Agers. Some estimates put the figure at 5 percent to 10 percent of our population, with the most robust support among the baby boomer generation.[87] The numbers may have grown rapidly, encouraged by Marilyn Ferguson's *Aquarian Conspiracy* and Shirley MacLaine's widely read books, especially *Out on a Limb*.[88] Today all the signs of a prospering subculture are visible. Bookstores, publications such as the hefty, ad-filled *New Age Journal* ("exploring the new frontiers of human potential"), radio stations, New Age music, and much more serve the diverse tastes of a world known for its desire to have a written as well as a more immediately experiential culture.[89]

The various manifestations of New Age spirituality (and spirituality, rather than religion, is the preferred term) are dazzling.[90] Some focus on nature,[91] some on forms of paganism; goddesses are especially popular. Others look to Eastern spiritual traditions, or interpret dreams, or believe in reincarnations, "channeling" (communication with spirits), the use of crystals, or special rituals of touching to heal by connecting with the larger universe.[92]

This vibrant diversity is one of the reasons why it may seem strange to include New Age beliefs as a significant illustration of the engagement of religion with community. Such diversity and a general resistance to the constrictions which definitions impose stand in the way of any generalizations we might make about New Age thought.[93] Moreover, so much of New Age thinking focuses on the potential of every person. The aura, so to say, is often highly individualistic. We are heralded as near gods who do not begin to realize those possibilities which lie within us.[94] We are called to respect and develop "our surprising capacities, our spectacular latent powers."[95] Such affirmations make talk of community appear to be no more than an afterthought. And in some cases it is just that at best. More often, though, community is basic to New Age beliefs and is celebrated fully by New Age intellectual voices.

Community is most frequently described in the language of wholeness. The search for personal wholeness involves a Greek-like unity of body, mind, and spirit—community of the self. Here the famous New Age emphasis on holistic medicine enters center stage and exemplifies how a skeptical secular world now increasingly welcomes New Age holistic ideas.[96] The holistic orientation also applies to other people and the world at large. Since God is in all, we are all one; we should live lives that reflect our earthly indeed our cosmic unity.[97] Moreover, all our communities from the most local to the most universal amount to nothing if they are not spirit-filled. For New Agers, any community worthy of the name must be infused and enveloped by spirit.[98]

The model of New Age public community is loose jointed, with more than a tinge of neoanarchistic resistance to any larger culture and any denial of "morality that derives from the innermost self."[99] Generous affirmation of individual autonomy is the characteristic perspective, in terms decidedly reminiscent of the Transcendentalists. Yet if rejection of governance by "great central power in society" is typical, sympathy for community remains much in force.[100] The assumption, and the encouraged practice, is that the growth of communities of similar souls and similar ways will in the end lead into the broadest of communities, "the planetary family." It will be a world made of real communities, not artificial nations or spiritless parts of a sacred whole.[101]

The New Age movement is an outgrowth of the 1960s and of California in the 1960s in particular. Its optimism, its spiritual idealism, and its predilection for community confirm its origins.[102] We know it is not especially political in an activist sense and thus it relates to those in the 1960s who lost considerable faith in politics as they searched for meaning and community. Yet its political undertones also remind us of its 1960s roots. New Age views on policy are indeed (if one can stand this mixed metaphor) "draped in the sacraments of political correctness,"[103] reflecting 1960s preferences: sweeping equality, direct democracy, hostility to U.S. foreign policy, all suitably updated by 1990s concerns about gender, ecology, and peace.[104] Confidence that politics can lead toward needed transformations in policy, however, is lacking. Politics is all but gone as the means to "harmonic convergence" and it has been replaced by New Age spirituality with its vague dreams of community.[105]

Of course to some intellectual sophisticates, New Age thought is nothing more than "an essentially harmless anthology of illusions."[106] Others are less sure and more critical, especially of the supposed egocentrism of New Age adherents.[107] One must grant that the New Age sentiments, however valuable, have not yet won intellectual respectability. Still, the New Age is decidedly a contemporary example of spiritual insistence on existence in a communal mode. That mode is not always or even often spatial, but it is real and routine for New Age communicants. To Christian communitarians New Age spirituality may seem strange or even dangerous, but the two groups have much in common. Above all, both tie religion and community together with a firm knot and both have vigorous intellectual subcultures that defend their thoughts on community.

From the age of the Constitution to the New Age, religion and community have often been connected in American intellectual thought and political debate. Indeed, religious and spiritual perspectives commonly affirm (varying ideals of) community. It is, in fact, the central organizing concept of religious political thought today, promulgated sometimes by those who are aware of the rigors of the struggle, sometimes not, but always by those confident of the sacredness of their mission. Thus while they often exemplify the mixture of caution and hope about community that is so recognizable in contemporary American political thought, their favorite word is hope. In this they are one with almost all those engaged with community in our time.

Chapter Nine

Reflections

The trumpet often sounds for community among contemporary American political intellectuals and produces many more notes than I can present. The diversity of images of community considered here—participatory, republican, global, traditional, and religious—is broad in itself. We have seen that community has its perimeters in contemporary discourse, but it is also wide-ranging (and contentious) in its adherents. Its tents are capacious.

Granted there are contemporary thinkers who do not fit in to the most expansively defined company of intellectual partisans of community. Even the most determined Hartzian efforts at synthesis would fail here. Community cannot begin to encompass easily the entire, cacophonous world of American political intellectuals. There is the somber world of modern economic thought, hardly a playing field for communitarians. This arena often reflects a genteel version of the broader, vigorous libertarian dimension in American political thought which does not have much patience with community, however it is dressed up. Libertarians, whether of the Left or Right, do not agree on an urgent need for community. Quite the contrary. And they fear zealots will sacrifice much liberty as they rush to instantiate community. [1]

Others spurn community as a soft-focused ideal which clouds the harsh problems of economics, gender, or race in America. Sometimes they are deconstructionists or postmoderns of one sort or another who see talk of community as interfering with the necessary breaking down of dominant forces and cultures. Some are more traditional radicals less solicitous of dreams of community and more interested in what

142

they see as justice. Still others are more likely to think a tough political realism about means and ends is what we need now and to scorn those who wander off reflecting on soft ideals such as community.[2]

A sharply contrasting perspective does not quite comprehend what the fuss is about in the first place. What leads so many American intellectuals to leap toward a vision of community? This view holds that the United States, as with any civilization, has its problems but it faces no great crisis except perhaps among a good many political intellectuals. Its basic message is straightforward: The values, institutions, and trends of the U.S. are proceeding nicely, and an obsession with community is hardly requisite.[3]

Finally, there are those who, though not exactly supposing all is well, cannot join in the cries of alarm or chants of community. For them one must be realistic. What we have is less than one might wish or expect to achieve, yet the United States is also a great gift in its freedoms, relative democracy, and pluralism. We must speed the day in which such benefits are everyone's, but there is no point in chasing after some impossible and questionably noble goal of community.[4]

Thus there are a host of other voices. Still, the community-oriented side of American political thought today is indisputable. Its sway is significant, if also diffuse. It cannot be dismissed as shallow either, though it has as generous an amount of empty rhetoric as does any other perspective. What I propose to discuss here are the continuities I find amidst the diversity, reaching to gain some overall perspective on community as an idea in contemporary American political theory and concluding with some personal reflections, resolving little but joining in the common struggle for understanding.

Four or five considerations deserve our attention, maybe more. One, surely, is the chastened mood of thinking regarding community today. Another is the question of purpose and motivation in the urge toward community, an issue quite related to the matter of communitarians in a mature stage. A third, of course, is the larger meaning of the turn toward community in American intellectual development, a daunting topic but especially so for our time. A fourth is the form of the critiques about the theory of community today. They concentrate on the charge that such a theory is an escape from politics and from social justice, a nostalgic refuge for intellectuals rather than a summons for engagement.

Slightly Chastened

Among some communitarian enthusiasts the days of the Port Huron Statement and the earlier 1960s live on.[5] The 1960s shadow hovers around the outlines of visions of contemporary community, most predictably around participatory democracy as community. This is not surprising since the 1960s was an era of praise for community as an ideal. What is more unexpected is that community is so popular a theme among a fair number of contemporary political intellectuals in the 1980s despite their generally restrained mood.

By this time it is fair to say that the commitment is much more than a superficial fad, not a summer romance and no longer a spring one. No doubt the engagement with community is related to the aura of anxiety in contemporary perceptions and analyses. There is a sober, worried perception of massive problems, which current proponents of the creation of community propose to face. Moving toward more human community is the answer, but it will not be easy. Michael Sandel articulates the sentiment clearly. We can no longer just profess the glories of (one version or another of) community; we must proceed with a reflective sense of past failures and the mixed odds for future success.[6] Glenn Tinder, the most somber contemporary communitarian, affirms this judgment. The days of the confident utopians in expectant search for the perfect community (as in the perfect wave) must be declared over.[7] Nancy Rosenblum counsels that we must step back from the romantic and unreflective image, the community of "direct relations," as if it could be composed of friends or even lovers.[8] Jane Mansbridge suggests caution;[9] the mood is chastened.

The reasons are multiple. Some are mundane, though still not to be ignored. Communities cannot make a go of it alone, the warnings often suggest. They need leaders, organizations, even well-thought-through strategies to exist in a larger world.[10] Put another way, good will is far from enough.[11] Moreover, coordination among communities will always be a major challenge. Communities can and do clash, and reflective consideration on how to facilitate coordination will be a permanent need.[12] Even more challenging and related to every other dilemma will be the powerful presence of human selfishness. Even communitarians who are unmistakably children of the 1960s such as Kirkpatrick Sale duly note that self-interest is a constant and not necessarily friendly companion on every journey toward community. It cannot be wished away but only confronted somehow. [13]

There are those, especially in the participatory tradition, who do want to have almost everything both ways. Thus they proclaim their limitless faith in small group community and simultaneously laud a society with "a broader, more pluralist appreciation for the great diversity of peoples and in our land." [14] The paradox is that too much internationalism in the local participatory democracy will lead us either to burned-out and disinterested participants or to a crisis of legitimacy. Politics simply cannot become too demanding given our current burdens if it wants to maintain a high level of participation. [15]

And yes, Nancy Rosenblum is correct when she complains of communitarians who do not ask what the personal costs might be if they encourage unrestrained personal expressiveness in the 1960s manner. "Contemporary communitarians are moved in part by romantic impulses, but they have not learned the lessons of chastened romanticism." [16] The costs of unchecked expressiveness can be real when it reaches too deeply to expose vulnerable people or interferes with private affections. In such intense and personal situations the opportunities for deep hurt are real. [17] This is especially true in face-to-face communities where there may be no refuge.

In short, the yearning for community that somehow reflects unfettered freedom is far from gone and the desire to have everything remains intense. Its presence is clearly expressed—and observed. [18] But it hardly reigns alone anymore; countercycles of awareness are now at work. The general situation reminds me more of the thought of the 1950s when community was considered in terms of limits and restraints and through the eye of existential hope. The easy air of (a certain) 1960s is gone now. Merelman questions just how loose bounded a culture one may have. [19] Bellah and his associates explicitly attack the idea that expressiveness is the answer, intent on impressing us with the notion that community will require limits. [20]

This is the message today. For the alarmed globalists it takes center stage; they warn that we have had enough expressiveness. Its wasteful irresponsibility may soon kill us. The republicans are all about creating (or rediscovering) a set of shared virtues to develop a mature common good. Although the varieties of religious communitarians are formidable, a consistent stance is the recognition that community involves choices made and options denied. The new mood is that community and limits should not be strangers to each other.

It is not merely the limits imposed by institutions and human beings that gain acknowledgement today. Current readings of our history find it far from a universally hospitable story. We know that much of the discussion by communitarians defends the possibility of community in the context of American history. This is the subtext of the work, for example, of many so-called republicans, yet their analysis heralds no basis for optimistic prospects. Pickings look thin. Much of American history—and especially contemporary U.S. history —yields modest inspiration for communitarian enthusiasts, though there are exceptional readings by the most determined optimists (such as Harry Boyte).[21] Complaints would not cover the ground so thickly if there were many promising seedlings of community—or well-tested expectations of seedlings forthcoming. The past is no obvious prologue.

Purposes

Considerations of the purposes of community today have also been significant. As we have seen, uncritical and unreflective concentration on expressiveness is over. So is the all but universal praise for community without addressing what it will take for it to flourish, as suggested by the argument of Lawrence Goodwyn that communities must have a purpose or mission if they are to live.[22] No wonder former high priests of community from the 1960s no longer reign untroubled, confronted now by sharp critics who think romantic effusions are irrelevant, impractical, and antipolitical.[23] Newer visions are likely to come in the form of Michael Walzer's conception of community: complex, pluralistic, restrained.[24] Sometimes they even explore how community and liberalism can be reconciled in America; one of the old verities is quite intact.[25]

Consider the matter of the purpose of community (however community is conceptualized). Often, as we have seen, the goal is mundane—survival—and its motivating energy is practical rather than grand or expressive.[26] At other times the focus is on the expansion of democratic community. This image is routine in the language of participatory politics, though nowadays it comes as a more modest and less flamboyant gospel than it did twenty-five years ago. The republican model of community invariably appears as a grounded vision, connected with history and avoiding dramatic claims and utopian dreams.

Religious voices for community are a more radical and a more demanding strain in contemporary thought. Even here, though, there are signs of the times, those such as Parker Palmer whose thought is no echo of the 1960s.[27] In their (relative) temperateness they unite with those who think strengthening community in terms of roots is practical. It must be so, they assert, for without the character and boundaries traditions foster we are lost as persons and as a society. Roots are natural to the human. For them modern liberalism has turned out to be dangerously utopian in its cavalier discarding of tradition and its reification of a stripped-down individual.

One may wonder though about the unrestrained expectations of some globalists who are more utopian from one angle than the most optimistic participatory democrats. In their way, after all, globalists are out to save the world—indeed the universe. Still, some skepticism here is appropriate. Globalists can be incautious in making predictions, and their language slips easily into the stridently moralistic, yet they seek to live not by faith but by reason. Their purposes may (or may not) be judged grand by us. However, survival is a distinctly practical, one wants to say mundane, aim. Their community is about this fundamental but also uncomplicated purpose. In general, then, the goals of much contemporary writing about community are restrained, practical, and down-to-earth. They are distinctly signs of the times.

Questions

A chastened mood is often apparent in the house of community as is a modest set of expectations regarding community's purposes. The latter is, of course, an example of the former. The mood has grown restrained, though what remains is at bottom a live faith invoked by a pressing sense of urgency. This conviction can insulate some community-oriented intellectuals. There are problems—intellectual, attitudinal, political, and structural—which require more attention than they get. One is the tendency to criticize, especially to indulge in a spree of liberal-bashing. It can be more emotionally satisfying (granted, some would say at least as important) to attack liberalism and/or liberal America than to ask some tough questions of oneself. But the cost can be high: neglecting problems of conceptualization, normative defense, and practical development of community.

Moreover, the barrage of criticism is not always more informed or particularly fair, though fairness is not to be expected in intellectual wars. As Nancy Rosenblum has contended, the sweeping excoriations of liberalism do not appreciate its complexity and richness. For example, liberalism too has theorists who incorporated the sentiment of community; John Stuart Mill is a classic nineteenth-century illustration.[28]

But let us concede the antiliberal chorus is right, that the philosophical, cultural, and institutional ground must be cleared as an essential first step forward. Equally apparent is that something must be put in its place. There have been some serious, meaty, provoking responses to this challenge; Benjamin Barber's *Strong Democracy* is a welcome recent example.[29] More often than one might like, though, there are less happy models. Vague calls for community obviously don't get us anywhere. And the better the critique, the more awkward the situation when no alternative appears, as in Bellah's classic *Habits of the Heart*.[30]

A cluster of difficulties, of course, surrounds the nature of any community. Some of these garner predictable attention, such as problems over property relations, who shall rule, and coordination. Others generate almost inexhaustible arguments. How much must any community proceed from consensus? How much must it be, so to say, a consensus by definition and how much can it be a haven for individual choice? Are communities necessarily about tight boundaries of culture and values? Or can they combine diversity and a range of freedom with a ground of shared community?

Advocates of various kinds of community must tackle this last conundrum far more rigorously than many do. Too many want it both ways, a free community which at the same time has shared meanings, values, and duties. Again, we are not entirely bereft of positive models. Michael Walzer is rewarding for the student of community in this regard as in others. Sensitive to complexity, diversity, freedom and agreement, boundary and choice, Walzer suggests that efforts to confront this issue seriously are worthwhile, but he stands out as an exception.[31]

Other problems, as Clarke Cochran has written, include the closely related matters of authority and obligation.[32] Community-oriented intellectuals do not especially honor either concept, and modern models of community are frequently loose bounded. Granted, there are others which incorporate many authorities or values or shared narratives or understandings of the good.[33] This is particularly true of traditionalists, but proponents of religiously oriented community necessarily stress divine authority and in principle support obligations. Globalists obviously tend to grant nature immense authority. Yet authority is an uneasy concept for an intellectual disposition so affected by the free and easy, even anarchistic, 1960s. Obligation and duty are still more in question. The connection between community and anything binding remains strangely uncertain in American thought. Thus whether there can be community without duty remains a major issue. Is such a community possible, conceptually, not to mention practically? Much more thinking is needed, above all much more tough-minded exploration.

Also, I am struck by the shared assumptions behind much communitarian thinking today. The energetic criticisms we explored in chapter two are only part of the (flexible) boundaries of this considerable agreement. Another instance will serve to illustrate others: the attraction of many communitarians to substantive equality in numerous, even all, possible areas of life. Community is often taken to imply equality without question. This tendency is not universal, of course, as theorists of tradition establish, but it is the ordinary assumption, one dominant even among globalists where a suspicious Heilbroner in *The Human Prospect* is unusual.[34] This pervasive and usually uncontested premise demands more argument than it usually gets.[35] More important, it forces one to examine the texts closely to discover whether community is the actual goal or whether equality is. The answer to this query is vital, for a very different society might easily result from the two visions. Among participatory democrats in particular it is necessary to distinguish those who quite frankly are much more interested in equality than in community.

Another consideration that gives pause about much of the current discussion of community is its modest intellectual fiber and creativity. For instance, although character is almost a totem among communitarian intellectuals, there is disappointingly little exploration of the concept and only scant new insight from that weak effort. Yet a focus on what people are like, could be like, or what one would want them to be like is essential for students of community in practice or in ideal. Nothing can be more important for any community.

It is true, on the other hand, that character is a concept of growing importance among community-minded intellectuals today.[36] For MacIntyre or Cochran, among others, it is the concept fittingly associated with community.[37] Those intrigued by republican community are particularly concerned with character or virtue. But the issue of character in contemporary theorizing about community often becomes a sectarian question, part of the contest between proponents of various ideas of community, an intramural weapon, for instance, to scold fellow communitarians who do not adequately grant character its primacy.[38] This gets us only so far—about as far as discussions of virtue or character couched in glittering and nearly empty terms such as "community-oriented," "free," "participatory," and the like. Also of limited value are invocations of character and its importance that fail to grapple with how it addresses problems of obligation or authority within community.

This is not to imply that highly optimistic understandings of people hold sway in the literature. They do not. As we have seen, the mood of modern American communitarian literature is frequently chastened and has tempered the more zealous utopian expectations regarding humans. Yet whatever the analysis of human beings, too little depth obtains in current thought about community. The shift toward discussion of character is welcome, but the problem remains. History and criticism are the popular languages; psychology is not, perhaps because it is so difficult a discipline to master and so disturbing to confront.

Larger Meanings: Community, Politics, and Justice

The widespread intellectual alarm that this book examines receives no automatic respect in certain realms. Many of my students cast

a jaundiced eye on it. Along with others, a number of them have
wondered if too many American political intellectuals do not suffer
from a bad case of nostalgia. In some expressions such as Bell's or
Bloom's nostalgia for times (often in their own lives) before the 1960s
may be at work. For the republicans nostalgia for a vaguely leftist 1960s
recast as a benign Revolutionary War may be present. For religious
communitarians perhaps there is nostalgia for another historical age
(though which one is in dispute). For those grasping for roots, nostalgia for a lost (but never experienced) past, indeed for an imaginary
past, may sometimes be lurking in the background. For some participatory democrats nostalgia for the 1960s, a communal youth experienced and now gone (or fantasized about but now impossible) may
be a factor.

This game of exposing signs of nostalgia is one everybody can
play. It is not self-evident that it is either patently unfair or false. But
the limitation of the critique of nostalgia is that it resolves nothing even
if it taps a truth. Knowing that nostalgia is present does not eliminate
the value of the quest for community, the arguments about which
model is better, or even the use of exploring history for guidance. Nor
should it. Why is nostalgia automatically an evil or a false instinct?

The interpretation of nostalgia directs us to another question:
Does the engagement with crisis and community tell us as much about
the United States as it does about political intellectuals in the United
States? As Herbert Gans asks pointedly about Robert Bellah's ideal, do
most people want all of this community? He doubts it and doubts on
this score are hardly confined to him.[39] This is not the place where the
legitimate query can be addressed, much less answered. But suspicions concerning the answer are natural. At the least one must be
skeptical of this and every crisis proclaimed by intellectuals.

This is the place, however, to discuss the view that the engagement with community among contemporary American intellectuals
represents a disturbing flight from politics. One might argue that
community is a replacement for politics, defined as conflict and consensus in the public realm. Such an interpretation draws from both the
present critical mood and the considerable affinity for history and
nostalgia. It also draws on the particular models of community now
afloat. The point is that the near obsession with complaint and the
perhaps too frequent journeys into history or nostalgia signal a flight

from political engagement, indeed, even that they are a substitute for politics.

It does not follow that these activities should be condemned. A fair number of contemporary intellectuals are merely following the path of such predecessors as Marx or Nietzsche. They are clearing the ground and exploring historical alternatives, both essential missions for theory and action. Why are such integral tasks to be dismissed?

I am more impressed with the proposition that the overall fascination with community as it appears in contemporary intellectual life reveals a disinclination for serious politics. On the one hand, community has become almost a mantra for some people and perhaps functions in a similar manner. It is often meant to be a radical idea, but in practice it quietens and calms and leads away from the conflicts inherent in politics.

On the other hand, we have to judge from the particular ideas of community current in contemporary intellectual circles. The fundamental issue is not whether focusing on community in general indicates a desire to escape from politics but whether the specific forms of community that appeal today do so. One properly wonders. Many of the globalists are certainly not interested in politics nor are many of the religious communitarians. The agendas of both are crowded, but more important than politics is the realization of truths which do not require politics for their discovery, articulation, or (in some versions) achievement. From at least one angle many participatory democrats are equally nonpolitical in their reach for consensus and even mutual identity, especially those whose hearts lie in the 1960s.

Yet this is a fiercely contested analysis. Participatory advocates ardently believe that they are the supreme exalters of politics in our disappointing time. They make politics—defined as dialectic and decision in the public realm—the highest of human activities, the way we can experience a communal life and enhanced personhood. From their perspective, they might understand why someone could accuse them of loving politics too much, but to suggest they are hostile to politics makes no sense. Perhaps they are right. But it is not so clear what the range of politics would be in a participatory setting. It never is, though as the sympathetic Jane Mansbridge reflects, participatory democracy may not be the best mechanism when disagreements are substantive. Participatory community celebrates political democracy, but it may simultaneously generate more pressures to conform than it might wish or expect—the ancient fear.[40]

A rich politics is central to advocates of republican community. Nothing excites them more than the cause of expanding the range and significance of public, political decision making. They favor politics in their theory of the good society, and their choice of historical models reaffirms and underlines their choice and their sincerity. Yet they too have a good deal of work to do in exploring what virtue, character, and community might mean in circumscribing the boundaries of what is open for political decision.

Some of those most involved in the discussion of roots appear to separate the political and the communal at the expense of the political. Sometimes a great deal may be fixed in tradition and traditionalists place far more emphasis on education than they do on politics. Some tradition-oriented thinkers are committed to a modest public and political realm, though even there they are likely to insist that politics cannot flourish without a foundation of private nonpolitical communities.

Taken as a whole, the record is mixed. There are those for whom community is, if not a substitute for politics, at least distinctly a priority over it. Were this view dominant, it would not astonish anyone. Politics has won few ardent adherents in the American public, and political intellectuals in our culture often share a similar distaste. Still, the main movement lies in another direction. What strikes me about many of the new communitarians is their affirmation of two unpopular ideas in America, community in a public, political sense (as distinguished from a private or a patriotic meaning) and politics itself. Community is less a replacement of politics than it is a new companion for it. Both are to supersede a feeble, apolitical liberalism and its fractured institutions and culture.

Another issue about communitarian thought often raised along with the status of politics is the importance of social justice. It is appropriate to ask of enthusiasts of community whether they routinely skirt awkward questions of justice.[41] Sometimes critics mean that many communitarian intellectuals do not care enough about the central economic dimensions of life, preferring matters of participation, communication, and expression. More often, the critique comes specifically from the Left where pursuit of egalitarian distribution is either as important a value as community—or a much more important one. That such a judgment has its adherents fits with chapter four's discussion that economic democrats often care less about community than about equal distribution of income and wealth.

I do not think the claim that community-oriented intellectuals neglect social justice is persuasive. It concentrates too much on several of the most prominent proponents of community on the American intellectual scene today at the expense of the larger, more diverse communitarian movement. Even if, let us agree for the sake of argument, Michael Sandel is uninterested in issues of justice, others of equal prominence, Michael Walzer for instance, care very much about it. Moreover, justice is integral to religious communitarians; and among many participatory communitarians, of course, the story is the same.

Again, the distinctions must be made. Community theorists usually do consider justice; frequently it is central to their enterprise, as Walzer's work illustrates. This is not to say that justice is the primary concern except where an identity between community and justice is assumed, nor is there unanimity in seeing justice defined as egalitarian distribution. This is hardly the case. But it is simply inaccurate to fault the political intellectuals who focus on community for ignoring issues of justice or even less plausibly, for antipathy to its considerations. Sometimes it is true, but it is hardly the whole truth.

Existential Community

Analytic reflections can take us only so far. The problematics of the revival of (interest in) community are inescapable but they hardly obviate its major motivation, unease over the health and practice of community in the United States. Here I do not plan to recapitulate the strong tide of complaints that washes against American life, pulling in with it the ideal of community. Nor do I propose to assess the often bewildering and frequently conflicting particular complaints or the variety of possible communities that have their devotees. But even for an intellectual historian such as myself there is room for more personal reflection and argument.

There is, I think, another image of the good community besides those so popular today, one at times almost indistinct since it often lies in the shadows of the present discussions. I will call it the existential model of community, a model which emphasizes paradox, tension, even contradiction. Those intrigued by it muse about the possibilities of expanded individualism as well as expanded community, about a shared culture filled with free minds, and about democracy and authority bonded together. In the hands of Glenn Tinder it has moved from academic discourse to discussion among a broader, informed public audience.[42]

Existential thinkers self-consciously distinguish themselves from the fallacies they perceive in others. Most of all, they have no taste for what they consider the abstract optimism which accompanies a good deal of the enthusiasm for some kind of revival of community today. Existentialists' reality includes sin (if, as is often true, they are religious) or selfishness or whatever it is that ensures discord and tribulation in any community. They acknowledge the paradox that they are committed to a goal in community that may not be possible and would, if realized, guarantee perpetual danger. Finally, these modest champions of community share the considerable engagement with the idea of community defined in terms of individual character above all else. What matters to them is the individual who nourishes community, who thrives in community, the person whom community creates. The individual is the story in community, not in isolation to be sure, but not homogenized and destroyed by absorption into a character-denying community either.

The variations among existential communities are numerous. They are different from each other in their specific, or existential, concreteness. They are the same, however, in valuing this specificity, community fitted to diverse and particular people, conditions, and circumstance. They are also alike in a corresponding skepticism of abstraction, of community visualized apart from the earthy, fallible, real people, and of most other ideals of community. Everything in their approach is governed by a spirit infused with both hope and sadness, the hope of aspiration, the sadness of restricted possibility. This spirit, and the role of spirit overall, is very much in the existential mode. Thinkers interested in existential community in no way constitute a movement or affirm one or another's partisan history; nor are they prophets sounding dogmatic calls to arms. They often have no program at all. The spirit is the thing, the hope and sadness about the human prospect for developing a character more authentic and communal now and in the future.

Contemporary students of community give passing credit to one or another thinkers or traditions that gave birth or rebirth to the ideal community. The search for community in history, especially American history, is serious business, as chapter three illustrates. The same applies in writing about existential community. The path leads to the great era of existential thought, the West in the 1950s, as the sometimes unacknowledged historical ground for contemporary existential community theorists. In that age existential themes included, necessarily it would seem, the invocation of community defined as aspiration, the vitalness of hope, and the approval of courageous choice against overpowering and negative winds of despair and meaninglessness.

Camus is an obvious exemplar here,[43] as is Martin Buber, whose greatest vogue in his long career was in the 1950s. Indeed, Buber is perhaps the more congenial since his language of community is both existential and religious in the modern mode.[44] In approaching him one approaches the themes of the existential community.

Buber begins in the existential fashion with human selfishness as our fate and, more than that, with a recognition of the essential mystery of the universe and of each of us alone and in relation with others. These realities of human life forbid him to think in a "soft, expressionistic" mode.[45] He is, to say the least, neither a Carl Rogers nor an Abraham Maslow, and he offers no possibility of romantic affirmation or free self-actualization. Such faith is innocent and fatuous.[46] Only the most naive could believe the result of rampant individualism will somehow be community or unity. "Unity is not a property of the world but its task. To form unity out of the world is our never-ending work."[47]

And then there is the power of mystery. "Man is not to be seen through, but to be perceived ever more completely in his openness and his headiness."[48] No solution can be considered, therefore, which does not involve our "standing and withstanding in the abyss of the real reciprocal relation with the mystery of man."[49] To deny such a view is to block out not just reality but the spirit and dignity of every person.

Yet Buber did not believe we were lost, surrounded only by the dark truths of sin or mystery. We also had God, even though we could speak only of "the mystery of God."[50] And we had capacity for dialogue and education and potential for the risk of trust. "Let us dare, despite all to trust!"[51] Above all, there was our ability to love—and thus to strive for community. Love for God and for one's neighbor led to community[52]—in Buber's favorite exemplification, the Israeli kibbutzim. Such was the goal, understanding that every experiment to realize it was, of course, always promise, always in process, always partial. It tottered on Buber's "narrow ridge," as all else did.[53]

Everything filtered in between false dualism. Community could not be nourished in an individual-denying environment or in a naively individualistic one, not in an irrational world or a nonmysterious one, not in capitalism or socialism. It could grow only where dialogue and openness sprouted. It had to be realistic and respond to pragmatic imperatives— including the communal. And of course community had to be chosen by each person, as existentialists always prescribe, chosen in both faith and uncertainty, belief and risk.[54]

Patrons of existential community are uncertain and complex advocates. We know they are earnest supporters of an ideal that cannot occur in existential reality. They are wedded to an ideal which if existentially limited is encompassing beyond measure. Its paradoxes include the understanding that community must not be interpreted as the other part of a lame dualism with the liberal individual—despite what so many other community-oriented intellectuals believe or suspect. Existentialists rightly fear this dualism. They refuse to welcome community grounded in the "all-consuming public spirit such as ancient Greek citizenship or revolutionary republicanism with its Jacobin fervor."[55] Community can never pay empty lip service to human connections or to the collapse of all human distinctions. In Clarke Cochran's intriguing formulation, community is not the opposite of "tolerance" or "diversity" but is about their realization.[56] His defining concept is "hospitality." A community can and must be a place of hospitality, a generous and expansive aspiration as attractive as it is problematic.[57]

The centrality of paradox, I think, leads Carey McWilliams to want to edge us closer to the kind of community he prefers to describe as "fraternity" but which I call existential. The Bellamys and Whitmans of our American past make McWilliams uncomfortable, and their modern descendants do not represent exactly what he has in mind. They incline to understandings of community which are too monistic, too simple. Community is not about the merger of the individual into an army (Bellamy's Industrial Army, or Whitman's Union Army for that matter) or into nature, or whatever. Paradoxes, tensions, and problematics do not and should not disappear in community.

It follows that McWilliams is pulled toward the existential perception that human pain and death are not somehow in conflict with or a denial of community. On the contrary, they are givens which can and should constitute powerful spurs toward human community. Community in this view is not an escape from individualism or from death but the coming to terms with existential realities in a fraternal setting.[58]

It is not surprising that Mark Twain serves as a hero for McWilliams. Twain might seem both too superficial and too corrosive for serious, community-minded intellectuals. But McWilliams's Twain saw the paradoxes, the ironies, the necessary incompleteness in his own and in human experience and responded by fostering fraternity through his humor. It enabled people to confess to their "fears and pretensions" and to their often painful situations. It freed them to hear the universal call we all have, which for McWilliams's Twain "is the moral sense."[59] In short, Twain nourished community by helping us to share our limited and universal selves—our existential selves.

Thus at no juncture do existential echoes reverberate more poignantly than when thinkers confront the ideal of community with human frailty as they comprehend it. With Glenn Tinder, for instance, one is instantly back in time and community is confronted, in effect, with the combination of Camus and, since religious motifs haunt this perspective, St. Augustine. It is not the findings of social science or even a particular reading of history that pave the main highway. More than anything else, it is ontology that we must know about, human ontology as it inevitably confronts existence.

This is again the paradox for Tinder. He tells us our being yearns for community and consolation with our brothers and sisters in the deepest reaches of our soul. Yet we cannot satisfy our thirst because of ourselves as well as our circumstances. We are inextricably lonely, separated beings in a world which perpetually conspires to keep us that way. There is no escape. For an existentialist such as Tinder this condition is the heart of our tragedy.[60] And it is a tragedy that we cannot avoid through the false reconciliations of the evils of either idealism or cynicism.[61]

There is nothing necessarily wrong with efforts to expand those features of our lives which are communal. On the contrary, this is laudable if we accept from the start the existential limits (one hears Camus) on politics, on all human life, that ensure community will be ever elusive. Politics must also and always be where we remind ourselves, where we reexperience the truth that community is beyond us. We must never leap to the illusory and fatal belief that somehow through political action we can break the existential chains that permanently bind our existence. The human costs will be too high, the guaranteed failure too painful. Yet politics is a worthy place to work for community, understanding the inescapable truth that it "cannot be a political creation."[62] Thus it is proper to describe politics as a place to relearn that we are communal humans alive in a world of stillborn community.[63]

Against the chorus lauding community today—participatory, global, republican, traditional, and others—the existentialist view is sober, maybe even grim. In its most pessimistic expressions, its exponents are driven to assert the power of its drawbacks as "a crucial and neglected truth."[64] The truth is that "man is not capable of community—not, at least, in any full and stable form."[65]

Religious and existential vocabularies mix easily. For a writer in this genre, Clarke Cochran for instance, one might as well talk directly of human sin as the decisive constraint.[66] In religious vocabulary it is our selfishness which is the ontological defect we cannot fully conquer. Augustine is the teacher, one might say, of so much of the ontological heritage. It may be expressed in some other fashion; one may discourse on "man's spacial, temporal, and mortal nature," but the conclusive reality constantly cited is human alienation and separation.[67] Its origins are one thing, subject to alternative explanation and varying languages. For existentialists it is a given, fixed forever.

Thus there is a tone, sometimes of puzzlement, sometimes of annoyance, among existential communitarians as they experience the enthusiasm for community today. Enthusiasm appears to precede reality. There is too much invocation of community with too little probing of the human condition and not enough recognition that "entry into community is unnatural and difficult." "The most serious and widespread fault in the existing literature on community is an unrealistic optimism."[68] For these existentialists the answer is not an entity called community. Whatever its forms (or meanings), its possibilities look slim. The answer is to continue nevertheless to encourage bonds among men and women for the communal good. For McWilliams this means encouraging fraternity among people whenever possible. Cochran urges us toward his society of hospitality. Tinder advises us to place ourselves in as many communal relationships as possible, granting there will be no community.

It is predictable that those whom I would describe as existential intellectuals concerned with community discuss the kind of people they want to encourage more than they do the forms and practices of community. For them community is at least as much a matter of life lived and attitudes facilitated as it is anything else. The result is their great interest in the matter of character. As with Plato, so with them; it is in our particular virtues and character that community exists. Indeed, admirable character sometimes becomes the substitute for (spatial) community, its goal, and the means to it. Character is everywhere the closest to community that men and women will come.

Clarke Cochran provides an excellent illustration of this focus. He spends much of his effort exploring the formulation of character since in it lies the basis and the reality of community. He singles out such traits as warmth, hospitality, and responsibility to others. Faith is central; so is commitment and tolerance. All these are relevant, of course, to fostering closer human relations and in that sense all are political. Yet conventional political virtues often endorsed by many other communitarian enthusiasts receive fewer affirmations here. Missing, for example, is political participation as crucial to development of character.[69]

Emphasis on character does not mean a politics fixated on character building or support for a politics concerned with human formation alone. Yet formation of character is clearly the premier objective because existential community, whether religious or not, is its own good. It is not about any other goal, either of policy or of a more sweeping objective, nor is it about building utopias or applying political truths. Rather, this view seeks to construct community in the polis certainly, but even more in the soul, the only place where community will ever succeed.[70]

My own sympathies lie with the existentialists. Community is not a place or a thing; it is a calling, a struggle, a journey. It is worth engaging, but its form is not obvious now nor will it be tomorrow. Thus I am not uncomfortable with the profusion of ideas about community in contemporary thought. The concept is too rich to be pinned down tightly. The diversity and disagreement are, in my mind, all to the good. They are the basis for the dialectics or the conversation that may lead us closer to community and may remind us that vibrant community is always open, always in process. I maintain, though, that the various worlds of community explored here are part of a movement. Grounded in dissatisfaction with modern liberalism (though not necessarily with its traditional values), modern communitarian thinkers are trying to reconceptualize the world as a more united, more sharing, more meaningful, and more affective place. Innumerable emphases, analyses, and dreams are at work. Yet the project is common, just as it is never ending and ultimately elusive.

Notes

Preface

    1. E.g., Alasdair MacIntyre, *After Virtue: A Study in Moral Theory* (Notre Dame, Ind.: University of Notre Dame Press, 1981), pp. 244–45. Thomas A. Spragens, Jr., *The Irony of Liberal Reason* (Chicago: University of Chicago Press, 1981), ch. 1.

Chapter One. Introduction: The Meaning of Community

    1. Sara M. Evans and Harry C. Boyte, *Free Spaces: The Sources of Democratic Change in America* (New York: Harper and Row, 1986), p. 185.
    2. Harry C. Boyte, Heather Booth, and Steve Max, *Citizen Action and the New American Populism* (Philadelphia: Temple University Press, 1986), p. 43.
    3. E.g., Michael Harrington, *The Politics at God's Funeral: The Spiritual Crisis of Western Civilization* (New York: Penguin, 1985); Joshua Cohen and Joel Rogers, *On Democracy* (New York: Penguin, 1983); Robert A. Dahl, *A Preface to Economic Democracy* (Berkeley: University of California Press, 1985).
    4. E.g., J. G. A. Pocock's *The Machiavellian Moment: Florentine Political Thought and the Atlantic Republican Tradition* (Princeton, N.J.: Princeton University Press, 1975) is the founding work in the movement, though Pocock is historian more than advocate; Gordon Wood's *The Creation of the American Republic, 1776–1787* (New York: Norton, 1972) is the most influential work on republican history in our Founding period; Wood is more openly sympathetic. There are, as we shall see, a host of advocates more open than either of these Founding masters.
    5. E.g., Christopher Lasch, *Haven in a Heartless World: The Family Besieged* (New York: Basic Books, 1977); Allan Bloom, *The Closing of the American Mind* (New York: Simon and Schuster, 1987).
    6. E.g., Robert L. Heilbroner, *An Inquiry into the Human Prospect* (New York: Norton, 1974); Jonathan Schell, *The Fate of the Earth* (New York: Knopf, 1982).

163

7. E.g., Parker Palmer, *The Company of Strangers: Christians and the Renewal of America's Public Life* (New York: Crossroads, 1981); Jim Wallis, *The Call to Conversion* (New York: Harper and Row, 1981).

8. Fran Schumer, "A Return to Religion," *New York Times Magazine*, April 15, 1984, pp. 90–94, 98.

9. E.g., Glenn Tinder, *Community: Reflections on a Tragic Ideal* (Baton Rouge: Louisiana State University Press, 1980).

10. George A. Hillery, Jr., "Definitions of Community: Areas of Agreement," *Rural Sociology* 20 (July 1955): 111–23.

11. W. B. Gallie, "Essentially Contested Concepts," *Proceedings of the Aristotelian Society* 56 (1955–1956), quoted in William E. Connolly, *The Terms of Political Discourse* (Lexington, Mass.: D. C. Heath, 1974), ch. 1, p. 10.

12. E.g., Robert Nisbet, "The Concept of Community: A Reexamination," *Sociological Review* 21 (August 1973): 397–416.

13. Michael J. Sandel, *Liberalism and the Limits of Justice* (Cambridge: Cambridge University Press, 1982), p. 150.

14. Ibid., p. 173.

15. Hillery, "Definitions of Community."

16. Erik Olsen's discussions with me about the nature of community have been of great value.

Chapter Two. Present Discontents

1. Alasdair MacIntyre, *After Virtue: A Study in Moral Theory* (Notre Dame, Ind.: University of Notre Dame Press, 1981), p. 263.

2. Joshua Cohen and Joel Rogers, *On Democracy* (New York: Penguin, 1983), p. 176.

3. See Allan Megill, *Prophets of Extremity: Nietzsche, Heidegger, Foucault, Derrida* (Berkeley: University of California Press, 1985).

4. Charlene Spretnak, *The Spiritual Dimension of Green Politics* (Santa Fe, N.Mex.: Bear and Co., 1986), p. 16.

5. Daniel Bell, *The Cultural Contradictions of Capitalism* (New York: Basic Books, 1978), p. 28; Richard Rorty, "That Old-Time Philosophy: Straussianism, Democracy, and Allan Bloom," *New Republic*, April 4, 1988, pp. 28–33.

6. Richard John Neuhaus, *The Naked Public Square: Religion and Democracy in America* (Grand Rapids, Mich.: Eerdmans, 1984), pp. 21, 61, 64.

7. Glenn Tinder, *Community: Reflections on a Tragic Ideal* (Baton Rouge: Louisiana State University Press, 1980), p. 149.

8. Michael Harrington, *The Politics at God's Funeral: The Spiritual Crisis of Western Civilization* (New York: Penguin, 1985), p. 128.

9. Ibid., p. 197.

10. Bell, *Cultural Contradictions.*

11. Benjamin Barber, *Strong Democracy: Participatory Politics for a New Age* (Berkeley: University of California Press, 1984), pp. 47–49.

12. Bell, *Cultural Contradictions*, pp. 108–19.

13. Alasdair MacIntyre, *After Virtue: A Study in Moral Theory* (Notre Dame, Ind.: University of Notre Dame Press, 1981).

14. Michael J. Sandel, *Liberalism and the Limits of Justice* (Cambridge: Cambridge University Press, 1982), ch. 3.

15. MacIntyre, *After Virtue*, p. 238.

16. Allan Bloom, *The Closing of the American Mind* (New York: Simon and Schuster, 1987), Introduction and p. 125.

17. Ibid., p. 221.

18. Irving Kristol, *Two Cheers for Capitalism* (New York: Meridian, 1977), p. 235 and ch. 30.

19. Thomas Dumm, *Democracy and Punishment: Disciplinary Origins of the United States* (Madison: University of Wisconsin Press, 1987).

20. Bloom, *American Mind*, p. 155.

21. Bell, *Cultural Contradictions*, p. 171; Bloom, *American Mind*, p. 67.

22. Barber, *Strong Democracy*, p. 231.

23. Robert Bellah, Richard Madsen, William M. Sullivan, Ann Swidler, Steven M. Tipton, *Habits of the Heart: Individualism and Commitment in American Life* (Berkeley: University of California Press, 1985).

24. Bloom, *American Mind*, p. 141.

25. Bell, *Cultural Contradictions*, ch. 1.

26. Bellah et al., *Habits of the Heart*, pp. 281–86.

27. Bloom, *American Mind*, p. 117.

28. Neuhaus, *Naked Public Square*, pp. 111–12.

29. Michael Sandel, *Liberalism and Its Critics* (New York: New York University Press, 1984), p. 6.

30. Richard M. Merelman, *Making Something of Ourselves: On Culture and Politics in the United States* (Berkeley: University of California Press, 1984), pp. 1–2.

31. Bloom, *American Mind*, pp. 47–61.

32. Herbert J. Gans, *Middle American Individualism: The Future of Liberal Democracy* (New York: Free Press, 1988), ch. 5.

33. Bloom, *American Mind*, pp. 89–90.

34. Bellah et al., *Habits of the Heart*, pp. 23–25.

35. E.g., Andrew Oldenquist, *The Non-Suicidal Society* (Bloomington: Indiana University Press, 1986), chs. 1, 2, 6.

36. E.g., James Oliver Robertson, *American Myth, American Reality* (New York: Hill and Wang, 1980).

37. Bell, *Cultural Contradictions*, pp. 232–36.

38. E.g., Oldenquist, *Non-Suicidal Society*, ch. 15.

39. Christopher Lasch, *Haven in a Heartless World: The Family Besieged* (New York: Basic Books, 1977).

40. Bellah et al., *Habits of the Heart*, ch. 3.

41. Ibid., pp. 75–81.

42. Ibid., pp. 27, 32–35.

43. Ibid., ch. 4; Bloom, *American Mind*, p. 122.

44. Clarke E. Cochran, *Character, Community, and Politics* (University: University of Alabama Press, 1982), p. 3.

45. Peter Berger, "On the Obsolescence of the Concept of Honor," *European Journal of Sociology* 11 (1970): 339–47.

46. Sandel, *Liberalism and the Limits of Justice*, p. 183; idem, *Liberalism and Its Critics*, p. 153.

47. Barber, *Strong Democracy*, p. 231.

48. Sheldon Wolin, "Democracy in the Discourse of Postmodernism," *Social Research* 57 (Spring 1990): 5–30.

49. Bell, *Cultural Contradictions*, p. xxiv.

50. Sandel, *Liberalism and Its Critics*; MacIntyre, *After Virtue*.

51. Bloom, *American Mind*, p. 28.

52. Alasdair MacIntyre, *Whose Justice? Which Rationality?* (Notre Dame, Ind.: University of Notre Dame Press, 1988), pp. 344–45.

53. C. B. Macpherson, *Democratic Theory: Essays in Retrieval* (Oxford: Oxford University Press, 1973), p. 21 and ch. 2.

54. Sandel, *Liberalism and the Limits of Justice*, p. 175.

55. MacIntyre, *After Virtue*, ch. 18 and p. 259.

56. Sandel, *Liberalism and Its Critics*, p. 10.

57. Sandel, *Liberalism and the Limits of Justice*, pp. 179–83.

58. Nancy L. Rosenblum, *Another Liberalism: Romanticism and the Reconstruction of Liberal Thought* (Cambridge, Mass.: Harvard University Press, 1987), p. 153.

59. William M. Sullivan, *Reconstructing Public Philosophy* (Berkeley: University of California Press, 1982), p. 15.

60. Samuel Bowles and Herbert Gintis, *Democracy and Capitalism: Property, Community, and the Contradictions of Modern Social Thought* (London: Routledge and Kegan Paul), 1986, pp. 15–16.

61. Sandel, *Liberalism and the Limits of Justice*, p. 174.

62. Bloom, *American Mind*, pp. 130–31.

63. Thomas L. Pangle, "The Constitution's Human Vision," *Public Interest* 86 (Winter 1987): 77–90.

64. John Patrick Diggins, *The Lost Soul of American Politics: Virtue, Self-Interest, and the Foundations of Liberalism* (Chicago: University of Chicago Press, 1984), p. 6, passim.

65. Wilson Carey McWilliams, *The Idea of Fraternity in America* (Berkeley: University of California Press, 1974), p. 5; Sullivan, *Reconstructing Public Philosophy*, p. 18.

66. Sullivan, *Reconstructing Public Philosophy*, p. 73.

67. Ibid., p. 39.

68. Barber, *Strong Democracy*, pp. 110–11.

69. Clarke E. Cochran, "The Thin Theory of Community: The Communitarians and Their Critics," *Political Studies* 37 (1989): 13.

70. Cochran, *Character, Community, and Politics*, p. 8.

71. Bell, *Cultural Contradictions*, p. xxix.

72. Mason Drukman, *Community and Purpose in America: An Analysis of American Political Theory* (New York: McGraw-Hill, 1971), p. 6.

73. Bell, *Cultural Contradictions*, ch. 3; Bloom, *American Mind*, pp. 313–35.

74. Christopher Lasch, *The Minimal Self: Psychic Survival in Troubled Times* (New York: Norton, 1984), ch. 1.

75. E.g., McWilliams, *The Idea of Fraternity*, pp. 65, 69; Drukman, *Community and Purpose*, pp. 10–13.

76. Russell Kirk, *A Program for Conservatives*, rev. ed. (Chicago: Regnery, 1962), p. 141.

77. Cohen and Rogers, *Democracy*, chs. 3, 2.

78. Lawrence Goodwyn, *The Populist Moment: A Short History of the Agrarian Revolt in America* (New York: Oxford University Press, 1978), p. 322.

79. Harrington, *Politics at God's Funeral*, p. 81.

80. R. Jeffrey Lustig, *Corporate Liberalism: The Origins of Modern American Political Theory, 1890–1920* (Berkeley: University of California Press, 1982).

81. Bellah et al., *Habits of the Heart*, ch. 5, pp. 47–48.

82. Ibid., pp. 71–75.

83. Herve Varenne, *Americans Together: Structure and Diversity in a Midwestern Town* (New York: Columbia University Press, 1977).

84. Michael W. McCann, *Taking Reform Seriously: Perspectives on Public Interest Liberalism* (Ithaca, N.Y.: Cornell University Press, 1986), pp. 190–91.

85. E.g., Lasch, *Haven in a Heartless World*, ch. 7.

86. E.g., Bloom, *American Mind*, pp. 118–20, 58.

87. Lasch, *Haven in a Heartless World*, pp. 91, 174.

88. Bell, *Cultural Contradictions*, pp. 244, 77.

89. Lasch, *Haven in a Heartless World*, pp. 183, 189.

90. Lustig, *Corporate Liberalism*, pp. 234, 229.

91. Bellah et al., *Habits of the Heart*, p. 207.

92. Kirkpatrick Sale, *Human Scale* (New York: Coward, McCann and Geoghegan, 1980), p. 107.

93. Paul Kennedy, "Fin-de-Siecle America," *New York Review of Books*, June 28, 1990, pp. 31–40.

94. James Fishkin, *Justice, Equal Opportunity, and the Family* (New Haven, Conn.: Yale University Press, 1983); Amy Gutmann, *Liberal Equality* (Cambridge: Cambridge University Press, 1980); idem, *Democratic Education* (Princeton, N.J.: Princeton University Press, 1987).

95. John Rawls, *A Theory of Justice* (Cambridge, Mass.: Harvard University Press, 1971).

96. Peter Clecak, *America's Quest for the Ideal Self: Dissent and Fulfillment in the 60s and 70s* (New York: Oxford University Press, 1983), pp. 107, 5–9, 226, 326, and chs. 9, 12.

97. Richard Reeves, *American Journey* (New York: Simon and Schuster, 1982), p. 206 and chs. 15–17.

98. Ibid., pp. 92, 337–38, 357.

99. Daniel Boorstin, *The Genius of American Politics* (Chicago: University of Chicago Press, 1953); idem, *The Americans: The Democratic Experience* (New York: Vintage, 1974); idem, *The Americans: The National Experience* (New York: Vintage, 1965).

100. Boorstin, *Genius of American Politics; Americans: Democratic Experience; Americans: National Experience*.

101. Robert Nisbet, *The Present Age: Progress and Anarchy in Modern America* (New York: Harper and Row, 1988).

102. Alan Wolfe, *Whose Keeper? Social Science and Moral Obligation* (Berkeley: University of California Press, 1989).

103. Kristol, *Two Cheers*, p. 65.

104. Don Herzog, "Some Questions for Republicans, *Political Theory* 14 (August 1986): 473–93.

Chapter Three. Rummaging through American History

1. E.g., Jane J. Mansbridge, *Beyond Adversary Democracy* (Chicago: University of Chicago Press, 1983), pp. 134–35.
2. Samuel P. Huntington, *American Politics: The Promise of Disharmony* (Cambridge, Mass.: Harvard University Press, 1981).
3. Don Herzog, "Some Questions for Republicans," *Political Theory* 14 (August 1986): 473–93.
4. Louis Hartz, *The Liberal Tradition in America* (New York: Harcourt, Brace and World, 1955).
5. Mason Drukman, *Community and Purpose in America: An Analysis of American Political Theory* (New York: McGraw-Hill, 1971), pp. 25–45, 100.
6. Ibid., pp. 109–10.
7. J. G. A. Pocock, *The Machiavellian Moment: Florentine Political Thought and the Atlantic Republican Tradition* (Princeton, N.J.: Princeton University Press, 1975).
8. For a succinct summary of the debate and a view which stresses the renewed strength of the nonrepublican interpretation, see Michael Lienesch, *New Order of the Ages: Time, the Constitution, and the Making of Modern American Political Thought* (Princeton, N.J.: Princeton University Press, 1988).
9. Bernard Bailyn, *Ideological Origins of the American Revolution* (Cambridge, Mass.: Harvard University Press, 1967); Robert Bellah, Richard Madsen, William M. Sullivan, Ann Swidler, Steven M. Tipton, *Habits of the Heart: Individualism and Commitment in American Life* (Berkeley: University of California Press, 1985); William M. Sullivan, *Reconstructing Public Philosophy* (Berkeley: University of California Press, 1982).
10. Sullivan, *Reconstructing Public Philosophy*, p. 12.
11. Gordon S. Wood, "The Fundamentalists and the Constitution," *New York Review of Books*, February 18, 1988, p. 38.
12. Forrest McDonald, *Novus Ordo Seclorum: The Intellectual Origins of the Constitution* (Lawrence: University Press of Kansas, 1985), p. 291.
13. Sullivan, *Reconstructing Political Philosophy*, pp. 13–14.
14. Wood, "The Fundamentalists," p. 38.
15. McDonald, *Novus Ordo*, p. 292.
16. Ibid., p. 235.
17. A point made by Charles Anderson, among others. Anderson was a considerable help to me in thinking about this chapter.
18. Gordon S. Wood, *The Creation of the American Republic 1776–1787* (New York: Norton, 1972).
19. Ibid., p. 395.
20. Ibid., pp. 120–21.
21. Ibid., ch. 2.
22. Ibid., pp. 608–12.
23. James T. Kloppenberg, "The Virtues of Liberalism: Christianity, Republicanism, and Ethics in Early American Political Discourses," *Journal of American History* 74 (June 1987): 11, 17, 21.
24. Ibid., pp. 14–17.
25. Joyce Appleby, *Capitalism and a New Social Order: The Republican Vision of the 1790s* (New York: New York University Press, 1984).

26. E.g., Wilson Carey McWilliams, *The Idea of Fraternity in America* (Berkeley: University of California Press, 1974), ch. 5; see also John Patrick Diggins, *The Lost Soul of American Politics: Virtue, Self-Interest and the Foundation of Liberalism* (Chicago: University of Chicago Press, 1984).

27. Sara M. Evans and Harry C. Boyte, *Free Spaces: The Sources of Democratic Change in America* (New York: Harper and Row, 1986), pp. 7–8.

28. Diggins, *Lost Soul*, pp. 212–17.

29. Drukman, *Community and Purpose*, ch. 5.

30. Diggins, *Lost Soul*, p. 191.

31. Rowland Berthoff, *An Unsettled People* (New York: Harper and Row, 1971).

32. Drukman, *Community and Purpose*, pp. 178–89.

33. Russell L. Hanson, *The Democratic Imagination in America* (Princeton, N.J.: Princeton University Press, 1985), p. 120; Diggins, *Lost Soul*, ch. 9.

34. Richard Hofstadter, *The Age of Reform* (New York: Knopf, 1955).

35. Lawrence Goodwyn, *The Populist Moment: A Short History of the Agrarian Revolt in America* (New York: Oxford University Press, 1978), p. 212.

36. Ibid., p. 295.

37. Ibid., p. 66.

38. Ibid., p. 270.

39. David E. Price, "Community and Control: Critical Democratic Theory in the Progressive Period," *American Political Science Review* 68 (December 1974): 1663–78. An interesting earlier discussion is Eric Goldman's *Rendezvous with Destiny: A History of Modern American Reform* (New York: Knopf, 1952).

40. E.g., McWilliams, *Idea of Fraternity*, ch. 17.

41. Goldman, *Rendezvous with Destiny*.

42. Both a valuable guide and a good example is Robert M. Crunden's *Ministers of Reform: The Progressives' Achievement in American Civilization* (New York: Basic Books, 1982); or contrast John D. Buenker's *Urban Liberalism and Progressive Reform* (New York: Scribner's 1973) with Dewey W. Grantham's *Southern Progressivism: The Reconciliation of Progress and Tradition* (Knoxville: University of Tennessee Press, 1983).

43. Joseph Ratner, ed., *Intellectuals in the Modern World: John Dewey's Philosophy* (New York: Modern Library, 1939); Charlotte Perkins Gilman, *Women and Economics* (New York: Harper, 1966); Herbert Croly, *The Promise of American Life* (New York: Macmillan, 1909).

44. Some useful places to start: Howard Zinn, *A People's History of the United States* (New York: Harper and Row, 1980); Staughton Lynd, *Intellectual Origins of American Radicalism* (New York: Random House, 1969); Arthur Schlesinger, Jr., ed., *The Writings and Speeches of Eugene V. Debs* (New York: Hermitage, 1948).

45. Christopher Lasch, *The New Radicalism in America 1889–1963* (New York: Vintage, 1965), ch. 9.

46. Richard Flacks, *Making History: The Radical Tradition in American Life* (New York: Columbia University Press, 1988).

47. See Aileen Kraditor, *The Radical Persuasion 1890–1917* (Baton Rouge: Louisiana State University Press, 1981).

48. E.g., Russell L. Hanson, *Democratic Imagination*.

49. Philip Abbott, *Seeking Many Inventions: The Idea of Community in America* (Knoxville: University of Tennessee Press, 1987), p. 176.

50. Drukman, *Community and Purpose*, p. 4.

51. Bellah et al., *Habits of the Heart*, pp. 20–21, passim.

52. Alexis de Tocqueville, trans. Henry Reeve, *Democracy in America* (New York: Vintage, 1957).

53. Hartz, *The Liberal Tradition*.

54. As developed throughout Bellah's *Habits of the Heart*.

Chapter Four. Participatory Community

1. E.g., Carole Pateman, *Participation and Democratic Theory* (Cambridge: Cambridge University Press, 1970), ch. 2.

2. Contrast Robert Booth Fowler's *Believing Skeptics: American Political Intellectuals 1945–1965* (Westport, Conn.: Greenwood, 1978) with the story told in Mitchell Cohen and Dennis Hale, eds., *The New Student Left* (Boston: Beacon, 1966).

3. E.g., Roberto M. Unger, *Knowledge and Politics* (New York: Free Press, 1975), p. 262; and Michael W. McCann, *Taking Reform Seriously: Perspectives on Public Interest Liberalism* (Ithaca, N.Y.: Cornell University Press, 1986), p. 190.

4. Unger, *Knowledge and Politics*, p. 262.

5. Pateman, in *Participation and Democratic Theory*, discussed the theory, past and modern, of participatory politics.

6. As Eric Gorham put it to me nicely.

7. E.g., McCann, *Taking Reform Seriously*, p. 198.

8. Kirkpatrick Sale, *Human Scale* (New York: Coward, McCann and Geoghegan, 1980), p. 428, pt. 2, p. 89.

9. Benjamin Barber, *Strong Democracy: Participatory Politics for a New Age* (Berkeley: University of California Press, 1984), pp. 235–37.

10. Ibid., p. 173.

11. Ibid., p. 157.

12. Ibid., p. 132.

13. William M. Sullivan, *Reconstructing Public Philosophy* (Berkeley: University of California Press, 1982), p. 164.

14. Ibid., p. 168.

15. Barber, *Strong Democracy*, p. xv.

16. Ibid., p. 65.

17. Clarke E. Cochran, "The Thin Theory of Community: The Communitarians and Their Critics," *Political Studies* 37 (1989): 422–35.

18. Marx is a case in point.

19. Pateman, *Participation and Democratic Theory*, p. 47.

20. This is the burden of the entire second half of Pateman.

21. E.g., Samuel Bowles and Herbert Gintis, *Democracy and Capitalism: Property, Community, and the Contradictions of Modern Social Thought* (London: Routledge and Kegan Paul, 1986), p. 178.

22. Barber, *Strong Democracy*, p. 155.

23. Ibid., p. 132.

24. Bowles and Gintis, *Democracy and Capitalism*, p. 140.

25. Pateman, *Participation and Democratic Theory*, p. 63.

26. Bowles and Gintis, *Democracy and Capitalism*, p. 83.

27. Jane J. Mansbridge, *Beyond Adversary Democracy* (Chicago: University of Chicago Press, 1983).

28. Ibid., p. 295.

29. Ibid., pp. 276–77, 135, 147–48.

30. Ibid., ch. 2.

31. Ibid., ch. 4.

32. Barber, *Strong Democracy*.

33. Ibid., pp. 238–40.

34. Ibid., pp. 118, 128.

35. Barbara Ehrenreich, "Liberalism and 'Community': Another Communitarianism," *New Republic*, May 9, 1988, p. 21.

36. Sale, *Human Scale*, p. 37.

37. Ibid., p. 41.

38. Ibid., pp. 188, 404.

39. Ibid., pp. 411, 352–92.

40. Ibid., pp. 38–39.

41. E.g., Arthur Stein, *Seeds of the Seventies: Values, Work, and Commitment in Post-Vietnam America* (Hanover, N.H.: University Press of New England, 1985); Corinne McLaughlin and Gordon Davidson, *Builders of the Dawn: Community Lifestyles in a Changing World* (Shutesbury, Mass.: Sirius, 1986); there are many more.

42. McLaughlin and Davidson, *Builders of the Dawn*, p. 2.

43. Ibid., ch. 12–14.

44. Ibid., ch. 5.

45. Ibid., pp. 26 ff.

46. Ibid., ch. 4.

47. Ibid., p. 8 and ch. 6.

48. Stein, *Seeds of the Seventies*.

49. McLaughlin and Davidson, *Builders of the Dawn*, p. 60.

50. Ibid., ch. 10.

51. Ibid., ch. 3, pp. 68–78.

52. Richard Hofstadter, *The Age of Reform* (New York: Knopf, 1955); Michael Ansara and S. M. Miller, "Democratic Populism," in *The New Populism: The Politics of Empowerment*, ed. Harry C. Boyte and Frank Riessman (Philadelphia: Temple University Press, 1986), p. 149.

53. Harry C. Boyte, "Beyond Politics as Usual," in Boyte and Riessman, eds., *New Populism*, pp. 3–15.

54. E. P. Thompson, *The Making of the English Working Class* (New York: Pantheon, 1964); Sara M. Evans and Harry C. Boyte, *Free Spaces: The Sources of Democratic Change in America* (New York: Harper and Row, 1986), p. ix.

55. E.g., Evans and Boyte, *Free Spaces*.

56. Lawrence Goodwyn, *The Populist Moment: A Short History of the Agrarian Revolt in America* (New York: Oxford University Press, 1978).

57. Harry C. Boyte, Heather Booth, and Steve Max, *Citizen Action and the New America* (Philadelphia: Temple University Press, 1986), p. 34.

58. Goodwyn, *The Populist Moment*, p. vii.

59. Harry C. Boyte, *Community Is Possible: Repairing America's Roots* (New

York: Harper and Row, 1984), ch. 3; Boyte, Booth, and Max, *Citizen Action*, ch. 3.

60. Evans and Boyte, *Free Spaces*, p. viii.
61. Ansara and Miller, "Democratic Populism," p. 146.
62. Goodwyn, *The Populist Moment*, p. 302.
63. Boyte, Booth, and Max, *Citizen Action*, ch. 2; Boyte, *Community Is Possible*, ch. 5.
64. E.g., Evans and Boyte, *Free Spaces*, p. viii; Robert N. Bellah, "Populism and Individualism," in Boyte and Riessman, eds., *New Populism*, pp. 101–102.
65. Boyte and Riessman, eds., *New Populism*.
66. Charlene Spretnak, "Postmodern Populism: The Greening of Technocratic Society," in Boyte and Riessman, eds., *New Populism*, pp. 156–64.
67. Boyte, Booth, and Max, *Citizen Action*, p. 22.
68. Evans and Boyte, *Free Spaces*, p. 186.
69. E.g., Glenn Tinder, *Community: Reflections on a Tragic Ideal* (Baton Rouge: Louisiana State University Press, 1980), p. 64.
70. Carey McWilliams raised this issue most pointedly with me. For two perspectives, see McLaughlin and Davidson, *Builders of the Dawn*, pp. 62–66; and Barber, *Strong Democracy*, p. 249.
71. E.g., Tinder *Community*, p. 71.
72. Barber, *Strong Democracy*; Bowles and Gintis, *Democracy and Capitalism*, ch. 4.
73. Compare Barber with Pateman.
74. Two examples of those who take it that the really contested issue is not normative but practical/empirical: Pateman, *Participation and Democratic Theory*; and Robert Dahl, *A Preface to Economic Democracy* (Berkeley: University of California Press, 1985).
75. Mansbridge, *Beyond Adversary Democracy*, pp. 4–5, 147–48, 276–77, ch. 20, passim.
76. Ibid., pp. 230–95.
77. See Pateman, *Participation and Democratic Theory*; and Barber, *Strong Democracy*, ch. 10.
78. Pateman, *Participation and Democratic Theory*, pp. 102, 111; contrast with John Witte, *Democracy, Authority, and Alienation in Work: Workers' Participation in an American Corporation* (Chicago: University of Chicago Press, 1980).
79. Pateman, *Participation and Democratic Theory*, ch. 5.
80. Bowles and Gintis, *Democracy and Capitalism*, pp. 201–02.
81. Barber, *Strong Democracy*, p. 247.
82. Goodwyn, *The Populist Moment*, pp. 98–100.
83. Roberto M. Unger, *Passion: An Essay on Personality* (New York: Free Press 1984), pp. 73–74.
84. Unger, *Passion*, pp. 193, 258.
85. Unger, *Passion*, pp. 246, 96, 211.
86. Unger, *Knowledge and Politics*, pp. 272–74; idem, *Passion*, p. 76.
87. Unger, *Knowledge and Politics* p. 266.
88. Ibid.

89. Roberto M. Unger, *Politics: A Work in Constructive Social Theory* (Cambridge: Cambridge University Press, 1987).

90. See Bernard Yack, "Toward a Free Marketplace of Social Institutions," *Harvard Law Review* 101 (June 1988): 1961–77.

91. Ibid.

92. Sale, *Human Scale*, p. 345; Barber, *Strong Democracy*, p. 160.

93. Barber, *Strong Democracy*, p. 215.

94. Ibid., p. 37.

95. A point my colleague Eric Gorham made to me.

96. Herbert J. Gans, *Middle American Individualism: The Future of Liberal Democracy* (New York: Free Press, 1988), ch. 6.

97. Ansara and Miller, "Democratic Populism," p. 151.

98. Pateman, *Participation and Democratic Theory*, p. 2.

99. Barber, *Strong Democracy*, p. 259.

100. Mansbridge, *Beyond Adversary Democracy*, p. vii.

101. E.g., Pateman, *Participation and Democratic Theory*; Unger, *Knowledge and Politics*; Joshua Cohen and Joel Rogers, *On Democracy* (New York: Penguin, 1983); Bowles and Gintis, *Democracy and Capitalism*.

102. Patemen, *Participation and Democracy Theory*, ch. 4; Bowles and Gintis, *Democracy and Capitalism*, p. 150; Cohen and Rogers, *On Democracy*, ch. 6.

103. E.g., Unger, *Knowledge and Politics*, pp. 264–65.

104. Ibid.

105. Sullivan, *Reconstructing Public Philosophy*, p. 224.

106. E.g., Pateman, *Participation and Democratic Theory*, p. 45; Sullivan, *Reconstructing Public Philosophy*, p. 225.

107. True of Bowles and Gintis, *Democracy and Capitalism*.

108. Michael Harrington, *The Politics at God's Funeral: The Spiritual Crisis of Western Civilization* (New York: Penguin, 1985), p. 217.

109. E.g., Sale, *Human Scale*, pp. 352–92.

110. Bruce Stokes, *Helping Ourselves: Local Solutions to Global Problems* (New York: W. W. Norton, 1981), ch. 2.

111. See C. B. MacPherson, *The Real World of Democracy* (Oxford: Oxford University Press, 1966), especially pp. 64, 67.

112. Ibid., p. 33.

113. C. B. MacPherson, *Democratic Theory: Essays in Retrieval* (Oxford: Oxford University Press, 1973), ch. 1.

114. MacPherson, *The Real World*, ch. 4.

115. Ibid., ch. 2.

116. Ibid., p. 29.

117. Robert Dahl, *Economic Democracy*.

118. Robert Dahl, *Democracy and Its Critics* (New Haven, Conn.: Yale University Press, 1989), chs. 6, 7.

119. Ibid., ch. 21.

120. Ibid., chs. 21–23.

121. Robert Dahl, "Worker's Control of Industry and the British Labor Party," *American Political Science Review* 41 (October 1947): 899–900, an article my friend Leon Epstein first told me about; Dahl makes his return in *Democracy and Its Critics*, of course.

122. Bowles and Gintis, *Democracy and Capitalism*, pp. 3, 12, 176.
123. As my colleague Eric Gorham puts the argument.
124. Harrington, *Politics at God's Funeral.*
125. Michael Walzer, *Spheres of Justice: A Defense of Pluralism and Equality* (New York: Basic Books, 1983).
126. Ibid., ch. 1.
127. Ibid., chs. 8, 7, 3, 4, 2.
128. Ibid., ch. 1.
129. John R. Wallach, "Liberals, Communitarians, and the Tasks of Political Theory," *Political Theory* 15 (November 1987): 595.
130. Ibid., ch. 13 and p. 310.
131. Ibid., p. 319.

Chapter Five. The Republican Community

1. William M. Sullivan, *Reconstructing Public Philosophy* (Berkeley: University of California Press, 1982), p. 10.
2. E.g., Ralph Ketcham, *Individualism and Public Life—A Modern Dilemma* (New York: Basil Blackwell, 1987), p. 163.
3. E.g., Sullivan, *Reconstructing Public Philosophy*, p. 55; for a less ardent view see William Lee Miller, *The First Liberty: Religion and the American Republic* (New York: Knopf, 1986), pp. 343–53.
4. Two partisan but thorough discussions are Thomas L. Pangle's *The Spirit of Modern Republicanism: The Moral Vision of the American Founders and the Philosophy of Locke* (Chicago: University of Chicago Press, 1988); and John Patrick Diggins's *The Lost Soul of American Politics: Virtue, Self-Interest, and the Foundations of Liberalism* (Chicago: University of Chicago Press, 1984).
5. Gordon S. Wood, *The Creation of the American Republic 1776–1787* (New York: Norton, 1972); Garry Wills, *Inventing America* (Garden City, N.Y.: Doubleday, 1978).
6. Forrest McDonald, *Novus Ordo Seclorum: The Intellectual Origins of the Constitution* (Lawrence: University Press of Kansas, 1985), p. 235.
7. Michael Lienesch, *New Order of the Ages: Time, the Constitution, and the Making of Modern American Political Thought* (Princeton, N.J.: Princeton University Press, 1988).
8. Ibid., p. 291.
9. One should judge for oneself. J. G. A. Pocock, *The Machiavellian Moment: Florentine Political Thought and the Atlantic Republican Tradition* (Princeton, N.J.: Princeton University Press, 1975).
10. Ibid., pp. 545–46.
11. Ibid., pp. 546–47.
12. Ibid., pp. 526–27. I read Pocock as having this view but grant there are other readings which downplay his analysis as having a normative tinge.
13. Gordon S. Wood, "The Fundamentalists and the Constitution," *New York Review of Books*, February 18, 1988, p. 36.
14. E.g., Richard K. Matthews, "Liberalism, Civic Humanism, and the American Political Tradition: Understanding Consensus," *Journal of Politics* 49

(Nov. 1987): 1127–53; Joyce Appleby, *Capitalism and a New Social Order: The Republican Vision of the 1790s* (New York: New York University Press, 1984).

15. Wood, "The Fundamentalists and the Constitution," pp. 35–39.

16. Richard Beeman, "Introduction," in *Beyond Confederation: Origins of the Constitution and American National Identity*, ed. Richard Beeman, Stephen Botein, and Edward C. Carter II (Chapel Hill: University of North Carolina Press, 1987).

17. Wood, *Creation of the American Republic*; idem, "Hellfire Politics," *New York Review of Books*, February 28, 1985, p. 30; idem, "Ideology and the Origins of Liberal America," *William and Mary Quarterly* 44 (July 1987): 628–40.

18. See Gordon Wood, "Interests and Disinterestedness in the Making of the Constitution," in Beeman et al., eds., *Beyond Confederation*, pp. 69–109.

19. Don Herzog, "Some Questions for Republicans," *Political Theory* 14 (August 1986): 478.

20. See Lance Banning, "The Practicable Sphere of a Republic: James Madison, the Constitutional Convention, and the Emergence of Revolutionary Federalism," in Beeman et al., eds., *Beyond Confederation*, pp. 162–87; "Republican Ideology and the Triumph of the Constitution, 1789–1793," *William and Mary Quarterly*, 31 (1974): 167–88.

21. Russell L. Hanson, *The Democratic Imagination in America* (Princeton, N.J.: Princeton University Press, 1985), ch. 2, p. 65, ch. 12.

22. Drew McCoy, *The Elusive Republic: Political Economy in Jeffersonian America* (Chapel Hill: University of North Carolina Press, 1980); Lance Banning, "Jeffersonian Ideology Revisited: Liberal and Classical Ideas in the New American Republic," *William and Mary Quarterly* 43 (January 1986): 3–19.

23. John W. Murrin, "Gordon S. Wood and the Search for Liberal America," *William and Mary Quarterly* 44 (July 1987): 597–601.

24. Rogers M. Smith, "The 'American Creed' and American Identity: The Limits of Liberal Citizenship in the United States," *Western Political Quarterly* 41 (June 1988): 225–51.

25. This is Erik Olsen's argument in his soon-to-be-completed Ph.D. dissertation at the University of Wisconsin-Madison.

26. Robert Bellah, Richard Madsen, William M. Sullivan, Ann Swidler, Steven M. Tipton, *Habits of the Heart: Individualism and Commitment in American Life* (Berkeley: University of California Press, 1985), p. 218.

27. Sullivan, *Reconstructing Public Philosophy*, p. 21.

28. R. Jeffrey Lustig, *Corporate Liberalism: The Origins of Modern American Political Theory, 1890–1920* (Berkeley: University of California Press, 1982), ch. 9; Hanson, *Democratic Imagination*, chs. 11, 9.

29. E.g., Sullivan, *Reconstructing Public Philosophy*.

30. Ibid., p. 90.

31. Ibid., p. 35.

32. Lustig, *Corporate Liberalism*, ch. 9; Sullivan, *Reconstructing Public Philosophy*, p. 158.

33. Sullivan, *Reconstructing Public Philosophy*, p. 161.

34. Ibid., ch. 7. Compare Bellah et al., *Habits of the Heart*, with Joshua Cohen and Joel Rogers, *On Democracy* (New York: Penguin, 1983).

35. Peter Clecak, *America's Quest for the Ideal Self: Dissent and Fulfillment*

in the 60s and 70s (New York: Oxford University Press, 1983), pp. 393–401; Sullivan, *Reconstructing Public Philosophy*, p. 181.

36. Hanson, *Democratic Imagination*. Ch. 12 is a good case by way of illustration but Bellah or Sullivan might serve just as well.

37. Joyce Appleby, "Republicanism in Old and New Contexts," *William and Mary Quarterly* 43 (January 1986): 20–34.

38. Edward Countryman, "Of Republicanism, Capitalism, and the American Mind," *William and Mary Quarterly* 44 (July 1987): 556–62.

39. Ralph Ketcham, "Publius: Sustaining the Republican Principle," *William and Mary Quarterly* 44 (July 1987): 576–82.

40. Robert H. Webking, *The American Revolution and the Politics of Liberty* (Baton Rouge: Lousiana State University Press, 1988).

41. Diggins, *Lost Soul*, ch. 1.

42. Ibid., ch. 2.

43. Ibid., Conclusion and p. 16.

44. McDonald, *Novus Ordo Seclorum*, p. viii.

45. Pangle, *Modern Republicanism*, p. 28.

46. Ibid., p. 35.

47. Ibid., p. 30.

48. Ibid., pp. 73, 61, 47, and ch. 8.

49. Ibid. p. 35.

50. Ibid., pp. 21–24.

51. Louis Hartz, *The Liberal Tradition in America* (New York: Harcourt, Brace and World, 1955).

52. Pangle, *Modern Republicanism*, pp. 25–27.

53. Claude S. Fischer, "Finding the 'Lost' Community: Facts and Fictions," *Tikkun* 3 (November/December 1988): 69–72.

54. A good case study is J. Anthony Lukas's *Common Ground: A Turbulent Decade in the Lives of Three American Families* (New York: Knopf, 1985).

55. E.g., Andrew Oldenquist, *The Non-Suicidal Society* (Bloomington: Indiana University Press, 1986), ch. 17; Eric Gorham has done interesting work on the republican weakness, as he sees it, for a national service arrangement. See his Ph.D. dissertation, "National Service: Citizenship and Political Education," University of Wisconsin–Madison, 1990.

56. Ketcham, *Individualism and Life*, pp. 147–87.

57. Ibid., p. 151.

58. Jean Bethke Elshtain, "Liberalism and 'Community': The Barrier of Law," *New Republic*, May 9, 1988, p. 22.

59. Benjamin Barber, *Strong Democracy: Participatory Politics for a New Age* (Berkeley: University of California Press, 1984).

60. Ibid.

61. Diggins, *Lost Soul*, pp. 332–33.

62. John H. Schaar, ed., "The Case for Patriotism," *Legitimacy in the Modern State* (New Brunswick, N.J.: Transaction Books, 1981), ch. 14.

63. Mary Dietz, "Patriotism," in *Political Innovation and Conceptual Change*, ed. Terence Ball (Cambridge: Cambridge University Press, 1988); Mary Dietz, "Context Is All: Feminism and Theory of Citizenship," *Daedalus* 116 (Fall 1987): 1–24; Mary Dietz, "Populism, Patriotism, and the Need for Roots," in *The New Populism: The Politics of Empowerment*, ed. Harvey C. Boyte and Frank

Riessman (Philadelphia: Temple University Press, 1987); Mary Dietz, "Citizenship with a Feminist Face: The Problem with Maternal Thinking," *Political Theory* 13 (February 1985): 19–37.

64. In truth, we need to know much, much more here.

65. Wilson Carey McWilliams, *The Idea of Fraternity in America* (Berkeley: University of California Press, 1974).

66. Ibid., p. 34.

67. Ibid., p. 569.

68. Ibid., p. 621.

69. Ibid., p. 355.

70. Christopher Lasch, "Fraternalist Manifesto," *Harper's*, April 1987, p. 20.

71. Erik Olsen has educated me over and over on this and other topics.

72. Bellah et al., *Habits of the Heart*.

73. Christopher Lasch, *The Minimal Self: Psychic Survival in Troubled Times* (New York: Norton, 1984).

Chapter Six. Community and Roots

1. George H. Nash, *The Conservative Intellectual Movement in America since 1945* (New York: Basic Books, 1979), p. xvi.

2. Russell Kirk, ed., *The Portable Conservative Reader* (New York: Penguin, 1982), pp. xv–xix; idem, *The Conservative Mind from Burke to Santayana* (Chicago: Henry Regnery, 1953), pp. 414–15. Excellent contemporary sources for Kirk include his occasional writing in *National Review* and his publication *The University Bookman*, which, though he does not write it, expresses his concerns.

3. Nash, *Conservative Intellectual Movement*, pp. 171–85; Frank S. Meyer, "The Recrudescent American Conservatism," in *American Conservative Thought in the Twentieth Century*, ed. William F. Buckley, Jr. (Indianapolis: Bobbs-Merrill, 1970), ch. 4.

4. Buckley, *American Conservative Thought*, ch. 5 and pp. xv–xxi.

5. Russell Kirk, *A Program for Conservatives*, rev. ed. (Chicago: Henry Regnery, 1962), p. 140.

6. Ibid., pp. 49, 47.

7. Kirk, *Conservative Reader*, xv–xix; idem, *Program for Conservatives*, p. 160.

8. Kirk, *Program for Conservatives*, p. 159.

9. Kirk, *Conservative Reader*, p. xxii.

10. Kirk, *Conservative Mind*, p. 62.

11. Kirk, *Program for Conservatives*, pp. 156–59, 79–81, and ch. 5.

12. Kirk, *Conservative Mind*, p. 7.

13. E.g., ibid.; and Kirk, *Program for Conservatives*, p. 76.

14. Kirk, *Program for Conservatives*, p. 41.

15. Russell Kirk, "Promises and Perils of Christian Politics," in *Churches on the Wrong Road*, ed. the Rt. Rev. Stanley Atkins and the Rev. Theodore McDonnell (Lake Bluff, Ill.: Henry Regnery, 1986), ch. 6.

16. Nash, *Conservative Intellectual Movement*, ch. 3.

17. Russell Kirk, "Defending Culture and Conservatism," *Conservative Digest* May/June 1988, pp. 57–62.

18. Kirk, *Conservative Mind*, p. 397.

19. Kirk, *Program for Conservatives*, p. 278; idem, *Conservative Mind*, p. 8.

20. Peter Steinfels has written the classic book on neoconservatism, though one must note that his lack of sympathy sometimes gets in the way of his analysis. See Steinfels, *The Neo-Conservatives* (New York: Simon and Schuster, 1979).

21. Brigitte Berger and Peter L. Berger, "Our Conservatism and Theirs," *Commentary* 82 (October 1986): 62–67.

22. Ibid., pp. 64–65.

23. Ibid., p. 64.

24. Irving Kristol, *Two Cheers for Capitalism* (New York: Meridian, 1977), p. xiii.

25. Ibid., ch. 10.

26. See Daniel Bell, *The Cultural Contradictions of Capitalism* (New York: Basic Books, 1978).

27. Kristol, *Two Cheers*, ch. 1.

28. Consider Berger and Berger, "Our Conservatism," and Kristol, *Two Cheers*. Also see Peter Steinfels, "Neo-conservatism in the United States," in *Neo-Conservatism: Social and Religious Phenomenon*, ed. Gregory Baum (New York: Seabury, 1981).

29. Michael Novak, "Toward a Liberal Morality: Liberalism and 'Community': A Symposium," *New Republic*, May 9, 1988, p. 22; idem, "Errand into the Wilderness," in *Political Passages: Journeys of Change Through Two Decades 1968–1988*, ed. John H. Bunzel (New York: Free Press, 1988), pp. 239–72.

30. Leo Strauss, *Natural Right and History* (Chicago: University of Chicago Press, 1965); idem, *What is Political Philosophy and Other Studies* (Glencoe, Ill.: Free Press, 1959), chs. 2, 3.

31. Richard Rorty, "The Old-Time Philosophy: Straussianism, Democracy, and Allan Bloom, I," *New Republic*, April 4, 1988, p. 29.

32. Allan Bloom, *The Closing of the American Mind* (New York: Simon and Schuster, 1987).

33. Ibid., p. 85.

34. Ibid., pp. 167–72.

35. Ibid., p. 58.

36. Ibid., pp. 126–27.

37. Ibid., pp. 118–20.

38. Ibid., p. 51.

39. Harvey C. Mansfield, Jr., "Democracy and the Great Books: Straussianism, Democracy, and Allan Bloom, II," *New Republic*, April 4, 1988, p. 34.

40. Ibid., p. 37.

41. Ibid.

42. Bloom, *American Mind*, p. 58.

43. Mansfield, "Democracy and the Great Books," p. 35.

44. Bloom, *American Mind*, p. 56.

45. Ibid., p. 73.

46. Ibid., p. 81.

47. Ibid., p. 41.

48. See Herbert Marcuse's discussion, "Repressive Tolerance," in *A Critique of Pure Tolerance*, ed. Robert Paul Wolff, Barrington Moore, Jr., and Herbert Marcuse (Boston: Beacon, 1965), pp. 81–117.

49. Bloom, *American Mind*, p. 82.

50. Ibid., pp. 132–34.

51. Ibid., pp. 228–29.

52. Ibid., pp. 61–99.

53. Ibid., pp. 66–67.

54. Ibid., p. 34.

55. Mansfield, "Democracy and the Great Books," p. 34.

56. Bloom, *American Mind*, p. 381 and the chapter "From Socrates' Apology . . ."

57. Mansfield, "Democracy and the Great Books," p. 34.

58. Though Suzanne Jacobitti, who helped me enormously in thinking about the Straussians, disagrees.

59. Eric Voegelin, *The New Science of Politics* (Chicago: University of Chicago Press, 1952); Nash, *Conservative Intellectual Movement*, ch. 2.

60. Alasdair MacIntyre, *After Virtue: A Study in Moral Theory* (Notre Dame, Ind.: University of Notre Dame Press, 1981); idem, *Whose Justice? Which Rationality?* (Notre Dame, Ind.: University of Notre Dame Press, 1988).

61. See, e.g., Stephen Holmes, "The Polis State," *New Republic*, June 6, 1988, pp. 32–39.

62. MacIntyre, *After Virtue*, ch. 4.

63. MacIntyre, *Whose Justice?* p. 353.

64. MacIntyre, *After Virtue*, p. 252.

65. MacIntyre, *Whose Justice?* pp. 344–45.

66. MacIntyre, *After Vitue*, pp. 204–5.

67. Ibid., p. 263.

68. Ibid., pp. 216–20.

69. MacIntyre, *Whose Justice?*

70. Ibid., p. 156.

71. Ibid., p. 253.

72. This is obvious in MacIntyre's *Whose Justice?*; see also MacIntyre, *After Virtue*, p. 259.

73. See Holmes, "The Polis State," pp. 32–39.

74. MacIntyre, *After Virtue*, pp. 273, 219.

75. MacIntyre, *Whose Justice?* pp. 385–86.

76. MacIntyre, *After Virtue*, pp. 221–22; MacIntyre, *Whose Justice?* p. 353.

77. MacIntyre, *After Virtue*, p. 165, passim; MacIntyre, *Whose Justice?* p. 321.

78. E.g., MacIntyre, *After Virtue*, p. 276.

79. MacIntyre, *Whose Justice?* p. 12.

80. Ibid., pp. 387–88, 364.

81. John R. Wallach, "Liberals, Communitarians, and the Tasks of Political Theory," *Political Theory* 15 (November 1987): 581–611.

82. MacIntyre, *After Virtue*, p. 263.

83. Wallach, "Liberals, Communitarians, and the Tasks of Political Theory," p. 598.

84. Charles Taylor, "Hegel, History and Politics," in *Liberalism and Its*

Critics, ed. Michael Sandel (New York: New York University Press, 1984), pp. 196–97. Taylor is Canadian but much admired in the United States.

85. Richard Merelman, *Making Something of Ourselves: On Culture and Politics in the United States* (Berkeley: University of California Press, 1984), pp. 25–26.

86. E.g., Thomas L. Pangle, "The Constitution's Human Vision," *Public Interest* 86 (Winter 1987): 77–90; Christopher Lasch, *Haven in A Heartless World: The Family Besieged* (New York: Basic Books, 1977).

87. Daniel Bell, *Cultural Contradictions,* ch. 6.

88. Lasch, *Haven in A Heartless World,* p. 91.

89. Ibid., p. 174.

90. Robert Bellah, Richard Madsen, William M. Sullivan, Ann Swidler, and Steven M. Tipton, *Habits of the Heart: Individualism and Commitment in American Life* (Berkeley: University of California Press, 1985), chs. 4 and 5.

91. Phyllis Schlafly, *The Power of the Christian Woman* (Cincinnati: Standard, 1981), pp. 9–11.

92. Ibid., pp. 11, 31, 52, passim.

93. Ibid., p. 147.

94. Ibid., p. 57.

95. Ibid., p. 23.

96. George Gilder, *Naked Nomads: Unmarried Men in America* (New York: Quadrangle, 1974).

97. Bloom, *American Mind,* p. 113.

98. Ibid., p. 122.

99. Ibid., p. 123.

100. Ibid., p. 105.

101. E.g., Myra Max Ferree and Beth B. Hess, *Controversy and Coalition: The New Feminist Movement* (Boston: Twayne, 1985), pp. 41–43, 104–12; Linda J. Nicholson, *Gender and History: The Limits of Social Theory in the Age of the Family* (New York: Columbia University Press, 1986), ch. 1.

102. Barbara Ehrenreich, "Another Communitarianism: Liberalism and 'Community': A Symposium," *New Republic,* May 9, 1988.

103. Nicholson, *Gender and History.*

104. Jean Grimshaw, *Philosophy and Feminist Thinking* (Minneapolis: University of Minnesota Press, 1986), pp. 13–14, 87.

105. Zillah R. Eisenstein, *Feminism and Sexual Equality: Crisis in Liberal America* (New York: Monthly Review Press, 1984), Introduction and ch. 1; idem, *The Radical Future of Liberal Feminism* (New York: Longman, 1981), ch. 9.

106. Jane Flax, "The Family in Contemporary Feminist Thought: A Critical Review," in *The Family in Political Thought,* ed. Jean Bethke Elshtain (Amherst: University of Massachusetts Press, 1982), p. 250.

107. Grimshaw, *Feminist Thinking,* p. 14.

108. Ibid., ch. 2.

109. E.g., Mary Dietz, "Citizenship with a Feminist Face: The Problem with Maternal Thinking," *Political Theory* 13 (February 1985): 19–37.

110. Grimshaw, *Feminist Thinking,* pp. 153–58.

111. Ibid., ch. 6.

112. Eisenstein, *Feminism and Sexual Equality,* ch. 8.

113. E.g., Susan Griffin, *Women and Nature: The Roaring inside Her* (New York: Harper, 1978); Ferree and Hess, *Controversy and Coalition*, pp. 38–39.

114. Dietz, "Citizenship"; idem, "Populism, Patriotism, and the Need for Roots," in *The New Populism: The Politics of Empowerment,* ed. Harry C. Boyte and Frank Riessman (Philadelphia: Temple University Press, 1986), pp. 261–71.

115. Jean Bethke Elshtain, "Feminists against the Family," *Nation,* November 17, 1979, pp. 497–98.

116. Ibid., p. 500.

117. Ibid., p. 1.

118. Ibid., p. 497.

119. Ibid., p. 1.

120. Ibid., p. 499.

121. Ibid., p. 497.

122. Ibid., p. 500.

123. Jean Bethke Elshtain, "The Feminist Movement and the Question of Equality," *Polity* 7 (Summer): 452–77; idem, *Public Man, Private Woman: Woman in Social and Political Thought,* (Princeton, N.J.: Princeton University Press, 1981).

124. Betty Friedan, *The Second Stage* (New York: Summit Books, 1981), pp. 58, 84.

125. Ibid., p. 51.

126. Ibid.

127. Sylvia Ann Hewlett, *A Lesser Life: The Myth of Women's Liberation in America* (New York: William Morrow, 1986), pt A.

128. Ibid., ch. 8, "Afterword."

129. Susan M. Okin, *Justice, Gender, and the Family* (New York: Basic Books, 1989).

130. Ibid., p. 42.

131. Ibid., ch. 3.

132. Ibid., p. 17.

133. Ibid., ch. 2 and p. 15.

134. Ibid., p. 171, chs. 7 and 8.

135. Barbara Rowland and Peregrine Schwartz-Shea, "Empowering Women: Self, Autonomy, and Responsibility." Paper for American Political Science Association, Chicago, Sept. 1989.

136. Rowland and Schwartz-Shea, "Empowering Women," pp. 8–10.

137. Ibid., p. 14; Carol Gilligan, *In a Different Voice: Psychological Theory and Women's Development* (Cambridge, Mass.: Harvard University Press, 1982).

Chapter Seven. Survival and Community

1. Kirkpatrick Sale, *Human Scale* (New York: Coward, McCann and Geoghegan, 1980), pp. 16, 20.

2. Mihajlo Mesarovic and Eduard Pestel, *Mankind at the Turning Point: The Second Report to the Club of Rome* (New York: Dutton, 1974), ch. 2.

3. Paul R. Ehrlich and Anne H. Ehrlich, *The Population Explosion* (New York: Simon and Schuster, 1990); Lester Brown, *The Twenty-Ninth Day: Accommodating Human Needs and Numbers to the Earth's Resources* (New York: Norton, 1978), ch. 4; Donella H. Meadows, Dennis L. Meadows, Jorgen Randers, and William W. Behrens III, *The Limits to Growth* (New York: Universe Books, 1972).

4. *The Global 2000 Report to the President: Entering the Twenty-First Century* (New York: Penguin, 1981), p. 1; Mesarovic and Pestel, *Mankind*, p. 1; Meadows et al., *Limits*, p. 25.

5. *Global 2000*.

6. Meadows et al., *Limits*, ch. 1.

7. Brown, *Twenty-Ninth Day*, p. 48 and ch. 1.

8. William Ophuls, *Ecology and the Politics of Scarcity: Prologue to a Political Theory of the Steady State* (San Francisco: W. H. Freeman, 1977), pp. 143–52; Brown, *Twenty-Ninth Day*, pp. 15–37.

9. Jonathan Schell, *The Fate of the Earth* (New York: Knopf, 1982).

10. Ibid., p. 148.

11. L. S. Stavrianos, *Global Rift: The Third World Comes of Age* (New York: William Morrow, 1981), p. 24.

12. Ophuls, *Ecology*, p. 1.

13. Brown, *Twenty-Ninth Day*, p. 201.

14. Ophuls, *Ecology*, p. 3.

15. Ibid., p. ix.

16. Joe Bowersox made this point to me. See his "Moral and Spiritual Potential of Environmentalism: Reclaiming Historical Foundations of Western Liberal Philosophical and Religious Thought." Unpublished manuscript, 1989.

17. *Global 2000*.

18. Ibid.

19. Ibid.

20. Ibid., p. 4.

21. Bruce Stokes, *Helping Ourselves: Local Solutions to Global Problems* (New York: Norton, 1981), ch. 1.

22. Ophuls, *Ecology*, pp. 228–29.

23. Ibid., p. 197.

24. Brown, *Twenth-Ninth Day*, pp. 310, 263, 96, passim; Ophuls, *Ecology*, ch. 6.

25. Robert L. Heilbroner, *An Inquiry into the Human Prospect* (New York: Norton, 1974).

26. Ophuls, *Ecology*, pp. 155–56.

27. Sale, *Human Scale*.

28. Ophuls, *Ecology*, p. 38.

29. Stokes, *Helping Ourselves*, ch. 9.

30. Ibid.

31. Ibid., pp. 5, 3.

32. Sale, *Human Scale*, pp. 156–64.

33. See, for instance, Murray Bookchin, *Municipalization: Community Ownership of the Economy* (Burlington, Vt.: Green Program Project, 1986).

34. E.g., Randall Rothenberg, *The Neoliberals: Creating the New American Politics* (New York: Simon and Schuster, 1984).

35. Mesarovic and Pestel, *Mankind*, pp. viii, 3–7; Stavrianos, *Global Rift*, ch. 1, pp. 23–27.

36. Mesarovic and Pestel, *Mankind*, p. 147; Brown, *Twenty-Ninth Day*, p. 305.

37. Charlene Spretnak, *The Spiritual Dimension of Green Politics* (Santa Fe, N.Mex.: Bear and Co., 1986), p. 22.

38. Ophuls, *Ecology*, pp. 218–19.

39. Brown, *Twenty-Ninth Day*, pp. 305, 300.

40. Mesarovic and Pestel, *Mankind*, pp. 97, 100.

41. Meadows et al., *Limits to Growth*, ch. 2; Ophuls, *Ecology*, p. 11.

42. Schell, *Fate*, pp. 174–75, ch. 3.

43. Ibid., ch. 1.

44. Ophuls, *Ecology*, p. 7.

45. Heilbroner, *Inquiry*.

46. As Joe Bowersox argued in his "Moral and Spiritual Potential of Environmentalism."

47. Warren Johnson, *Muddling toward Frugality* (Boulder, Colo.: Shambhala, 1979), p. 19; Brown, *Twenty-Ninth Day*, p. 242.

48. Christopher Lasch, *The Minimal Self: Psychic Survival in Troubled Times* (New York: Norton, 1984).

49. Ibid., chs. 2 and 3. In this discussion and elsewhere in this chapter Adolph Kirst-Gunderson has been of great help to me.

50. Walter Truett Anderson, *To Govern Evolution: Further Adventures of the Political Animal* (Boston: Harcourt Brace Jovanovich, 1987).

51. Ophuls, *Ecology*.

52. Mesarovic and Pestel, *Mankind*, p. 147.

53. Ophuls, *Ecology*, pp. 21, 229–32, passim.

54. Ibid., p. 7.

55. Brown, *Twenty-Ninth Day*, pp. 6–7.

56. Ophuls, *Ecology*, p. x; Mesarovic and Pestel, *Mankind*, p. ix.

57. Schell, *Fate*, p. 111.

58. Lynn White, "The Historic Roots of Our Ecologic Crisis," *Science* 155 (March 10, 1967): 1203–7.

59. Roderick F. Nash, *The Rights of Nature: A History of Environmental Ethics* (Madison: University of Wisconsin Press, 1989), ch. 4; Bowersox, "The Moral and Spiritual Potential of Environmentalism."

60. Nash, *Rights of Nature*, ch. 4.

61. Ibid., p. 120.

62. H. Paul Santmire, *The Travail of Nature: The Ambiguous Ecological Promise of Christian Theology* (Philadelphia: Fortress Press, 1985); Nash, *Rights of Nature*, ch. 4; Bowersox, "Moral and Spiritual Potential of Environmentalism."

63. Bowersox is especially good here; see his "Moral and Spiritual Potential of Environmentalism"; Nash, *Rights of Nature*, ch. 4.

64. Tim Stafford, "Animal Lib," *Christianity Today*, 34 (June 18, 1990), 19–23.

65. Spretnak, *Spiritual Dimensions*, pp. 27, 30, 52–53.

66. Anderson, *To Govern Evolution*, ch. 8.

67. Ibid., pp. 17–18.

68. See, for example, Hwa Yol Jung, "A Note on *Habits of the Heart:* An Eco-Criticism," *Soundings* 72 (Summer/Fall 1989): 473–76.

69. Ibid., pp. 68–69.

70. Later published as Christopher Stone, *Should Trees Have Standing? Toward Legal Rights for Natural Objects* (Los Altos, Calif.: William Kaufman, 1974).

71. Peter Singer, *Animal Liberation* (New York: Random House, 1975); Tom Regan, *The Case for Animal Rights* (London: Routledge and Kegan Paul, 1983).

72. Nash, *Rights of Nature*, ch. 5.

73. Stafford, "Animal Lib," p. 19.

74. J. Baird Callicott, *In Defense of the Land Ethic: Essays in Environmental Philosophy* (Albany: State University of New York Press, 1989); John Rodman, "The Liberation of Nature?" *Inquiry* 20 (1977): 83–131; Nash, *Rights of Nature*, chs. 5, 6.

75. Bowersox's analysis is excellent; see his "Moral and Spiritual Potential of Environmentalism"; Nash, *Rights of Nature*, chs. 5, 6.

76. Meadows et al., *Limits to Growth*, pp. 170–71; Ophuls, *Ecology*, pp. 2, 25.

77. Johnson, *Muddling toward Frugality*.

78. Julian L. Simon and Herman Kahn, eds., *The Resourceful Earth: A Response to Global 2000* (New York: Basil Blackwell, 1984), ch. 16.

79. Johnson, *Muddling toward Frugality*, p. 97.

80. Simon and Kahn, *Resourceful Earth*, pp. 2–3.

81. Ibid., p. 1.

82. Johnson, *Muddling toward Frugality*, p. 100.

83. Ibid., ch. 13.

84. Simon and Kahn, *Resourceful Earth*, ch. 10.

85. Ibid., ch. 13.

86. Ibid., p. 334.

87. Patricia M. Mische, *Star Wars and the State of Our Souls: Deciding the Future of Planet Earth* (Minneapolis, Minn.: Winston Press, 1985), p. 115.

Chapter Eight. Varieties of Religious Community

1. For an interesting discussion of the secularization thesis, see Rodney Stark and William Sims, *The Future of Religion: Secularization, Revival and Cult Formation* (Berkeley: University of California Press, 1985).

2. Fran Schumer, "A Return to Religion," *New York Times Magazine*, April 15, 1984, pp. 90–98.

3. One example of a broad interpretation is Richard Neuhaus's *The Naked Public Square* (Grand Rapids, Mich.: Eerdmans, 1984); he also illustrates a self-conscious awareness of the larger stakes.

4. Daniel Bell, *The Cultural Contradictions of Capitalism* (New York: Basic Books, 1978); Robert Bellah, Richard Madsen, William M. Sullivan, Ann Swidler, and Steven M. Tipton, *Habits of the Heart: Individualism and Commitment in American Life* (Berkeley: University of California Press, 1985).

5. This chapter offers a discussion of several examples.

6. See, for example, Patricia U. Bonomi, *Under the Cope of Heaven: Religion, Society, and Politics in Colonial America* (New York: Oxford University Press, 1986); Ruth H. Bloch, "The Constitution and Culture," *William and Mary Quarterly* 44 (July 1987): 550 55; John Howe, "Gordon S. Wood and the Analysis of Political Culture in the American Revolutionary Era," *William and Mary Quarterly* 44 (July 1987): 569–82.

7. E.g., John W. Whitehead, *The Second American Revolution* (Elgin, Ill.: David C. Cook, 1984); Franky Schaeffer, *Bad News for Modern Man: An Agenda for Christian Action* (Westchester, Ill.: Crossway, 1984).

8. Thomas J. Curry, *The First Freedoms: Church and State in America to the Passage of the First Amendment* (New York: Oxford University Press, 1986), p. 159.

9. William Lee Miller, *The First Liberty: Religion and the American Republic* (New York: Knopf, 1986), p. 127.

10. Victor Ferkiss, "Pluralism and the Relationship between Religion and the Government." Paper delivered at the Convention of the American Political Science Association, Sept. 1987, pp. 7–8.

11. Miller, *First Liberty*, pp. 133–34.

12. Ibid., p. 48.

13. Leo Pfeffer, *Religion, State and the Burger Court* (Buffalo, N.Y.: Prometheus, 1984).

14. Robert L. Cord, *Separation of Church and State: Historical Fact and Current Fiction* (New York: Lambeth Press, 1982).

15. Ibid., ch. 2.

16. Ibid.

17. Michael J. Malbin, *Religion and Politics: The Intentions of the Authors of the First Amendment* (Washington, D.C.: American Enterprise Institute, 1978), ch. 1; Pfeffer, *Religion*; Cord, *Separation of Church and State*, ch. 1.

18. Leonard W. Levy, "The Original Meaning of the Establishment Clause of the First Amendment," in *Religion and the State: Essays in Honor of Leo Pfeffer*, ed. James E. Wood, Jr. (Waco, Tex.: Baylor University Press, 1985), pp. 43–83.

19. Curry, *First Freedoms*.

20. Ibid., p. 222.

21. Ibid., pp. 209–13, 133, 175, passim.

22. Mark Tushnet, "The Constitution of Religion," *Connecticut Law Review* 18 (Summer 1986): 701–38.

23. Nathan O. Hatch, *The Democratization of American Christianity* (New Haven, Conn.: Yale University Press, 1989).

24. Alexis de Tocqueville, *Democracy in America*, trans. Henry Reeve (New York: Vintage, 1957), vol 2, p. 27.

25. Ibid., p. 23.

26. Robert N. Bellah, "Civil Religion in America," in *American Civil Religion*, ed. Russell E. Richey and Donald G. Jones (New York: Harper and Row, 1974), pp. 21–44; John Wilson, *Public Religion in American Culture* (Philadelphia: Temple University Press, 1979); Martin Marty, "Two Kinds of Civil Religion," in Richey and Jones, eds., *American Civil Religion*; Sanford Levinson, *Constitutional Faith* (Princeton, N.J.: Princeton University Press, 1988).

27. For some other versions of civil religion in the U.S., see Sidney Mead, *The Lively Experiment* (New York: Harper and Row, 1963); William Clebsch, *From Sacred to Profane: The Role of Religion in American History* (New York: Harper and Row, 1968); Marshall Frady, *Billy Graham; A Parable of American Righteousness* (Boston: Little, Brown, 1979).

28. Bellah, "Civil Religion in America."

29. Ferkiss, "Pluralism," pp. 27–28.

30. Besides the examples below, see also Robert Booth Fowler, *Unconventional Partners: Religion and Liberal Culture in the United States* (Grand Rapids, Mich.: Eerdmans, 1989).

31. Ibid., pp. 21, 59, 64, passim.

32. Richard Reeves, *American Journey* (New York: Simon and Schuster, 1982).

33. Miller, *First Liberty*, pp. 343–53; Neuhaus, *Naked Public Square*, p. vii.

34. Miller, *First Liberty*, pp. 266–67.

35. *Ibid.*, pp. 311–23.

36. Ibid. See the long discussion of Roger Williams.

37. Neuhaus, *Naked Public Square*.

38. Bell, *Cultural Contradictions*, pp. 30, 166, xxix, passim.

39. Bellah et al., *Habits of the Heart*; John Patrick Diggins, *The Lost Soul of American Politics: Virtue, Self-Interest, and the Foundations of Liberalism* (Chicago: University of Chicago Press, 1984).

40. Alasdair MacIntyre, *After Virtue: A Study in Moral Theory* (Notre Dame, Ind.: University of Notre Dame Press, 1981); idem, *Whose Justice? Which Rationality?* (Notre Dame, Ind.: University of Notre Dame Press, 1988).

41. Glenn Tinder, *Community: Reflections on a Tragic Ideal* (Baton Rouge: Louisiana State University Press, 1980).

42. Diggins, *Lost Soul*; Tinder, *Community*.

43. Tinder, *Community*, pp. 85, 199; Diggins, *Lost Soul*, p. 296.

44. Bellah et al., *Habits of the Heart*, ch. 9.

45. Diggins, *Lost Soul*, p. 296.

46. Tinder, *Community*, pp. 145–59.

47. Stanley Hauerwas, *A Community of Character: Toward a Constructive Christian Social Ethic* (Notre Dame, Ind.: University of Notre Dame Press, 1981), p. 6.

48. Ibid., pp. 2, 74 and chs. 2 and 3.

49. Ibid., p. 73.

50. Ibid., pp. 11, 10.

51. Ibid., p. 86.

52. Ibid., p. 101.

53. Ibid., pp. 98, 18.

54. Ibid., p. 12.

55. Ibid., pp. 219, 106–7, 75–76.

56. Ibid., chs. 7, 8.

57. Ibid., pp. 2–3.

58. Ibid., pp. 25–26.

59. Ibid., p. 14.

60. E.g., *Sojourners*, February 1988.

61. Parker Palmer, *The Company of Strangers: Christians and the Renewal of America's Public Life* (New York: Crossroad, 1981).

62. Jim Wallis, *Agenda for a Biblical People* (New York: Harper, 1976); idem, *The Call to Conversion* (New York: Harper and Row, 1981).

63. Wallis, *Agenda*, pp. 6, 10, 12.

64. Wallis, "Post-American Christianity," *Post American* 1, no. 1 (Fall 1971): 2–3.

65. Wallis, *Agenda*, p. 108.

66. William Stringfellow, *An Ethic for Christians and Other Aliens in a Strange Land* (Waco, Tex.: Word Books, 1976).

67. Wallis, *Call to Conversion*, pp. xi, xii.

68. The politics and political attitudes of *Sojourners* are discussed in more detail in Robert Booth Fowler's *Religion and Politics in America* (Metuchen, N.J.: Scarecrow Press, 1985), pp. 90–93.

69. Palmer, *Company of Strangers*, chs. 4, 7, and p. 123.

70. Dave Jackson and Neta Jackson, "Living in Community, Being the Church," *The Other Side* (May–June 1973): 8–13; (editors), "A Sign and a Choice: The Spirituality of Community. An Interview with Jean Chittister," *Sojourners* (June 1987): 14–19.

71. Graham Pulkingham, "The Shape of the Church to Come," *Sojourners* (November 1976): 13; idem, "The Shape of the Church to Come," *Sojourners* (December 1976): 11; idem, "Interview," *Sojourners* (January 1977): 21–23.

72. Palmer, *Company of Strangers*, p. 105.

73. Some randomly selected articles from a randomly selected recent year: Danny Collum, "Trident Resistance Actions South and North," *Sojourners* (March 1986): 12; Art Laffin, "The Final Verdict," *Sojourners* (March 1986): 35; Steven Hall-Williams, "Pledge Says 'No' to *Contra* Aid," *Sojourners* (June 1986): 10; Bob Campagna and Susan K. Delbner, "Faith and Resistance in Missouri," *Sojourners* (June 1986): 11; the issue celebrating Martin Luther King, Jr.: Vincent Harding, "Getting Ready for the Hero," *Sojourners* (January 20, 1986): 14–20; Sojourners Peace Ministry, "The Gospel Compels," *Sojourners* (March 1986): 6.

74. Palmer, *Company of Strangers*, ch. 8, p. 70.

75. Ibid., ch. 9.

76. Ibid., ch. 9.

77. Wallis, *Call to Conversion*; Palmer, *Company of Strangers*.

78. Saul Alinsky, *Reveille for Radicals* (Chicago: University of Chicago Press, 1946); idem, *Rules for Radicals: A Practical Primer for Realistic Radicals* (New York: Random House, 1971). For a study of Alinsky that does not stress the religious side of the movement, see Sanford D. Horwitt, *Let Them Call Me Rebel: Saul Alinsky, His Life and Legacy* (New York: Knopf, 1989).

79. See Sean Wilentz, "Local Hero," *New Republic*, December 25, 1989, pp. 30–38.

80. Richard N. Ostling, "Defrocking a Contentious Pastor," *Time*, March 25, 1985, p. 64; Peter Perl, "Supporters of Jailed Minister Defy Order to Leave Pennsylvania Church," *Washington Post*, January 3, 1985, p. A13; Susan Carey, "Pittsburgh Activist Is Promoting Tactics That Grab Attention with Shock Value," *Wall Street Journal*, February 13, 1985; William Robbins, "Bank and U.S. Steel Targets of Pittsburgh Protest," *New York Times*, July 23, 1984, p. A6.

81. Virtually every issue of the monthly *Confessing Synod Ministries Newsletter* echoes these similar themes. For these purposes, see the issue of March 1990.

82. Ibid.

83. Gregory F. Pierce, *Activism That Makes Sense: Congregation and Community Organization* (New York: Paulist, 1984).

84. Ibid., chs. 2–4.

85. Ibid., chs. 3–4.

86. Ibid., ch. 1; the remark about the NCC comes from a talk made by CSM activists and thinkers, David and Bert Honeywell, Madison, Wisconsin, June 17, 1990.

87. Richard Blow, "Moronic Convergence: The Moral and Spiritual Emptiness of the New Age," *New Republic*, January 25, 1988, pp. 24, 26.

88. Shirley MacLaine, *Out on a Limb* (New York: Bantam Books, 1983): Marilyn Ferguson, *The Aquarian Conspiracy: Personal and Social Transformation in the 1980s* (Los Angeles: Tarcher, 1980); Blow, "Moronic Convergence," p. 24.

89. Otto Friedrich, "New Age Harmonies," *Time*, December 7, 1987, pp. 62–66, 69, 72.

90. Ferguson, *Aquarian Conspiracy*, ch. 11.

91. Corinne McLaughlin and Gordon Davidson, *Builders of the Dawn: Community Lifestyles in a Changing World* (Shutesbury, Mass.: Sirius, 1986), ch. 9.

92. Douglas R. Groothuis, *Unmasking the New Age* (Downers Grove, Ill.: Intervarsity, 1986), ch. 7; Friedrich, "New Age Harmonies," pp. 24, 64.

93. Friedrich, "New Age Harmonies," p. 64.

94. Blow, "Moronic Convergence," p. 24; Friedrich, "New Age Harmonies," p. 64.

95. Ferguson, *Aquarian Conspiracy*, p. 279.

96. Ibid., p. 196.

97. Groothuis, *Unmasking the New Age*, pp. 18–31 and ch. 3; Friedrich, "New Age Harmonies," p. 69.

98. McLaughlin and Davidson, *Builders of the Dawn*, ch. 9.

99. Ferguson, *Aquarian Conspiracy*, p. 316 and ch. 3.

100. Ibid., p. 196.

101. Ibid., chs. 12–13.

102. Ferguson, *Aquarian Conspiracy*, ch. 7; Blow, "Moronic Convergence," p. 24; Groothuis, *Unmasking the New Age*, ch. 2.

103. Blow, *Moronic Convergence*," p. 27.

104. Groothuis, *Unmasking the New Age*, ch. 6.

105. Friedrich, "New Age Harmonies," pp. 25–27; Blow, "Moronic Convergence," p. 24.

106. Friedrich, "New Age Harmonies," p. 72.

107. Groothuis, *Unmasking the New Age*, ch. 4.

Chapter Nine. Reflections

1. Murray N. Rothbard, *For a New Liberty* (New York: Libertarian Review Press, 1985); Jerome Tuccille, *Radical Libertarianism* (New York: Harper, 1970);

see also Conrad Waligorski, *The Political Theory of Conservative Economists* (Lawrence: University Press of Kansas, 1990).

2. Some of the best examples today come from radical feminist thought: Susan Brownmiller, *Against Our Will* (New York: Simon and Schuster, 1975); Andrea Dworkin, *Pornography: Men Possessing Women* (New York: Pedigree Books, 1981); Andrea Dworkin, *Intercourse* (New York: Free Press, 1987).

3. E.g., Ben Wattenberg, *The Good News Is the Bad News Is Wrong* (New York: Simon and Schuster, 1984).

4. E.g., Richard Reeves, *American Journey* (New York: Simon and Schuster, 1982).

5. E.g., Arthur Stein, *Seeds of the Seventies: Values, Work, and Commitment in Post-Vietnam America* (Hanover, N.H.: University Press of New England, 1985).

6. Michael J. Sandel, *Liberalism and the Limits of Justice* (Cambridge: Cambridge University Press, 1982), p. 183.

7. Glenn Tinder, *Community: Reflections on a Tragic Ideal* (Baton Rouge: Louisiana State University Press, 1980), pp. 66–67.

8. Nancy L. Rosenblum, *Another Liberalism: Romanticism and the Reconstruction of Liberal Thought* (Cambridge, Mass.: Harvard University Press, 1987), pp. 176–85.

9. Jane J. Mansbridge, *Beyond Adversary Democracy* (Chicago: University of Chicago Press, 1983).

10. E.g., Sara M. Evans and Harry C. Boyte, *Free Spaces: The Sources of Democratic Change in America* (New York: Harper & Row, 1986).

11. A painful illustration is in J. Anthony Lukas, *Common Ground: A Turbulent Decade in the Lives of Three American Families* (New York: Knopf, 1985).

12. Ibid.

13. Kirkpatrick Sale, *Human Scale* (New York: Coward, McCann and Geoghegan, 1980), pp. 509–15.

14. Harry C. Boyte, Heather Booth, and Steve Max, *Citizen Action and the New American Populism* (Philadelphia: Temple University Press, 1986), p. 171.

15. As Joe Bowersox pointed out to me.

16. Rosenblum, *Another Liberalism*, p. 186.

17. Ibid., pp. 183–89.

18. Boyte, Booth, and Max, *Citizen Action*, p. 171; Evans and Boyte, *Free Spaces*, p. 5; Rosenblum, *Another Liberalism*, p. 189.

19. Richard M. Merelman, *Making Something of Ourselves: On Culture and Politics in the United States* (Berkeley: University of California Press, 1984).

20. Robert Bellah, Richard Madsen, William M. Sullivan, Ann Swidler, and Steven M. Tipton, *Habits of the Heart: Individualism and Commitment in American Life* (Berkeley: University of California Press, 1985).

21. Evans and Boyte, *Free Spaces*.

22. Lawrence Goodwyn, *The Populist Moment: A Short History of the Agrarian Revolt in America* (New York: Oxford University Press, 1978), p. 307.

23. Peter Clecak, *America's Quest for the Ideal Self: Dissent and Fulfillment in the 60s and 70s* (New York: Oxford University Press, 1983), p. 323.

24. Michael Walzer, *Spheres of Justice: A Defense of Pluralism and Equality* (New York: Basic Books, 1983).

25. Rosenblum, *Another Liberalism*, pp. 165–76.

26. E.g., Stein, *Seeds*.

27. E.g., Parker Palmer, *The Company of Strangers: Christians and the Renewal of America's Public life* (New York: Crossroad, 1981).

28. The burden of Rosenblum's interesting book; *Another Liberalism*.

29. Benjamin Barber, *Strong Democracy: Participatory Politics for a New Age*. (Berkeley: University of California Press, 1984).

30. Clarke E. Cochran, "The Thin Theory of Community: The Communitarians and Their Critics," *Political Studies* 37 (1989): 4.

31. Walzer, *Spheres of Justice*.

32. Cochran, "Thin Theory," p. 22.

33. An example is Andrew Oldenquist, *The Non-Suicidal Society* (Bloomington: Indiana University Press, 1986), p. 157.

34. Robert Heilbroner, *An Inquiry into the Human Prospect* (New York: Norton, 1974).

35. See ch. 7 of this book.

36. Cochran, "Thin Theory," p. 1.

37. Alasdair MacIntyre, *After Virtue: A Study in Moral Theory* (Notre Dame, Ind.: University of Notre Dame Press, 1981); Cochran, "Thin Theory."

38. E.g., Cochran, "Thin Theory," pp. 12, 15.

39. Herbert J. Gans, *Middle American Individualism: The Future of Liberal Democracy* (New York: Free Press, 1988); Mansbridge, *Beyond Adversary Democracy*.

40. Alexis de Tocqueville, *Democracy in America*, trans. Henry Reeve (New York: Vintage, 1957).

41. E.g., Clarke Cochran, "Thin Theory."

42. See Glenn Tinder, "Can We Be Good without God?" *Atlantic Monthly*, December 1989, pp. 69–85.

43. Albert Camus, *The Plague*, trans. Stuart Gilbert (New York: Vintage, 1972).

44. Kathy Sell first suggested the connections here with Martin Buber.

45. Ronald C. Arnett, *Communication and Community: The Implications of Martin Buber's Dialogue* (Carbondale: Southern Illinois University Press, 1986), 40–42.

46. Ibid., p. 71.

47. Martin Buber, *Pointing the Way: Collected Essays*, trans. Maurice Friedman (London: Routledge and Kegan Paul), 1957, p. 30.

48. Ibid., p. 227.

49. Ibid., p. 113.

50. Ibid.

51. Ibid., pp. 232–39.

52. Martin Buber, "An Experiment That Did Not Fail," in *The Writings of Martin Buber*, ed. Will Herberg (New York: Meridian, 1956), pp. 132–41; Arnett, *Communication and Community*, p. 35.

53. Ibid., pp. xii, 30.

54. Ibid., pp. viii–x, 6, 109.

55. Rosenblum, *Another Liberalism*.

56. Clarke E. Cochran, *Character, Community, and Politics* (University: University of Alabama Press, 1982).

57. Ibid., p. 41.

58. Wilson Carey McWilliams, *The Idea of Fraternity in America* (Berkeley: University of California Press, 1974), p. 427.

59. Ibid., p. 468.

60. Glenn Tinder, *Community*, p. 5.

61. For a fuller discussion see Glenn Tinder, *The Political Meaning of Christianity* (Baton Rouge: Lousiana State University Press, 1989).

62. Tinder, *Community*, p. 45.

63. Ibid., ch. 3.

64. Ibid., p. 2.

65. Ibid.

66. Cochran, *Character, Community, and Politics*, pp. 135–37, 118–21.

67. Ibid., pp. 118–21.

68. Ibid., p. 155.

69. Ibid., pp. 118–21, 22–28, ch. 4, pp. 152–153, 42–51.

70. As Plato says at the end of book nine, "The Republic," *The Portable Plato*, trans. Benjamin Jowett (New York: Viking, 1984), pp. 656–57.

Bibliography

Abbott, Philip. *Seeking Many Inventions: The Idea of Community in America.* Knoxville: University of Tennessee Press, 1987.

Alinsky, Saul. *Reveille for Radicals.* Chicago: University of Chicago Press, 1946.

———. *Rules for Radicals: A Practical Primer for Realistic Radicals.* New York: Random House, 1971.

Anderson, Walter Truett. *To Govern Evolution: Further Adventures of the Political Animal.* Boston: Harcourt Brace Jovanovich, 1987.

Ansara, Michael, and S. M. Miller. "Democratic Populism." In Harry C. Boyte and Frank Riessman, eds., *The New Populism: The Politics of Empowerment.* Philadelphia: Temple University Press, 1986, pp. 143–55.

Appleby, Joyce. *Capitalism and a New Social Order: The Republican Vision of the 1790s.* New York: New York University Press, 1984.

———. "Republicanism in Old and New Contexts." *William and Mary Quarterly* 43 (January 1986): 20–34.

Arnett, Ronald C. *Communication and Community: The Implications of Martin Buber's Dialogue.* Carbondale: Southern Illinois University Press, 1986.

Bailyn, Bernard. *Ideological Origins of the American Revolution.* Cambridge, Mass.: Harvard University Press, 1967.

Banning, Lance. "Jeffersonian Ideology Revisited: Liberal and Classical Ideas in the New American Republic." *William and Mary Quarterly* 43 (January 1986): 3–19.

———. "The Practicable Sphere of a Republic: James Madison, the Constitutional Convention, and the Emergence of Revolutionary Federalism." In Richard Beeman, Stephen Botein, and Edward C. Carter II, eds., *Beyond Confederation: Origins of the Constitution and American National Identity.* Chapel Hill: University of North Carolina Press, 1987.

———. "Republican Ideology and the Triumph of the Constitution, 1789–1793." *William and Mary Quarterly* 31 (April 1974): pp.167–88.

Barber, Benjamin. *Strong Democracy: Participatory Politics for a New Age.* Berkeley: University of California Press, 1984.

Baumol, William J., and Wallace E. Oates. "Long-Run Trends in Environmental Quality." In Julian L. Simon and Herman Kahn, eds., *The Resourceful*

Earth: A Response to Global 2000. New York: Basil Blackwell, 1984, pp. 439–75.

Beeman, Richard, Stephen Botein, and Edward C. Carter II, eds. *Beyond Confederation: Origins of the Constitution and American National Identity.* Chapel Hill: University of North Carolina Press, 1987.

———. "Introduction." In Richard Beeman et al. *Beyond Confederation: Origins of the Constitution and American National Identity.* Chapel Hill: University of North Carolina Press, 1987.

Bell, Daniel. *The Cultural Contradictions of Capitalism.* New York: Basic Books, 1978.

Bellah, Robert N. "Civil Religion in America." In Russell E. Richey and Donald G. Jones, eds., *American Civil Religion,* pp. 21–24. New York: Harper and Row, 1974.

———. "Populism and Individualism." In Harry C. Boyte and Frank Riessman, eds., *The New Populism: The Politics of Empowerment.* Philadelphia: Temple University Press, 1986, pp. 100–107.

Bellah, Robert N., Richard Madsen, William M. Sullivan, Ann Swidler, and Steven M. Tipton. *Habits of the Heart: Individualism and Commitment in American Life.* Berkeley: University of California Press, 1985.

Berger, Brigitte, and Peter L. Berger. "Our Conservatism and Theirs." *Commentary* 82 (October 1986): pp. 62–67.

Berger, Peter. "On the Obsolescence of the Concept of Honor." *European Journal of Sociology* 11 (1970): 339–47.

Berthoff, Rowland. *An Unsettled People.* New York: Harper and Row, 1971.

Bloch, Ruth H. "The Constitution and Culture." *William and Mary Quarterly* 44 (July 1987): 550–55.

Bloom, Allan. *The Closing of the American Mind.* New York: Simon and Schuster, 1987.

Blow, Richard. "Moronic Convergence. The Moral and Spiritual Emptiness of the New Age." *New Republic,* January 25, 1988, p. 24.

Bonomi, Patricia U. *Under the Cope of Heaven: Religion, Society, and Politics in Colonial America.* New York: Oxford University Press, 1986.

Bookchin, Murray. *Municipalization: Community Ownership of the Economy.* Burlington, Vt.: Green Program Project, 1986.

Boorstin, Daniel. *The Americans: The Democratic Experience.* New York: Vintage, 1974.

———. *The Americans: The National Experience.* New York: Vintage, 1965.

———. *The Genius of American Politics.* Chicago: University of Chicago Press, 1953.

Bowersox, Joe. "The Moral and Spiritual Potential of Environmentalism: Reclaiming Historical Foundations of Western Liberal Philosophical and Religious Thought." Unpublished manuscript, 1989.

Bowles, Samuel, and Herbert Gintis. *Democracy and Capitalism: Property, Community, and the Contradictions of Modern Social Thought.* London: Routledge and Kegan Paul, 1986.

Boyte, Harry C. "Beyond Politics as Usual." In Harry C. Boyte and Frank Riessman, eds., *The New Populism: The Politics of Empowerment.* Philadelphia: Temple University Press, 1986, pp. 3–15.

————. *Community Is Possible: Repairing America's Roots.* New York: Harper and Row, 1984.

Boyte, Harry C., Heather Booth, and Steve Max. *Citizen Action and the New American Populism.* Philadelphia: Temple University Press, 1986.

Boyte, Harry C., and Frank Riessman, eds. *The New Populism: The Politics of Empowerment.* Philadelphia: Temple University Press, 1986.

Brown, Lester. *The Twenty-Ninth Day: Accommodating Human Needs and Numbers to the Earth's Resources.* New York: Norton, 1978.

Brown, William M. "The Outlook for Future Petroleum Supplies." In Julian L. Simon and Herman Kahn, eds., *The Resourceful Earth: A Response to Global 2000.* New York: Basil Blackwell, 1984.

Brownmiller, Susan. *Against Our Will.* New York: Simon and Schuster, 1975.

Buber, Martin. "An Experiment That Did Not Fail." In Will Herberg, ed., *The Writings of Martin Buber,* New York: Meridian, 1956.

————. *Pointing the Way: Collected Essays.* Trans. Maurice Friedman. London: Routledge and Kegan Paul, 1957.

Buckley, William F., Jr., ed. *American Conservative Thought in the Twentieth Century.* Indianapolis: Bobbs-Merrill, 1970.

Buenker, John D. *Urban Liberalism and Progressive Reform.* New York: Scribner's, 1973.

Callicott, J. Baird. *In Defense of the Land Ethic: Essays in Environmental Philosophy.* Albany: State University of New York Press, 1989.

Campagna, Bob, and Susan K. Delbner. "Faith and Resistance in Missouri." *Sojourners,* June 1986, p.11.

Camus, Albert. *The Plague.* Translated by Stuart Gilbert. New York: Vintage, 1972.

Carey, Susan. "Pittsburgh Activist Is Promoting Tactics That Grab Attention with Shock Value." *Wall Street Journal,* February 13, 1985.

Clebsch, William. *From Sacred to Profane: The Role of Religion in American History.* New York: Harper and Row, 1968.

Clecak, Peter. *America's Quest for the Ideal Self: Dissent and Fulfillment in the 60s and 70s.* New York: Oxford University Press, 1983.

Cochran, Clarke E. *Character, Community, and Politics.* University: University of Alabama Press, 1982.

————. "The Thin Theory of Community: The Communitarians and Their Critics." *Political Studies* 37 (1989): 422–35.

Cohen, Joshua, and Joel Rogers. *On Democracy.* New York: Penguin, 1983.

Cohen, Mitchell, and Dennis Hale, eds. *The New Student Left.* Boston: Beacon, 1966.

Collum, Danny. "Trident Resistance Actions South and North." *Sojourners,* March 1986, p. 12.

Confessing Synod Ministries Newsletter. Monthly, 1989–1990.

Connolly, William E. *The Terms of Political Discourse.* Lexington, Mass.: D.C. Heath, 1974.

Cord, Robert L. *Separation of Church and State: Historical Fact and Current Fiction.* New York: Lambeth Press, 1982.

Countryman, Edward. "Of Republicanism, Capitalism, and the American Mind." *William and Mary Quarterly* 44 (July 1987): 556–62.

Croly, Herbert. *The Promise of American Life*. New York: Macmillan, 1909.

Crunden, Robert M. *Ministers of Reform: The Progressives' Achievement in American Civilization*. New York: Basic Books, 1982.

Curry, Thomas J. *The First Freedoms: Church and State in America to the Passage of the First Amendment*. New York: Oxford University Press, 1986.

Dahl, Robert A. *Democracy and Its Critics*. New Haven, Conn.: Yale University Press, 1989.

———. *A Preface to Economic Democracy*. Berkeley: University of California Press, 1985.

———. "Workers' Control of Industry and the British Labor Party." *American Political Science Review* 41 (October 1947): 875–900.

Dietz, Mary. "Citizenship with a Feminist Face: The Problem with Maternal Thinking." *Political Theory* 13 (February 1985): 19–37.

———. "Context Is All: Feminism and Theory of Citizenship." *Daedalus* 116 (Fall 1987): 1–24.

———. "Patriotism." In Terence Ball, ed., *Political Innovation and Conceptual Change* Cambridge: Cambridge University Press, 1988.

———. "Populism, Patriotism, and the Need for Roots." In Harry C. Boyte and Frank Riessman, eds., *The New Populism: The Politics of Empowerment*. Philadelphia: Temple University Press, 1986, pp. 261–71.

Diggins, John Patrick. *The Lost Soul of American Politics: Virtue, Self-Interest, and the Foundations of Liberalism*. Chicago: University of Chicago Press, 1984.

Dolbeare, Kenneth. *American Political Thought*. Chatham, N.J.: Chatham, 1984.

Drukman, Mason. *Community and Purpose in America: An Analysis of American Political Theory*. New York: McGraw-Hill, 1971.

Dumm, Thomas. *Democracy and Punishment: Disciplinary Origins of the United States*. Madison: University of Wisconsin Press, 1987.

Dworkin, Andrea. *Intercourse*. New York: Free Press, 1987.

———. *Pornography: Men Possessing Women*. New York: Pedigree Books, 1981.

Ehrenreich, Barbara. "Liberalism and 'Community': Another Communitarianism." *New Republic*, May 9, 1988, p. 21.

Ehrlich, Paul R. *The Population Bomb*. New York: Ballantine, 1968.

Ehrlich, Paul, and Anne H. Ehrlich. *The Population Explosion*. New York: Simon and Schuster, 1990.

Eisenstein, Zillah R. *Feminism and Sexual Equality: Crisis in Liberal America*. New York: Monthly Review Press, 1984.

———. *The Radical Future of Liberal Feminism*. New York: Longman, 1981.

Elshtain, Jean Bethke. "Liberalism and 'Community': The Barrier of Law." *New Republic*, May 9, 1988, p.22.

———. *The Family in Political Thought*. Amherst: University of Massachusetts Press, 1982.

———. "The Feminist Movement and the Question of Equality." *Polity* 7 (Summer): 452–77.

———. "Feminists against the Family." *Nation*, November 17, 1979, pp.497–500, 1.

———. *Public Man, Private Woman: Women in Social and Political Thought*. Princeton, N. J.: Princeton, University Press, 1981.

Evans, Sara M., and Harry C. Boyte. *Free Spaces: The Sources of Democratic Change in America*. New York: Harper and Row, 1986.

Ferguson, Marilyn. *The Aquarian Conspiracy: Personal and Social Transformation in the 1980s*. Los Angeles: Tarcher, 1980.

Ferkiss, Victor. "Pluralism and the Relationship between Religion and the Government." Paper, American Political Science Association Convention, Sept. 1987.

Ferree, Myra Max, and Beth B. Hess. *Controversy and Coalition: The New Feminist Movement*. Boston: Twayne, 1985.

Fischer, Claude S. "Finding the 'Lost' Community: Facts and Fictions." *Tikkun* 3 (November/December 1988): 69–72.

Fishkin, James. *Justice, Equal Opportunity, and the Family*. New Haven, Conn.: Yale University Press, 1983.

Flacks, Richard. *Making History: The Radical Tradition in American Life*. New York: Columbia University Press, 1988.

Flax, Jane. "The Family in Contemporary Feminist Thought: A Critical Review." In Jean Bethke Elshtain, ed., *The Family in Political Thought*. Amherst: University of Massachusetts Press, 1982.

Fowler, Robert Booth. *Believing in Skeptics: American Political Intellectuals 1945–1965*. Westport, Conn.: Greenwood, 1978.

———. *Religion and Politics in America*. Metuchen, N. J.: Scarecrow Press, 1985.

———. *Unconventional Partners: Religion and Liberal Culture in the United States*. Grand Rapids, Mich.: Eerdmans, 1989.

Fox, Stephen. *The American Conservation Movement: John Muir and His Legacy*. Madison: University of Wisconsin Press, 1985.

Frady, Marshall. *Billy Graham: A Parable of American Righteousness*. Boston: Little, Brown, 1979.

Friedan, Betty. *The Second Stage*. New York: Summit Books, 1981.

Friedrich, Otto. "New Age Harmonies." *Time*, December 7, 1987, p. 62.

Gallie, W. B. "Essentially Contested Concepts." *Proceedings of the Aristotelian Society* 56 (1955–1956). Quoted in William E. Connolly. *The Terms of Political Discourse*. Lexington, Mass.: D.C. Heath, 1974.

Gans, Herbert J. *Middle American Individualism: The Future of Liberal Democracy*. New York: Free Press, 1988.

"Getting Ready for the Hero." *Sojourners*, January 20, 1986.

Gilder, George. *Naked Nomads: Unmarried Men in America*. New York: Quadrangle, 1974.

Gilligan, Carol. *In a Different Voice: Psychological Theory and Women's Development*. Cambridge, Mass.: Harvard University Press, 1982.

Gilman, Charlotte Perkins. *Women and Economics*. New York: Harper, 1966.

The Global 2000 Report to the President: Entering the Twenty-First Century. New York: Penguin, 1981.

Goldman, Eric. *Rendezvous with Destiny: A History of Modern American Reform*. New York: Knopf, 1952.

Goodwyn, Lawrence. *The Populist Moment: A Short History of the Agrarian Revolt in America*. New York: Oxford University Press, 1978.

Gorham, Eric. "National Service: Citizenship and Political Education." Ph.D. dissertation, University of Wisconsin-Madison, 1990.

Grantham, Dewey W. *Southern Progressivism: The Reconciliation of Progress and Tradition.* Knoxville: University of Tennessee Press, 1983.

Griffin, Susan. *Woman and Nature: The Roaring inside Her.* New York: Harper, 1978.

Grimshaw, Jean. *Philosophy and Feminist Thinking.* Minneapolis: University of Minnesota Press, 1986.

Groothuis, Douglas R. *Unmasking the New Age.* Downers Grove, Ill.: Intervarsity, 1986.

Gutman, Amy. *Democratic Education.* Princeton, N.J.: Princeton University Press, 1987.

———. *Liberal Equality.* Cambridge: Cambridge University Press, 1980.

Hall-Williams, Steven. "Pledge Says 'No' to *Contra* Aid." *Sojourners,* June 1986, p.10.

Hanson, Russell L. *The Democratic Imagination in America.* Princeton, N. J.: Princeton University Press, 1985.

Hardin, Garrett. "The Tragedy of the Commons." *Ekistics* 160 (1969): 168–70.

Harrington, Michael. *The Politics at God's Funeral: The Spiritual Crisis of Western Civilization.* New York: Penguin, 1985.

Hartz, Louis. *The Liberal Tradition in America.* New York: Harcourt, Brace and World, 1955.

Hatch, Nathan O. *The Democratization of American Christianity.* New Haven, Conn.: Yale University Press, 1989.

Hauerwas, Stanley. *A Community of Character: Toward a Constructive Christian Social Ethic.* Notre Dame, Ind.: University of Notre Dame Press, 1981.

Heilbroner, Robert L. *An Inquiry into the Human Prospect.* New York: Norton, 1974.

Herberg, Will, ed. *The Writings of Martin Buber.* New York: Meridian, 1956.

Herzog, Don. "Some Questions for Republicans." *Political Theory* 14 (August 1986): 473–93.

Hewlett, Sylvia Ann. *A Lesser Life: The Myth of Women's Liberation in America.* New York: William Morrow, 1986.

Hillery, George A., Jr. "Definitions of Community: Areas of Agreement." *Rural Sociology* 20 (July 1955): 111–23.

Hofstadter, Richard. *The Age of Reform.* New York: Knopf, 1955.

Holland, Joe. "Populism and America's Spiritual Crisis." In Harry C. Boyte and Frank Riessman, eds. *The New Populism: The Politics of Empowerment.* Philadelphia: Temple University Press, 1986, pp. 272–83.

Holmes, Stephen. "The Polis State." *New Republic,* June 6, 1988, pp. 32–39.

Horwitt, Sanford D. *Let Them Call Me Rebel: Saul Alinsky, His Life and Legacy.* New York: Knopf, 1989.

Howe, John. "Gordon S. Wood and the Analysis of Political Culture in the American Revolutionary Era." *William and Mary Quarterly* 44 (July 1987): 569–82.

Huntington, Samuel P. *American Politics: The Promise of Disharmony.* Cambridge, Mass.: Harvard University Press, 1981.

Jackson, Dave, and Neta Jackson. "Living in Community, Being the Church." *The Other Side,* May/June 1973, pp. 8–13.

Johnson, Warren. *Muddling toward Frugality.* Boulder, Colo.: Shambhala, 1979.

Jung, Hwa Yol. "A Note on *Habits of the Heart:* An Eco-Criticism." *Soundings* 72 (Summer/Fall 1989): 473–76.

Kann, Mark. "Individualism and Civic Virtue: Introduction." Unpublished essay.

Kennedy, Paul. "Fin-de-Siecle America." *New York Review of Books,* June 28, 1990, pp. 31–40.

Ketcham, Ralph. *Individualism and Public Life—A Modern Dilemma.* New York: Basil Blackwell, 1987.

———. "Publius: Sustaining the Republican Principle." *William and Mary Quarterly* 44 (July 1987): 576–82.

Kirk, Russell. *The Conservative Mind from Burke to Santayana.* Chicago: Henry Regnery, 1953.

———. "Defending Culture and Conservatism." *Conservative Digest,* May/June 1988, pp. 57–62.

———. *The Portable Conservative Reader.* New York: Penguin, 1982.

———. *A Program for Conservatives.* Rev. ed. Chicago: Regnery, 1962.

———."Promises and Perils of Christian Politics." In the Rt. Rev. Stanley Atkins and the Rev. Theodore McConnell, eds., *Churches on the Wrong Road.* Lake Bluff, Ill.: Regnery, 1986.

Kloppenberg, James T. "The Virtues of Liberalism: Christianity, Republicanism, and Ethics in Early American Political Discourses." *Journal of American History* (June 1987): 9–33.

Kraditor, Aileen. *The Radical Persuasion 1890–1917.* Baton Rouge: Louisiana State University Press, 1981.

Kristol, Irving. *Two Cheers for Capitalism.* New York: Meridian, 1977.

Laffin, Art. "The Final Verdict." *Sojourners,* March 1986, p. 35.

Landsberg, H. E. "Global Climatic Trends." In Julian L. Simon and Herman Kahn, eds., *The Resourceful Earth: A Response to Global 2000.* New York: Basil Blackwell, 1984.

Lasch, Christopher. "Fraternalist Manifesto." *Harper's,* April 1987, pp. 17–20.

———. *Haven in a Heartless World: The Family Besieged.* New York: Basic Books, 1977.

———. *The Minimal Self: Psychic Survival in Troubled Times.* New York: Norton, 1984.

———. *The New Radicalism in America 1889–1963.* New York: Vintage, 1965.

Leege, David. "The Parish as Community." *Notre Dame Study of Catholic Parish Life,* Report no. 10, March 1987.

Levin, Michael. *Feminism and Freedom.* New Brunswick, N.J.: Transaction, 1987.

Levinson, Sanford. *Constitutional Faith.* Princeton, N. J.: Princeton University Press, 1988.

Levy, Leonard W. "The Original Meaning of the Establishment Clause of the First Amendment." In James E. Wood, Jr., ed., *Religion and the State: Essays in Honor of Leo Pfeffer.* Waco, Tex.: Baylor University Press, 1985, pp. 43–83.

Lienesch, Michael. *New Order of the Ages: Time, the Constitution, and the Making of Modern American Political Thought.* Princeton, N. J.: Princeton University Press, 1988.

Lora, Donald. *Conservative Minds in America.* Chicago: Rand McNally, 1971.

Lukas, J. Anthony. *Common Ground: A Turbulent Decade in the Lives of Three American Families.* New York: Knopf, 1985.

Lustig, R. Jeffrey. *Corporate Liberalism: The Origins of Modern American Political Theory, 1890–1920.* Berkeley: University of California Press, 1982.

Lynd, Staughton. *Intellectual Origins of American Radicalism,* New York: Random House, 1969.

MacIntyre, Alasdair. *After Virtue: A Study in Moral Theory.* Notre Dame, Ind.: University of Notre Dame Press, 1981.

———. *Whose Justice? Which Rationality?* Notre Dame, Ind.: University of Notre Dame Press, 1988.

MacLaine, Shirley. *Out on a Limb.* New York: Bantam Books, 1983.

MacPherson, C. B. *Democratic Theory: Essays in Retrieval.* Oxford: Oxford University Press, 1973.

———. *The Real World of Democracy.* Oxford: Oxford University Press, 1966.

Malbin, Michael. *Religion and Politics: The Intentions of the Authors of the First Amendment.* Washington, D.C.: American Enterprise Institute, 1978.

Mansbridge, Jane J. *Beyond Adversary Democracy.* Chicago: University of Chicago Press, 1983.

Mansfield, Harvey C., Jr. "Democracy and the Great Books: Straussianism, Democracy, and Allan Bloom, II." *New Republic,* April 4, 1988, pp. 33–37.

Marcuse, Herbert. "Repressive Tolerance." In Robert Paul Wolff, Barrington Moore, Jr., and Herbert Marcuse, eds., *A Critique of Pure Tolerance.* Boston: Beacon, 1965, pp. 81–117.

Marty, Martin. "Two Kinds of Civil Religion." In Russell E. Richey and Donald G. Jones, eds., *American Civil Religion.* New York: Harper and Row, 1974.

Matthews, Richard K. "Liberalism, Civic Humanism, and the American Political Tradition: Understanding Consensus." *Journal of Politics* 49 (November 1987): 1127–53.

McCann, Michael W. *Taking Reform Seriously: Perspectives on Public Interest Liberalism.* Ithaca, N.Y.: Cornell University Press, 1986.

McCoy, Drew. *The Elusive Republic: Political Economy in Jeffersonian America.* Chapel Hill: University of North Carolina Press, 1980.

McDonald, Forrest. *Novus Ordo Seclorum: The Intellectual Origins of the Constitution.* Lawrence: University Press of Kansas, 1985.

McLaughlin, Corinne, and Gordon Davidson. *Builders of the Dawn: Community Lifestyles in a Changing World.* Shutesbury, Mass.: Sirius, 1986.

McWilliams, Wilson Carey. *The Idea of Fraternity in America.* Berkeley: University of California Press, 1974.

Mead, Sidney. *The Lively Experiment.* New York: Harper and Row, 1963.

Meadows, Donnella H., Dennis L. Meadows, Jorgen Randers, and William W. Behrens III. *The Limits to Growth.* New York: Universe Books, 1972.

Megill, Allan. *Prophets of Extremity: Nietzsche, Heidegger, Foucault, Derrida.* Berkeley: University of California Press, 1985.

Merelman, Richard M. *Making Something of Ourselves: On Culture and Politics in the United States.* Berkeley: University of California Press, 1984.

Mesarovic, Mihajlo, and Eduard Pestel. *Mankind at the Turning Point: The Second Report to the Club of Rome.* New York: Dutton, 1974.

Meyer, Frank S. "The Recrudescent American Conservatism." In William F.

Buckley, Jr., ed., *American Conservative Thought in the Twentieth Century*. Indianapolis: Bobbs-Merrill, 1970.

Miller, William Lee. *The First Liberty: Religion and the American Republic*. New York: Knopf, 1986.

Mische, Patricia M. *Star Wars and the State of Our Souls: Deciding the Future of Planet Earth*. Minneapolis, Minn.: Winston Press, 1985.

Murrin, John W. "Gordon S. Wood and the Search for Liberal America." *William and Mary Quarterly* 44 (July 1987): 597–601.

Nash, George H. *The Conservative Intellectual Movement in America since 1945*. New York: Basic Books, 1979.

Nash, Roderick F. *The Rights of Nature: A History of Environmental Ethics*. Madison: University of Wisconsin Press, 1989.

Neuhaus, Richard John. *The Naked Public Square: Religion and Democracy in America*. Grand Rapids, Mich.: Eerdmans, 1984.

Nicholson, Linda. *Gender and History: The Limits of Social Theory in the Age of the Family*. New York: Columbia University Press, 1986.

Nisbet, Robert. "The Concept of Community: A Reexamination." *Sociological Review* 21 (August 1973): 397–416.

————. *The Present Age: Progress and Anarchy in Modern America*. New York: Harper and Row, 1988.

Novak, Michael. "Errand into the Wilderness." In John Bunzel, ed., *Political Passages: Journeys of Change through Two Decades 1968–1988*. New York: Free Press, 1988.

————. "Toward a Liberal Morality: Liberalism and 'Community': A Symposium." *New Republic*, May 9, 1988, p. 22.

Ogilvy, James. *Many Dimensional Man: Decentralizing Self, Society, and the Sacred*. New York: Harper and Row, 1977.

Okin, Susan M. *Justice, Gender, and the Family*. New York: Basic Books, 1989.

Oldenquist, Andrew. *The Non-Suicidal Society*. Bloomington: Indiana University Press, 1986.

Ophuls, William. *Ecology and the Politics of Scarcity: Prologue to a Political Theory of the Steady State*. San Francisco: W. H. Freeman, 1977.

Ostling, Richard N. "Defrocking a Contentious Pastor." *Time*, March 25, 1985, p. 64.

Palmer, Parker. *The Company of Strangers: Christians and the Renewal of America's Public Life*. New York: Crossroad, 1981.

Pangle, Thomas L. "The Constitution's Human Vision." *Public Interest* 86 (Winter 1987): 77–90.

————. *The Spirit of Modern Republicanism: The Moral Vision of the American Founders and the Philosophy of Locke*. Chicago: University of Chicago Press, 1988.

Pateman, Carole. *Participation and Democratic Theory*. Cambridge: Cambridge University Press, 1970.

Perl, Peter. "Supporters of Jailed Minister Defy Order to Leave Pennsylvania Church." *Washington Post*, January 3, 1985, p. A 13.

Pfeffer, Leo. "An Autobiographical Sketch." In James E. Wood, Jr., ed., *Religion and the State: Essays in Honor of Leo Pfeffer*. Waco, Tex.: Baylor University Press, 1985, pp. 487–533.

————. *Religion, State and the Burger Court*. Buffalo, N.Y.: Prometheus, 1984.

Pierce, Gregory F. *Activism That Makes Sense: Congregation and Community Organization*. New York: Paulist, 1984.

Pocock, J. G. A. *The Machiavellian Moment: Florentine Political Thought and the Atlantic Republican Tradition*. Princeton, N.J.: Princeton University Press, 1975.

Price, David E. "Community and Control: Critical Democratic Theory in the Progressive Period." *American Political Science Review* 68 (December 1974): 1663–78.

Pulkingham, Graham. "Interview." *Sojourners*, January 1977, pp. 21–23.

————. "The Shape of the Church to Come." *Sojourners*, November 1976, p. 13.

————."The Shape of the Church to Come." *Sojourners*, December 1976, p.11.

Ratner, Joseph, ed. *Intellectuals in the Modern World: John Dewey's Philosophy*. New York: Modern Library, 1939.

Rawls, John. *A Theory of Justice*. Cambridge, Mass.: Harvard University Press, 1971.

Reeves, Richard. *American Journey*. New York: Simon and Schuster, 1982.

Regan, Tom. *The Case for Animal Rights*. London: Routledge and Kegan Paul, 1983.

Richey, Russell E., and Donald G. Jones, eds. *American Civil Religion*. New York: Harper and Row, 1974.

Robbins, William. "Bank and U.S. Steel Targets of Pittsburgh Protest."*New York Times*, July 23, 1984, p. A6.

Robertson, James Oliver. *American Myth, American Reality*. New York: Hill and Wang, 1980.

Rodman, John. "The Liberation of Nature?" *Inquiry* 20 (1977): 83–131.

Rorty, Richard. "That Old-Time Philosophy: Straussianism, Democracy, and Allan Bloom." *New Republic*, April 4, 1988, pp. 28–33.

Rosenblum, Nancy L. *Another Liberalism: Romanticism and the Reconstruction of Liberal Thought*. Cambridge, Mass.: Harvard University Press, 1987.

————."A Liberalism in Common: Liberalism and 'Community': A Symposium." *New Republic*, May 9, 1988, p. 23.

Rothbard, Murray N. *For a New Liberty*. New York: Libertarian Review Press, 1985.

Rothenberg, Randall. *The Neoliberals: Creating the New American Politics*. New York: Simon and Schuster, 1984.

Rowland, Barbara M., and Peregrine Schwartz-Shea. "Empowering Women: Self, Autonomy, and Responsibility." Paper read at American Political Science Association Convention, Sept. 1989, Chicago, Ill.

Sale, Kirkpatrick. *Human Scale*. New York: Coward, McCann and Geoghegan, 1980.

Sandel, Michael J. *Liberalism and Its Critics*. New York: New York University Press, 1984.

————. *Liberalism and the Limits of Justice*. Cambridge: Cambridge University Press, 1982.

Santmire, Paul H. *The Travail of Nature: The Ambiguous Ecological Promise of Christian Theology*. Philadelphia: Fortress Press, 1985.

Schaar, John H. "The Case for Patriotism." In John H. Schaar, ed., *Legitimacy in the Modern State*. New Brunswick, N.J.: Transaction Books, 1981.

Schaeffer, Franky. *Bad News for Modern Man: An Agenda for Christian Action.* Westchester, Ill.: Crossway, 1984.

Schell, Jonathan. *The Fate of the Earth.* New York: Knopf, 1982.

Schlafly, Phyllis. *The Power of the Christian Woman.* Cincinnati: Standard, 1981.

Schlesinger, Arthur, Jr., ed. *The Writings and Speeches of Eugene V. Debs.* New York: Hermitage, 1948.

Schumer, Fran. "A Return to Religion." *New York Times Magazine,* April 15, 1984, pp. 90–98.

"A Sign and a Choice. The Spirituality of Community. An Interview with Joan Chittister." *Sojourners.* June 1987, pp. 14–19.

Simon, Julian L., and Herman Kahn, eds. *The Resourceful Earth: A Response to Global 2000.* New York: Basil Blackwell, 1984.

Singer, Peter. *Animal Liberation.* New York: Random House, 1975.

Smith, Rogers M. "The 'American Creed' and American Identity: The Limits of Liberal Citizenship in the United States." *Western Political Quarterly* 41 (June 1988): 225–51.

Sojourners Peace Ministry. "The Gospel Compels." *Sojourners,* March 1986, p. 6.

Spragens, Thomas A., Jr. *The Irony of Liberal Reason.* Chicago: University of Chicago Press, 1981.

Spretnak, Charlene. "Postmodern Populism: The Greening of Technocratic Society." In Harry C. Boyte and Frank Riessman, eds., *The New Populism: The Politics of Empowerment.* Philadelphia: Temple University Press, 1986, pp. 156–64.

———. *The Spiritual Dimension of Green Politics.* Santa Fe, N.Mex.: Bear and Co., 1986.

Stafford, Tim. "Animal Lib." *Christianity Today,* June 18, 1990, pp. 19–23.

Stark, Rodney, and William Sims. *The Future of Religion: Secularization, Revival and Cult Formation.* Berkeley: University of California Press, 1985.

Stavrianos, L. S. *Global Rift: The Third World Comes of Age.* New York: William Morrow, 1981.

Stein, Arthur. *Seeds of the Seventies: Values, Work, and Commitment in Post-Vietnam America.* Hanover, N.H.: University Press of New England, 1985.

Steinfels, Peter. *The Neo-Conservatives.* New York: Simon and Schuster, 1979.

———. "Neo-Conservatism in the United States." In Gregory Baum, ed., *Neo-Conservatism: Social and Religious Phenomenon.* New York: Seabury, 1981.

Stokes, Bruce. *Helping Ourselves: Local Solutions to Global Problems.* New York: W. W. Norton, 1981.

Stone, Christopher. *Should Trees Have Standing? Toward Legal Rights for Natural Objects.* Los Altos, Calif.: William Kaufman, 1974.

Strauss, Leo. *Natural Right and History.* Chicago: University of Chicago Press, 1965.

———. *What Is Political Philosophy and Other Studies.* Glencoe, Ill.: Free Press, 1959.

Stringfellow, William. *An Ethic for Christians and Other Aliens in a Strange Land.* Waco, Tex.: Word Books, 1976.

Sullivan, William M. *Reconstructing Political Philosophy.* Berkeley: University of California Press, 1982.

Taylor, Charles. "Hegel: History and Politics." In Michael Sandel, ed., *Liberalism and Its Critics*. New York: New York University Press, 1984.

Thompson, E. P. *The Making of the English Working Class*. New York: Pantheon, 1964.

Tinder, Glenn. "Can We Be Good without God?" *Atlantic Monthly*, December 1989, pp. 68–85.

―――. *Community: Reflections on a Tragic Ideal*. Baton Rouge: Louisiana State University Press, 1980.

―――. *The Political Meaning of Christianity*. Baton Rouge: Louisiana State University Press, 1989.

Tocqueville, Alexis de. *Democracy in America*. Translated by Henry Reeve. New York: Vintage, 1957.

Tuccille, Jerome. *Radical Libertarianism*. New York: Harper, 1970.

Tushnet, Mark. "The Constitution of Religion." *Connecticut Law Review* 18 (Summer 1986): 701–38.

Unger, Roberto Mangabeira. *Knowledge and Politics*. New York: Free Press, 1975.

―――. *Passion: An Essay on Personality*. New York: Free Press, 1984.

―――. *Politics: A Work in Constructive Social Theory*. Cambridge: Cambridge University Press, 1987.

Varenne, Herve. *Americans Together: Structured Diversity in a Midwestern Town*. New York: Columbia University Press, 1977.

Voegelin, Eric. *The New Science of Politics*. Chicago: University of Chicago Press, 1952.

Waligorski, Conrad. *The Political Theory of Conservative Economists*. Lawrence: University Press of Kansas, 1990.

Wallach, John R. "Liberals, Communitarians, and the Tasks of Political Theory." *Political Theory* 15 (November 1987): 581–611.

Wallis, Jim. *Agenda for a Biblical People*. New York: Harper, 1976.

―――. *The Call to Conversion*. New York: Harper and Row, 1981.

―――. "Post-American Christianity." *Post-American* 1 (Fall): 2–3.

Walzer, Michael. *Spheres of Justice: A Defense of Pluralism and Equality*. New York: Basic Books, 1983.

―――. "Welfare, Membership and Need." In Michael Sandel, ed., *Liberalism and Its Critics*. New York: New York University Press, 1984.

Warren, Roland L. *The Community in America*. Chicago: Rand McNally, 1972.

Wattenberg, Ben. *The Good News Is the Bad News Is Wrong*. New York: Simon and Schuster, 1984.

Webking, Robert H. *The American Revolution and the Politics of Liberty*. Baton Rouge: Louisiana State University Press, 1988.

White, Lynn, "The Historic Roots of Our Ecologic Crisis." *Science* 155 (March 10, 1967): 1203–7.

Whitehead, John W. *The Second American Revolution*. Elgin, Ill.: David C. Cook, 1984.

Wilentz, Sean. "Local Hero." *New Republic*, December 25, 1989, pp. 30–38.

Wills, Garry. *Inventing America*. Garden City, N.Y.: Doubleday, 1978.

Wilson, John. *Public Religion in American Culture*. Philadelphia: Temple University Press, 1979.

Witte, John. *Democracy, Authority, and Alienation in Work: Workers' Participation in an American Corporation*. Chicago: University of Chicago Press, 1980.

Wolfe, Alan. *Whose Keeper? Social Science and Moral Obligation*. Berkeley: University of California Press, 1989.

Wolff, Robert Paul, Herbert Marcuse, and Barrington Moore, Jr., eds. *A Critique of Pure Tolerance*. Boston: Beacon, 1967.

Wolin, Sheldon. "Democracy in the Discourse of Postmodernism." *Social Research* 57 (Spring 1990): 5–30.

Wood, Gordon S. *The Creation of the American Republic 1776–1787*. New York: Norton, 1972.

———. "The Fundamentalists and the Constitution." *New York Review of Books*, February 18, 1988, pp. 33–40.

———. "Hellfire Politics." *New York Review of Books*, February 28, 1985, p. 30.

———. "Ideology and the Origins of Liberal America." *William and Mary Quarterly* 44 (July 1987): 628–40.

———. "Interests and Disinterestedness in the Making of the Constitution." In Richard Beeman, Stephen Botein, and Edward C. Carter II, eds., *Beyond Confederation: Origins of the Constitution and American National Identity*. Chapel Hill: University of North Carolina Press, 1987, pp. 69–109.

Wood, James E., Jr. *Religion and the State: Essays in Honor of Leo Pfeffer*. Waco, Tex.: Baylor University Press, 1985.

Yack, Bernard. "Toward a Free Marketplace of Social Institutions." *Harvard Law Review* 101 (June 1988): 1961–77.

Zagarell, Sandra A. "Narrative of Community: The Identification of a Genre." *Signs* 13 (Spring 1988): 498–527.

Zinn, Howard. *A People's History of the United States*. New York: Harper and Row, 1980.

Index